The New Roberts Court
and Our Failing Constitution

Stephen M. Feldman

The New Roberts Court, Donald Trump, and Our Failing Constitution

palgrave
macmillan

Stephen M. Feldman
College of Law
University of Wyoming
Laramie, WY
USA

ISBN 978-3-319-56450-0   ISBN 978-3-319-56451-7   (eBook)
DOI 10.1007/978-3-319-56451-7

Library of Congress Control Number: 2017938539

Cover credits: © Stocktrek Images, Inc. / Alamy Stock Photo
                © Josiah Romano / EyeEm

Printed on acid-free paper

This Palgrave Macmillan imprint is published by Springer Nature
The registered company is Springer International Publishing AG
The registered company address is: Gewerbestrasse 11, 6330 Cham, Switzerland

To Laura, as always

Acknowledgements

This book developed from a series of articles into an evolving book project. When I decided to transform the articles into a book, I began with a critique of the Roberts Court, including Justice Antonin Scalia. Justice Scalia's death changed that project. When Hillary Clinton appeared likely to win the 2016 presidential election, I reconceived the book as explaining where a new progressive Supreme Court might go. Then, when Donald Trump won the presidency, I again reconceived the book—into the current volume.

A number of people helped along the way with their comments on the various manuscripts (sometimes on more than one). I thank Alan Chen, Richard Delgado, Sam Kalen, Noah Novogrodsky, Alex Tsesis, Mark Tushnet, and Evan Zoldan for their insights. Parts of this book are derived from papers I presented at the 2013 and 2014 Yale Law School Freedom of Expression Scholars Conferences, a 2013 University of Virginia Constitutional History Conference, and the 2014 Law and Society Conference. I appreciate Jack Balkin's invitations to the Yale conferences, Mark Graber's invitation to the Virginia conference, and the many suggestions I received from the workshop participants. I especially thank Vincent Blasi, Mel Urofsky, and Thomas Healy for their detailed comments on my papers at the Yale and Virginia conferences.

I also want to thank Steve Siebert, Anne Putnam, and the staff of Nota Bene for Windows, an incredible word processing program designed for scholarly writing. I remain amazed that, in a world of

Microsoft and Apple, Steve and Anne keep Nota Bene not only alive but vital and up-to-date. Their suite of programs has facilitated my work for more than 25 years.

Related articles and essays have been published in the following journals: *Constitutional Commentary, Brooklyn Law Review, Rutgers University Law Review Commentaries, Ohio Northern University Law Review,* and *Wyoming Law Review.*

CONTENTS

Part III   The Early and New Roberts Courts

CHAPTER 1

Introduction: Democracy, Inc., and the Betrayal of the Constitution

We live in the age of Democracy, Inc.[1] Advertisements package candidates in 20-second sound bites echoing car and beer commercials. Corporations and billionaires wield herculean political power. A billionaire reality-star, real-estate mogul has even been elected president and has filled his cabinet with billionaires and multi-millionaires. Citizens still vote—at least occasionally—but corporate muscle manages elections and shapes government policy to increase profits. The private economic sphere has become so bloated with power that it has, in effect, subsumed the government sphere. Yet, conservatives proclaim that government overreach is destroying America.[2]

The 5 conservative justices of the early Roberts Court—John Roberts, Antonin Scalia, Clarence Thomas, Samuel Alito, and Anthony Kennedy—stamped Democracy, Inc., with a constitutional imprimatur. In numerous decisions, starting in the fall 2005 Supreme Court term when Roberts stepped in as chief justice and continuing until Justice Scalia's death (February 13, 2016), the Court promoted business, protected economic liberties, and shielded the marketplace from government power and regulation. But these judicial decisions manifested a startling betrayal of the Constitution. The conservative justices might not have intentionally broken faith with constitutional principles, yet the betrayal was just as real—and just as dangerous. The justices, for the most part, sincerely applied constitutional text, doctrines, and precedents in accord with their political views. Yet, the Court's decisions generated unintended and perverse consequences. The conservative justices

© The Author(s) 2017
S.M. Feldman, *The New Roberts Court, Donald Trump, and Our Failing Constitution*, DOI 10.1007/978-3-319-56451-7_1

believed they were upholding and protecting the American way of life, but they instead placed our democratic-capitalist system in its gravest danger since World War II. Democracy, Inc., threatens the very survival of American constitutionalism.[3]

A 2012 Roberts Court case, with a history stretching back more than a century, illustrates how the conservative bloc's fundamentalist protection of the marketplace can undermine democracy. Montana in the late-nineteenth century was the Wild West of politics, where bribery, extortion, and dirty dealing ruled the day. In 1880, Marcus Daly bought a mine, the Anaconda, located in the Montana territory. Needing money for development, he persuaded a group of California capitalists to invest. Within 4 years, the Anaconda Company had built the world's largest copper smelter, and Montana's floodgates to outside wealth and corporate control opened wide. When Montana became the 41st state in 1889, the primary source of wealth was mining, and copper led all the metals, surpassing silver and gold. Corporations rushed to the state to invest in copper, with Anaconda going public in 1893.[4] Daly's former friend turned copper-mining rival, William Clark, craved one of the state's two U.S. Senate seats. Defeated twice because of Daly's opposition, Clark finally just purchased a seat by bribing state legislators (the Constitution, at the time, vested state legislatures with the power to choose senators). None other than Mark Twain wrote that Clark "bought legislatures and judges as other men buy food and raiment. By his example he has so excused and so sweetened corruption that in Montana it no longer has an offensive smell."[5]

A tidal wave of corporate mergers swept over the nation in the 1890s and engulfed the copper-mining industry. Standard Oil, already a corporate giant, sought control of Anaconda along with additional mining companies, but the Montana Supreme Court blocked the merger. Anaconda's attorney helped shove a bill countering the judicial decision through the legislative process. The governor, however, vetoed the bill. Mixing his metaphors, he warned Montanans: "If you do not assert your independence now and defeat this measure, it will be too late when the tentacles of this octopus have fastened their fangs on the strong limbs of this fair commonwealth." Standard Oil was prepared for this resistance. It had already bought several state newspapers, which now pressured legislators to support the corporate interests. The legislature buckled and overrode the governor's veto. Standard Oil gained control of Anaconda and the other mining enterprises, and shifted them into a holding company, Amalgamated Copper.[6]

Soon, though, a charismatic mining engineer, Frederick Heinze, reached to grab a cut of the copper-mining profits. Exploiting his camaraderie with local judges, he used the state courts to attack Amalgamated's mining interests. In response, Amalgamated shut all of its Montana businesses except for the newspapers, and threw four-fifths of the state workers into unemployment. The Amalgamated newspapers blamed Heinze whose popularity withered like a rose in a Montana snowstorm. The governor succumbed to pressure and called a special session of the legislature, which accommodated Amalgamated by passing a statute allowing corporations to choose friendly trial court venues. The *Idaho State Tribune* lamented: "It took the Amalgamated Copper Company just 3 weeks to coerce Montana into falling on her knees with promises of anything that big corporation might want."[7]

The corrupt cheated the corrupt, and the legislature was bought and paid for. But Montana citizens fought back. Bypassing the legislature, voters approved an initiative in 1912 that prohibited corporations from spending money in the state on political campaigns.[8] For nearly a century, this law controlled corporate campaign financing in Montana. Citizens had wielded democratic power and successfully checked corporate interests bent on manipulating state institutions for profit. But in 2010, corporations challenged the law as violating the national and Montana constitutions. The state Supreme Court, emphasizing the sordid state history, rejected the challenge. According to the court, the law was narrowly tailored to achieve a compelling purpose, preventing corporate corruption of the Montana democratic process.[9] The corporations, though, did not quit. They expected the pro-business Roberts Court to look favorably on an appeal, and the conservative justices did not disappoint. In *American Tradition Partnership, Inc. v. Bullock*, the conservative bloc deemed the history irrelevant. The democratic desires of the Montana people were beside the point. In a brief one-paragraph opinion, the Court stated "[t]here can be no serious doubt" that the state restriction on corporate campaign spending was unconstitutional. For the first time since 1912, corporations could spend money to influence—or control—political campaigns in Montana.[10]

While this book culminates with the new Roberts Court—with Neil Gorsuch having filled the empty seat previously occupied by

Scalia—the narrative begins before the constitutional framing. During the Revolutionary War and under the Articles of Confederation, in the 1780s, most government power rested with the states, and most state constitutions assumed the people, following civic republicanism, would virtuously pursue the common good. American leaders of this time were political idealists. They conceptualized the citizen-self as predominantly virtuous. Virtue alone, they believed, would sustain the republican state governments.[11]

By 1787, however, the delegates to the Philadelphia (constitutional) convention had been disabused of their idealism. The experiences in the state governments, during the 1780s, had revealed that many, if not most, citizens were more concerned with their own advantages than with a communal or public good. State governments were corrupt, the nation's finances were in tatters, and property was insecure. As the delegates–framers evaluated matters, adherence to utopian ideals had led the United States to the edge of a precipice. If the nation did not change direction, it would likely fall into an abyss, amid the ruins of government decay. By necessity, then, the framers began with a more realistic outlook. They recognized that the citizen-self was driven by passions and interests, which could be controlled by reason and virtue, but only at certain times and under the right conditions. Beginning with this more complex view of human nature—of the citizen-self—the framers attempted to build a constitutional system.[12]

The framers distinguished two spheres: that of civil society and that of government. The people lived simultaneously in both spheres. The government sphere was the realm of public affairs, while civil society was the realm of private affairs, such as commercial intercourse and the accumulation of property. Passions and interests should have free rein in the private sphere, but not in the public realm. The framers thus sought to construct a stable and workable government system that would mediate the conflict between private passions and interests, on the one side, and public goods, on the other. They wanted to protect individual rights, especially rights to property, but they simultaneously wanted to promote the virtuous pursuit of the common good. The crux, then, of the constitutional scheme was pragmatic balance: balance between the public and private spheres—between government power and individual rights. Interestingly, though, the framers barely mentioned free speech and a free press during the constitutional convention. The Bill of Rights, including the First Amendment and its protection of free expression, would be added in 1791, 2 years after the nation began operating under its new Constitution.

The framers' republican democratic constitutional system proved remarkably resilient. The public–private balance would become central to the nineteenth-century notion of a well-ordered society. Yet, conceptions of virtue and the common good evolved through that century, and the system survived vehement political disputes and a Civil War. With regard to free expression, courts accorded speech and writing minimal constitutional protection throughout the republican democratic era. The government could punish any expression that supposedly contravened the common good or, in other words, engendered bad tendencies. In any event, by the early-twentieth century, the United States had changed so substantially that the republican democratic system had begun to crack. For most of the late-eighteenth and nineteenth centuries, the nation had been rural, agrarian, and populated by a relatively homogeneous people. But by the early-twentieth century, the nation had become urban, industrial, and heterogeneous, the burgeoning cities teeming with diverse immigrants. Moreover, consistent with the developments in other western industrialized nations, the United States increasingly stressed a laissez-faire approach to the economic marketplace. Citizens and government officials still talked of regulating for the common good, but the scope of the common good had shrunk to a point where any economic regulation had become constitutionally suspect—a significant change from much of the nineteenth century. Laissez-faire ideology declared that the best government was the least government, whether democratic or otherwise. Few seemed to recognize or care that this emphasis on the private sphere at the expense of the public sphere contravened the framers' pragmatic desire for balance.

During the first half of the twentieth century, democracy confronted a worldwide existential crisis. Most European democracies crumbled, as they experienced 2 world wars, an economic depression and the Holocaust. The collapse of democracy proved disastrous to international capitalism. Democracy and capitalism functioned best together, as a system based on human dignity and liberty. Regardless, American democracy persevered through its troubles, partly because of a deeply rooted democratic culture grounded on a rough and relative material equality. In the crucible of the 1930s, however, the American system dramatically transformed from a republican to a pluralist democracy. Under pluralist democracy, the people and officials were not to focus on the substance of a common good. Instead, the pluralist regime revolved around a democratic process that encouraged more widespread participation and legitimated the political pursuit of self-interest. Furthermore, the New Deal, the first political manifestation of pluralist democracy, repudiated laissez-faire and restored a balance between the public and private spheres. Government regulations of the economic marketplace were no longer immediately suspected. As pluralist democracy emerged, judicial treatments of speech and writing changed, too. Free expression became a constitutional lodestar because the discussion of political views and ideas appeared to be central to the pluralist democratic process.[13]

Like republican democracy before it, though, pluralist democracy evolved. Two major forces shaped its initial post-World War II evolution. First, a developing mass consumer culture intertwined with pluralist democracy to produce a consumers' democracy, entailing a pluralist democratic process that more strongly resembled the capitalist marketplace. Political campaigning for candidates, for instance, now often resembled commercial advertising for products. Unsurprisingly, then, the Supreme Court in the 1970s effectively overturned an earlier ruling and held that the First Amendment protected commercial advertising. The Court reasoned that such speech was central to democracy itself.[14] Second, the nation's Cold-War battle against the Soviet Union pervasively influenced American society. Specifically, the Cold War spurred the strengthening of civil rights and the capitalist economy. The federal government needed to protect civil rights, at least symbolically, to deflect Soviet denunciations of democracy. Meanwhile, the ostentatious exhibition and use of American consumer products contrasted American economic prosperity with Soviet struggles. During the Cold War, the government and the capitalist leaders were bonded together in struggle against the communist enemy. The overriding desire for Cold-War victory tempered any calls for laissez-faire and concomitant attacks on democratic government.

Consequently, the end of the Cold War, in the late-1980s and early-1990s, also profoundly influenced national development. The nation's Cold-War victory generated additional and unanticipated changes in pluralist democracy. In particular, corporate wealth was unleashed from its Cold-War strictures. The government and capitalists were no longer fighting together against a common foe. To the contrary, capitalists now viewed government as its enemy. Demands for laissez faire became common and insistent, as did denigration of democratic government.

The consumers' democracy transformed into Democracy, Inc., a democratic system dominated by wealthy individuals and corporations. The early Roberts Court bolstered Democracy, Inc., in a wide variety of cases, but *Citizens United v. Federal Election Commission* and its progeny, including *American Tradition Partnership*, might best emblematize the conservative justices' proclivities.[15] Based on the First-Amendment protection of free expression, these campaign finance cases prohibit most government restrictions on monetary spending on political campaigns. Corporations and other wealthy entities, including individuals, can now spend astronomical (unlimited) sums of money to influence elections and government officials. The Court seemed to conceive of the citizen-self as homo economicus, an economic self rationally maximizing the satisfaction of its own interests.

Conservatives often assert that originalism is the best (or only) method of legitimate constitutional interpretation. Originalism supposedly requires the justices to uphold either the original public meaning of the Constitution or the framers' intentions.[16] On the early Roberts Court, Scalia and Thomas were avowed originalists, though the other conservatives also used originalist arguments and joined originalist opinions.[17] Indeed, the *Citizens United* majority opinion, written by Kennedy, underscored that its holding corresponded with originalism. Ironically, then, the Roberts Court conservatives betrayed one of the most fundamental principles of the framers' constitutional scheme. The framers were pragmatic realists who rejected utopianism, whether in relation to government or economics. As realists, they understood the complexity of human nature, of the American citizen-self, and drafted a Constitution based on that foundation. They constructed a political-economic system with a balance between the public and private spheres.

The framers wanted virtuous citizens and government officials to pursue the common good in the public sphere, but they had learned that a government relying on virtue alone would fail. Many citizens would pursue their own passions and interests rather than virtue and reason. To be a self-interested striver in the private economic sphere, the framers believed, was legitimate and beneficial. Yet, they feared that the unrestrained pursuit of self-interest in the public sphere would scuttle the American experiment in republican government and market economics. Thus, the framers aimed for a balance between property rights and government power. Unlike the Roberts Court conservatives, they never treated wealth and property rights as sacrosanct. The framers were not market fundamentalists. To the contrary, they understood that the crucial public–private balance ultimately depended on government empowerment to control private interests when they threatened the common good—including when they threatened to twist the government for their own profit.

The conservative justices, therefore, not only misinterpreted the Constitution but also did so in a dangerous manner. Many of the framers chose to attend the constitutional convention precisely because they thought the unrestrained pursuit of private passion and interests had corrupted American government and threatened imminent national decay. The framers worried that the United States could not survive if the private sphere subsumed the public. And in fact, the tragic history of the early-twentieth century in the United States and other countries suggest that the framers were correct. Economic rights and government power must remain in balance. Neither the public nor the private should dominate the other. When laissez faire is ascendant, democratic government suffers. In the end, if either the public or private dominates the other for too long, neither will survive. In the twenty-first century, with massive multinational corporations controlling enormous wealth, the United States government must remain strong and large to maintain the public–private balance. The continuing existence of the American democratic-capitalist system requires no less.[18]

The election of Donald Trump as president is a *symptom* of Democracy, Inc. Most likely, without Democracy, Inc., and the Court's approval of it, Trump would not be president. But the ascendancy of the thin-skinned and authoritarian Trump only increases the vulnerability of our Constitution.[19] The one advantage of Trump's election is that it has shone a light on the weakness of American democratic capitalism. A week before Trump's election, few people recognized the precarious state of American democracy, but mere days after his inauguration, the media suddenly realized that our constitutional system is not bullet proof.[20] Even so, the threat of Trump might easily mislead people. Too many Americans might view Trump like a bad apple. Get rid of that apple, and all is well. In other words, if the nation survives Trump's presidency without a constitutional collapse, then we will likely breathe a sigh of relief and assume our democratic-capitalist system is healthy. But its underlying problems will remain.

The Senate confirmed Neil Gorsuch as the newest Supreme Court justice shortly before this book went to press. With Gorsuch having filled the seat vacated by Scalia's death, the Roberts Court potentially has a new alignment. To be sure, Gorsuch seems likely to continue following in Scalia's footsteps. Like Scalia, Gorsuch claims to be a constitutional originalist. "Ours is the job of interpreting the Constitution," Gorsuch has written. "And that document isn't some inkblot on which litigants may project their hopes and dreams ... but a carefully drafted text judges are charged with applying according to its original public meaning."[21] Indeed, shortly after Scalia's death, Gorsuch celebrated Scalia's "legacy," calling Scalia a "lion of the law." Gorsuch learned from Scalia that judges should strive "to apply the law as it is, focusing backward, not forward, and looking to text, structure, and history to decide what a reasonable reader at the time of the events in question would have understood the law to be—not to decide cases based on their own moral convictions or the policy consequences they believe might serve society best." Gorsuch does not seem concerned with justice, fairness, practical consequences, or a history of subjugation. Rather, he aims for "cold neutrality."[22] In a political science empirical ranking of the justices' political ideologies, Gorsuch ranks to the right of Roberts, Alito, and even Scalia. Quite possibly, Gorsuch will be one of the five most conservative justices from the past century.[23]

Still, change is possible on the Court. A new voice and shifting political circumstances might alter outlook. Ultimately, then, the new Roberts Court must decide: Will it continue bolstering Democracy, Inc., despite the imminent danger to our Constitution, or will it reverse direction and protect our democratic-capitalist system?

This book analyzes the evolution of government–market relations in our constitutional system. How did the nation travel the long distance from the framers' balanced constitutionalism to Democracy, Inc.? More important, why does Democracy, Inc., threaten American democracy and capitalism? And given the danger of Democracy, Inc., why did the early Roberts Court nonetheless endorse it? Finally, how might the new Roberts Court change direction, repudiate Democracy, Inc., and reinvigorate our democratic-capitalist system?

Chapter 2 focuses on the framing and the surrounding political context, including the Revolutionary background. This chapter demonstrates that the constitutional framers sought to create a political-economic system in which the public and private remained relatively balanced. Emphasis is placed on the American understandings of government and the market, including property, at the time of the framing.

This discussion requires an examination of the framers' decision to protect slavery as a legal institution. All of the framers were white men. Almost all were Protestant, and most were wealthy. Many owned slaves. How, then, did the framers' own interests and prejudices influence their conception of the political-economic system?

Chapters 3 through 6 primarily explore historical changes in the American political-economic system. Emphasis is placed on the development of corporations, the evolution of democracy, the influence of the Cold War and its end, and the rise, fall, and rise of laissez-faire ideology. A critical historical point is that during the early-twentieth century, when laissez faire reared its head in the United States and Europe—when the private dominated the public—serious problems arose not only for democratic governments but also for capitalist economies. Chapter 3 focuses on the evolution of republican democracy during the nineteenth and early-twentieth centuries. Chapter 4 explains the emergence of pluralist democracy during the 1930s and the concomitant development of free expression as a constitutional lodestar. Chapter 5 explores the evolution of pluralist democracy after World War II while paying particular attention to the influence of the Cold War. The role of Justice Powell in free-expression developments is highlighted. In the summer of 1971, Powell was still a corporate attorney with a prestigious Virginia law firm. He wrote a memorandum advising the prominent business organization, the U.S. Chamber of Commerce, to strive to increase corporate political power. Less than 6 months later, Powell sat as an associate justice on the Court deciding cases related to corporations and business in general. To what extent did Powell successfully implement his goals for corporate power? Chapter 6 focuses on the end of the Cold War and the rise of Democracy, Inc. This chapter also examines how the early Roberts Court conservatives endorsed Democracy, Inc.

Chapter 7 analyzes the early Roberts Court's betrayal of fundamental constitutional principles and how that betrayal contributes to the current endangerment of the American democratic-capitalist system. The critique in this chapter is threefold. First, the chapter draws on the earlier discussion of the framing to underscore that the Roberts Court's endorsement of Democracy, Inc. , cannot be squared with an originalist approach. Second, the chapter draws on political philosophy and social theory. In particular, numerous theorists reason that a democratic-capitalist system cannot survive if one sphere dominates the other—as is the case in Democracy, Inc. Emphasis is placed on the importance of democratic culture and the problem of income and wealth inequality in the United States. The racialized slant of inequality is underscored, but this section explains why all Americans should worry about increasing inequality regardless of attitudes concerning the racial divide. Third, the chapter concludes by showing how the history of the early-twentieth century pragmatically reinforces the theoretical argument. The first part of the twentieth century illustrates that the implementation of laissez-faire policies can endanger not only democracy but also, counterintuitively, capitalism. And as a practical matter, there are alarming parallels between the early-twentieth and early-twenty-first centuries.

Chapter 8, the conclusion, begins by exploring whether the early-twentieth and early-twenty-first centuries differ in any significant ways. In fact, the most important distinction between the two eras only exacerbates the current danger to the American democratic-capitalist system. In the early-twentieth century, for a variety of reasons, most Americans eventually recognized the enormity of the threat to the nation. In the twenty-first century, at least before the election of 2016, few Americans recognized the serious danger. While an increasing number of Americans realized that growing economic inequality is problematic, too many Americans remained oblivious to the overarching threat to the nation. In fact, recent surveys showed that a remarkable number of Americans distrust democracy and favor a more authoritarian form of government.[24] Given this, the election of Trump did not bode well for our constitutional system. Yet, his early actions in office, such as his travel ban on seven predominantly Muslim countries and his attacks against the judiciary, at least woke some Americans from their slumbers. More people now realize that we need to worry about democracy.

After further elaborating the current dangers to our democratic-capitalist system, Chap. 8 examines the potential remedies. A possible call for a new constitutional convention, with a rewrite of the Constitution, is discussed, but a new convention remains unlikely. At this point in time, if one considers various private and public institutions, the one best positioned to help the nation restore its balance and escape Democracy, Inc. , is the Court itself—not a comforting conclusion, by any measure. Nevertheless, with Gorsuch having filled Scalia's former seat, the new Roberts Court must confront a profound question: Will it abet in the possible demise of the American constitutional system? Or will the conservative majority on the Court act to resuscitate democratic government (thus simultaneously preserving American capitalism)? This chapter argues that the three-pronged critique of the early Roberts Court, articulated in Chap. 7, should serve as a roadmap for the new Court in a repudiation of Democracy, Inc.

Ultimately, then, this book is simultaneously historical and prospective. The framing of the Constitution provides the genesis and initial drive for the narrative. The delegates to the constitutional convention faced a conundrum: How could they maintain republican government while simultaneously protecting property and stabilizing the nation's economy? The framers tried to hammer out a practical solution that could achieve these goals. As the framers saw matters, national survival depended on a relative balance between public and private spheres of activity. But the American constitutional system has not remained static over its more than two centuries of life. Consequently, the book follows the historical development of our system as it eventually evolved into the perilous Democracy, Inc. These interrelated histories—the framing and the subsequent evolution of the constitutional system—are integral to understanding the future. We cannot envision where the new Roberts Court might go without firmly grasping the past. The new Court will need to choose: Will it follow the early Roberts Court in approving and bolstering Democracy, Inc., or will it restore the crucial balance between the public and private spheres in our democratic-capitalist system?

Three caveats are in order at the outset. First, although I discuss the framing at length, I am not an originalist. Contrary to the claims of originalists, historical materials illuminating the founders' intentions and original public meanings cannot provide fixed and objective constitutional meanings that resolve concrete constitutional issues. Even so, such historical or originalist evidence is an important source that can inform constitutional interpretation.[25] Second, given that this book emphasizes the relationship between the government and the economic marketplace, one might be surprised at the attention allocated to the constitutional doctrine of free expression. But the explanation for the extensive forays into First-Amendment law is simple. In the late-twentieth and early-twenty-first centuries, the Supreme Court has interpreted the First-Amendment protection of free expression as encompassing the spending of money, at least in certain contexts. The development of free-expression jurisprudence must therefore be a significant component of any historical exploration of the relations between government and the economy. Third, this book explains constitutional doctrine as developing from a law-politics dynamic. That is, neither pure law nor raw politics determines Supreme Court votes and decisions. Rather, in constitutional cases, whether involving free expression or otherwise, the justices for the most part sincerely interpret the constitutional text and other law, but the justices' respective political horizons always influence how they interpret the law. Consequently, I discuss the reasoning and the doctrines in the justices' opinions—because the law matters—but I also discuss the justices' political orientations—because politics matters.[26]

NOTES

On the Format of the Notes: The source of each quotation is identified in a note. If a series of quotations is from the same source, then one note is placed at the end of the final quotation (or at the next advantageous position). Some additional sources are cited in these quotation footnotes. As a general matter, though, additional sources are cited at advantageous points, whether at the end of a paragraph or otherwise.

1. *Democracy Incorporated* is the title of a book by Sheldon S. Wolin, Sheldon S. Wolin, Democracy Incorporated: Managed Democracy and the Specter of Inverted Totalitarianism (2008), while *Democracy, Inc.* is the title of a book by David S. Allen. David S. Allen, Democracy, Inc.: The Press and Law in the Corporate Rationalization of the Public Sphere (2005).
2. Don Lee, *Trump to Preside Over the Richest Cabinet in U.S. History*, L.A. Times, Jan. 16, 2017; Theda Skocpol and Alexander Hertel-Fenandez, *The Koch Network and Republican Party Extremism*, 14 Perspectives on Politics 681 (2016) (emphasizing that the "Koch network" has intensified "right-tilted partisan polarization and rising economic inequality").
3. Roberto Stefan Foa and Yascha Mounk, *The Danger of Deconsolidation: The Democratic Disconnect*, 27 Journal of Democracy 5 (2016) (emphasizing the current danger to democracy).
4. C.B. Glasscock, The War of the Copper Kings (1935); Michael P. Malone and Richard B. Roeder, Montana: A History of Two Centuries (1976); Kenneth Ross Toole, Montana: An Uncommon Land (1959).
5. Mark Twain, Mark Twain in Eruption 72 (1940); Toole, supra note 4, at 174, 186–194.
6. Toole, supra note 4, at 166; Malone and Roeder, supra note 4, at 170–172.
7. Glasscock, supra note 4, at 288 (quoting *Idaho State Tribune*); Malone and Roeder, supra note 4, at 172–175; Toole, supra note 4, at 208–209.
8. Sect. 1335225, MCA; Malone and Roeder, supra note 4, at 196–197.

9. Western Tradition Partnership, Inc., v. Attorney General of Montana, 363 Mont. 220 (2011), *reversed*, 132 S. Ct. 2490 (2012).

10. 132 S. Ct. 2490, 2491 (2012).

11. As I use the term 'self' in this book, it is defined primarily by its motives, concerns, and capabilities. How does one view oneself in relation to the external world? How much does one care for others? How significant is one's belonging to a community? How much does one dwell on material well-being? How much does one strive for religious salvation? What constitutes religious salvation or a religious life? These are just some of the questions that animate a conception of the self. An individual who focuses on salvation after death might live differently from one who focuses on happiness in this life. For extensive discussions of different conceptions of the self, see Philip Cushman, Constructing the Self, Constructing America (1995); John P. Hewitt, Dilemmas of the American Self (1989); Charles Taylor, Sources of the Self (1989). For a philosophical history of notions of the self, see Louis P. Pojman, Who Are We? (2006).

12. As I explain at the beginning of Chap. 2, I will use the terms 'framer' and 'delegate' interchangeably.

13. For a more extensive discussion of the interrelated histories of free expression and democracy, see Stephen M. Feldman, Free Expression and Democracy in America: A History (2008).

14. Virginia State Bd. of Pharmacy v. Virginia Citizens Consumer Council, 425 U.S. 748, 765 (1976), see Bigelow v. Virginia, 421 U.S. 809, 819–820 (1975) (distinguishing *Valentine v. Chrestensen*, 316 U.S. 52 (1942)).

15. 558 U.S. 310 (2010); McCutcheon v. FEC, 134 S.Ct. 1434 (2014).

16. Randy E. Barnett, *An Originalism for Nonoriginalists*, 45 Loyola Law Review 611 (1999); John O. McGinnis and Michael B. Rappaport, *Original Interpretive Principles as the Core of Originalism*, 24 Constitutional Commentary 371 (2007). Focusing on the original public meaning is referred to as 'new originalism,' while focusing on framers' intentions is 'old originalism.' Stephen M. Feldman, *Constitutional Interpretation and History: New Originalism or Eclecticism?* 28 Brigham Young University Journal of Public Law 283 (2014). In many cases, though, including *Citizens United*, the justices do not clearly identify which form of originalism is being followed.

17. District of Columbia v. Heller, 554 U.S. 570, 576–626 (2008); Antonin Scalia, A Matter of Interpretation 38 (1997). Alito "has described himself as a 'practical originalist.'" Neil S. Siegel, *The Distinctive Role of Justice Samuel Alito: From A Politics of Restoration to A Politics of Dissent*, 126 The Yale Law Journal Forum 164, 166 (2016).

18. For another argument linking the Roberts Court to the current endangerment of the constitutional system, see Stephen E. Gottlieb, Unfit for Democracy: The Roberts Court and the Breakdown of American Politics (2016).

19. Numerous articles discuss and conjecture about Trump's psychological state. Richard A. Friedman, *Is It Time to Call Trump Mentally Ill?* NY Times, Feb. 17, 2017; Susan Milligan, *Temperament Tantrum*, U.S. New & World Report, Jan. 27, 2017; Ruth Ben-Ghiat, *Trump Is Following Authoritarian Playbook*, CNN, Jan. 17, 2017; Richard Green, *Is Donald Trump Mentally Ill? 3 Professors Of Psychiatry Ask President Obama To Conduct 'A Full Medical And Neuropsychiatric Evaluation,'* Huffington Post, Dec. 17, 2016; Jason Stanley, *Beyond Lying: Donald Trump's Authoritarian Reality*, NY Times, Nov. 4, 2016; James Hamblin, *Donald Trump: Sociopath?* The Atlantic, July 20, 2016.

20. David Frum, *How to Build an Autocracy*, The Atlantic, March 2017; Tom Ashcroft, *Guarding Against Authoritarianism*, NPR On Point, Jan. 31, 2017; Daron Acemoglu, *We Are the Last Defense Against Trump*, Foreign Policy, Jan. 18, 2017.

21. Cordova v. City of Albuquerque, 816 F.3d 645, 661 (10th Cir. 2016) (Gorsuch, Circuit Judge, concurring in the judgment).

22. Neil Gorsuch, *Of Lions and Bears, Judges and Legislators, and the Legacy of Justice Scalia*, 66 Case Western Reserve Law Review 905, 905–906, 920 (2016).

23. Lee Epstein, Andrew D. Martin, and Kevin Quinn, *President-Elect Trump and his Possible Justices* (Dec. 15, 2016). For rankings of prior Supreme Court justices based on political ideology, see Lee Epstein et al., The Behavior of Federal Judges 106–116 (2013), which includes comparisons with the Martin-Quinn scores (accounting for changes over time) http://mqscores.wustl.edu/index.php, and the Segal-Cover scores (quantifying Court nominees' perceived political ideologies at the time of appointment) http://www.sunysb.edu/polsci/jsegal/qualtable.pdf (data drawn from Jeffrey Segal and Albert Cover, *Ideological Values and the Votes of Supreme Court Justices*, 83 The American Political Science Review 557–565 (1989); updated in Lee Epstein and Jeffrey A. Segal, Advice and Consent: The Politics of Judicial Appointments (2005)).

24. Foa and Mounk, supra note 3, at 8–13.

25. Stephen M. Feldman, *Constitutional Interpretation and History: New Originalism or Eclecticism?* 28 Brigham Young University Journal of Public Law. 283 (2014). Lawrence Solum refers approvingly to "the fixation thesis" as a key originalist point. Lawrence B. Solum, *We Are All Originalists Now, in* Constitutional Originalism: A Debate 1, 4 (2011); *e.g.*, Randy E. Barnett, *Interpretation and Construction*, 34 Harvard

Journal of Law and Public Policy 65, 66 (2011); Keith E. Whittington, *The New Originalism*, 2 Georgetown Journal of Law & Public Policy 599, 611 (2004). For a more complex conceptualization of originalism, see Jack M. Balkin, Living Originalism (2011).

26. Stephen M. Feldman, *Supreme Court Alchemy: Turning Law and Politics Into Mayonnaise*, 12 Georgetown Journal of Law & Public Policy 57 (2014); Stephen M. Feldman, *The Rule of Law or the Rule of Politics? Harmonizing the Internal and External Views of Supreme Court Decision Making*, 30 Law & Social Inquiry 89 (2005).

PART I

The Foundation for a Balanced Structure

The Constitutional Framing: Republican Democracy, Private Property, and Free Expression

In 1785 and 1786, Massachusetts fell into economic depression. When the state government responded with fiscal restraint, many landowning farmers, particularly in the central and western portions of the state, fell behind on loan and tax payments and faced possible foreclosures. Town meetings produced demands for legislative action to protect the vulnerable landowners. The government instead pressed the debtors to fulfill their obligations, with imprisonment the penalty for non-payment. In desperation, groups of farmers formed armed vigilante bands. One of the leaders was Daniel Shays, a former Revolutionary War militia captain. No pauper, Shays owned a farm of more than 100 acres, yet he already had been dragged into court twice for small unpaid debts. Shays and the other armed insurrectionists, numbering somewhere between 2000 to 3000 men, forcefully closed local county courts, terrorized sheriffs, and even threatened an armory at Springfield, the main federal arsenal for all of New England.[1]

The Continental Congress asked Henry Knox to investigate in the fall of 1786. The corpulent Knox, a wartime confidant of George Washington and also a major landowner in Massachusetts, responded with a report wildly exaggerating the danger. In a letter to Washington, who had gladly retired in 1783 to his Mount Vernon estate in Virginia, Knox claimed the Shaysites were "determined to annihilate all debts public and private." By Knox's estimate, "12 or 15,000 desperate and unprincipled men" were on the verge of "a formidable rebellion against reason, the principles of all government, and against the very name of liberty."[2] Knox's inflammatory

© The Author(s) 2017
S.M. Feldman, *The New Roberts Court, Donald Trump, and Our Failing Constitution*, DOI 10.1007/978-3-319-56451-7_2

report frightened Congress and other political leaders. Washington reacted with suitable concern but refused to intercede directly in the conflict. In fact, Congress lacked the necessary funds for supplying federal troops that might have intervened. The Massachusetts governor nonetheless raised money from private donors and formed a state militia of 4400 men. In late-January and early-February 1787, a time of bitter cold and violent snowstorms, the militia routed Shays and his forces in and around Springfield, leaving at least four insurgents dead. Shays and several of his cohorts were caught, tried, and sentenced to hang for treason. Political sympathies intruded into debates over leniency. In the end, some Shaysites were executed, though Shays himself and others were pardoned. Shays's Rebellion appeared to be finished.[3]

The rebellion, however, continued by other means. In a republic, supporters of the Shaysites could exercise their strength in a more peaceful manner, through the vote. Soon they had elected enough new legislators that the Massachusetts assembly enacted many of the desired reforms and protections. In fact, the electoral aftermath of Shays's Rebellion seemed to disturb many national political leaders even more than the threat of armed insurgency. John Jay wrote to Washington: "Private rage for property suppresses public considerations, and personal rather than national interests have become the great objects of attention. Representative bodies will ever be faithful copies of their originals, and generally exhibit a checkered assemblage of virtue and vice, of abilities and weakness."[4] Washington replied pessimistically, lamenting that he and other Revolutionary leaders "probably had too good an opinion of human nature in forming our confederation.... Perfection falls not to the share of mortals." Washington worried most about the implications of the Massachusetts developments for the future of republican government. "What a triumph for the advocates of despotism to find, that we are incapable of governing ourselves, and that systems founded on the basis of equal liberty are merely ideal and fallacious!"[5]

The alarm and insecurity expressed by Jay and Washington typified the attitudes of the delegates who arrived in Philadelphia in 1787 for what became the constitutional convention. While Massachusetts had struggled through the most violent unrest, other states also had dealt with political conflicts revolving around debt, property, and control of government. As James Madison wrote, "The late turbulent scenes in

Massachusetts and infamous ones in Rhode Island [involving the state printing of paper money], have done inexpressible injury to the republican character."[6] The convention was, in other words, a political reaction to a perceived political crisis. During the Revolutionary years, American leaders had believed in the righteousness of civic republican government. They had been political idealists, conceptualizing the citizen-self—at least the American citizen-self—as predominantly virtuous. Virtue alone, the Revolutionaries had assumed, would sustain the republican state governments.[7] But when the delegates came to the constitutional convention, a decade of experience, climaxing with Shays's Rebellion, had deflated their idealism. The United States was not a utopia. From their perspective, many state governments were corrupt, the nation had plunged into dire economic straits, and private property was insecure. If the republic was to survive, the delegates believed, they would need to construct new institutions that would maintain republican government while also bolstering private property and the national economy. Complicating the problem, the delegates represented their respective states, many of which had diverse and conflicting interests. The delegates would need to be politically astute and realistic if they were to achieve their goal: no less than saving the nation.[8]

Fifty-five delegates participated in the convention, but only 39 would sign the proposed Constitution. Several delegates left early because they did not like the general direction of the convention: the drafting of a new Constitution rather than the amending of the Articles of Confederation. Of the delegates who contributed extensively to the discussions, only Edmund Randolph and George Mason of Virginia and Elbridge Gerry of Massachusetts refused to sign.[9] Thus, throughout this book, I will for the most part use the terms 'framer' and 'delegate' interchangeably to refer to those at the convention because, with the exceptions just noted, the most important delegates were the ones who signed on as framers. Of course, when a particular delegate expresses a unique viewpoint, not widely shared among the others, I will specify the speaker. Quotations and other primary source materials are drawn predominantly from Madison's convention notes and *The Federalist*, essays written by Madison, Alexander Hamilton, and Jay in support of ratification. Finally, one should recognize the homogeneity of the delegates: They were all white Protestant men, except for two Roman Catholics, and most were relatively wealthy.[10]

THE REVOLUTIONARY BACKGROUND

Civic republican ideology, Lockean philosophy, and Protestant theology influenced Americans during the Revolution as well as a decade later, during the framing and ratification of the Constitution. In the 1760s and 1770s, as Americans grew unhappy with English rule, they found sustenance and justification in the civic republican writings of the British Country (or Opposition) theorists, such as John Trenchard and Thomas Gordon, the authors of the renowned early-eighteenth-century *Cato's Letters*. Although Americans certainly knew other writers from the civic humanist (republican) tradition, Revolutionary-era newspapers repeatedly reprinted *Cato's Letters*. From the civic republican perspective, citizens and government officials were to be virtuous. Civic virtue required individuals to pursue the common good rather than private or partial interests. If citizens or officials sought instead to satisfy their own (private or partial) interests through government institutions, then government was corrupt. And, indeed, the British government during these decades was rife with corruption—at least from the perspective of many Americans. When the moment arrived to declare independence, however, Thomas Jefferson and the American political leaders drew inspiration from John Locke's writings legitimating resistance to unjust rulers. As filtered through the Enlightenment philosophy of Locke, civic virtue appeared to demand that the Americans rebel against British tyranny and corruption of republican government.[11]

From the American perspective, in other words, the Revolution was not the product of avarice or economic desperation. Compared to the rest of the western (European) world, the Americans—at least, white Protestant American men—were freer and less constrained by feudal hierarchies. They were not an economically oppressed people. Property ownership was far more widespread than in Europe.[12] Therefore, the Declaration of Independence was, first and foremost, a rational justification for rebellion. It began by proclaiming "self-evident" truths, derived from Lockean philosophy, "that all men are created equal, that they are endowed by their Creator with certain unalienable Rights, that among these are Life, Liberty and the pursuit of Happiness."[13] After articulating these fundamental natural rights, the Americans delineated an exhaustive list of corrupt actions perpetrated by the British government. From the outset, then, America arose as "the empire of reason," as Joel Barlow would soon phrase it.[14]

Of course, while Jefferson and other leaders might have been intimately familiar with the writings of Locke and other Enlightenment philosophers, most Americans were not so well educated. To be sure, some read the newspapers and pamphlets spreading civic republican ideology, but perhaps, equally important, Protestantism united and motivated many ordinary Americans. Approximately 90% of the populace had religious roots in Calvinist Protestantism.[15] Clergy generated revolutionary fervor by invoking millennial themes: "Was it possible that this was 'the Time, in which Christ's Kingdom is to be thus gloriously set up in the World?'" By successfully rebelling, Americans could prove that God had chosen the United States to be a "model of the glorious kingdom of Christ on earth."[16] And clergy were not the only ones appealing to religion. The political leader, Samuel Adams, declared that the nation could be a "Christian Sparta."[17] As the historian Gordon Wood has aptly phrased it, "[r]evolution, republicanism, and regeneration all blended in American thinking."[18]

The early state constitutions, many of which were adopted during the Revolution, strongly reflected the commitment to civic republican ideals. These constitutions presumed that the people were virtuous and emphasized that government must be for the common good rather than for partial or private interests. The Massachusetts constitution declared: "Government is instituted for the common good, for the protection, safety, prosperity of the people, and not for the profit, honor, or private interest of any one man, family, or class of men." Other state constitutions would echo these sentiments, often with only stylistic variations. For instance, the 1784 New Hampshire constitution stated that the government was "being instituted for the common benefit, protection, and security of the whole community, and not for the private interest or emolument of any one man, family or class of men."[19] Elected officials were, of course, to be virtuous: "disinterested men, who could have no interest of their own to seek."[20] The 1776 Virginia Bill of Rights emphasized that "virtue" was crucial to the preservation of "free government" and "the blessings of liberty." In fact, because of the presumed virtue of the citizens, the state constitutions tended to concentrate power in the legislatures, which would most closely represent the will of the sovereign people. Thus, in typical fashion, the Maryland constitution declared that "the right in the people to participate in the Legislature, is the best security of liberty, and the foundation of all free government."[21] Moreover, of great significance, the Articles of Confederation displayed a strong distrust of any centralized government—which would resonate too closely with the British monarchy—and therefore left most government power with the states, as the paragons of virtuous republicanism. Indeed, one can reasonably describe the Articles as little more than "a peace treaty among thirteen separate and sovereign states."[22]

Lockean philosophy also influenced the early state constitutions, most evidently in the universal declarations that the sovereign people were the source of state power. Locke had reasoned that, in a state of nature, each individual enjoys "perfect freedom," an "uncontrollable liberty to dispose of his person or possessions." Because life in a state of nature entails fear and uncertainty, however, people voluntarily agree to a social contract. They consent to join civil society for the "mutual preservation of their lives, liberties, and estates." Subsequently, the people likely would consent, by majority vote, to form a government for the same reasons, to protect their natural rights to life, liberty, and property.[23] The 1776 North Carolina constitution similarly invoked the sovereignty of the people. "[A]ll political power," it explained, "is vested in and derived from the people only." Likewise, the Massachusetts constitution proclaimed that "[a]ll power residing originally in the people, and being derived from them, the several magistrates and officers of government ... are the substitutes and agents, and are at all times accountable to them."[24] This ultimate reliance on the reason and power of the individual—the people—typified Enlightenment thought. God no longer appeared to bestow government power on a monarch or other divine representative who then ruled a subordinate people. Instead, government depended upon the consent of the governed. Citizens were the source of sovereign power, and together they pursued the good of the entire political community.[25]

Meanwhile, these early state constitutions bolstered Protestant practices and beliefs in multiple ways. Most state constitutions protected freedom of conscience (or the free exercise of religion), which was understood to be a distinctly Protestant doctrine. During the Reformation, Jean Calvin emphasized conscience as an irresistible conviction, an inner awareness of one's own inescapable depravity in relation to the greatness of the truth of Jesus Christ. Freedom of conscience, then, meant a freedom to follow the dictates of one's conscience to Jesus but did not, in any sense, connote an individual freedom to choose among different religions. Governmental and religious institutions–the state and the church—were not to coerce faith because genuine spiritual faith could not be compelled. Each individual was to remain free so that his or her conscience could inwardly experience Christ and Christian faith. The 1776 Virginia Bill of Rights illustrated the constitutional protection of this Protestant doctrine. "That religion, or the duty which we owe to our Creator, and the manner of discharging it, can be directed only by reason and conviction, not by force or violence; and therefore all men are equally entitled to the free exercise of religion, according to the dictates of conscience; and that it is the mutual duty of all to practise Christian forbearance, love, and charity towards each other."[26]

Given this understanding of freedom of conscience, numerous states also expressly maintained Protestant (or more generally Christian) establishments. The government support or establishment of a church seemed consistent with freedom of conscience (free exercise) because, in the American context, both establishment and freedom of conscience harmonized with or bolstered Protestantism. And regardless of the existence (or non-existence) of official establishments, America was de facto Protestant. Most Americans, whether they attended church or not, viewed the nation as being an inherently Protestant dominion.[27] Unsurprisingly, then, state constitutions and statutes often burdened non-Christians with civil disabilities, such as prohibitions on voting and public office holding. Even in Pennsylvania, which long had no official establishment, the state constitution demanded that state legislators swear to an oath that would exclude many non-Christians, including Jews, Muslims, and atheists.[28]

The three strands of thought that shaped the Revolution and early state constitutions would continue to exert influence during the framing and ratification years. Civic republican ideology (from the civic humanist tradition), Lockean philosophy (from the Enlightenment movement), and Protestant theology all remained important, though the relative importance of Lockean theory would increase.

EXPERIENCE DEFEATS IDEALISM

American state governments of the 1780s were built on two interrelated premises. First, Americans believed themselves to be especially virtuous, fully committed to liberty, equality, and republican government. They were, in other words, an exceptional people. Second, if the people were virtuous, and the state legislatures represented the people, then government should inevitably pursue the common good. The early state constitutions embodied this republican enthusiasm.

The experiences of the 1780s, however, had led many political elites—men like James Wilson, Alexander Hamilton, and James Madison—to question these premises. From their perspective, demagogues had won far too many state elections. And all too often, democratic majorities and their officials had used government power to satisfy their own interests, thus contravening the common good and frequently threatening the property rights of others. That was the lesson of Shays's Rebellion and its electoral aftermath, as indebted landowners sought government refuge for money owed.[29]

To be clear, state government corruption appeared to threaten both republican government, on the one hand, and liberty and property rights, on the other. When individuals and factions pursued their own interests rather than the common good, then property could be taken arbitrarily. Debtor relief laws, such as those at stake in the Shays dispute, appeared to victimize creditors. Moreover, the state and national governments still carried heavy debts from the Revolutionary War. As the ineffective governments could not meet those debts, public securities lost value and public credit vanished. In short, property and other forms of wealth were no longer secure. Without wise or virtuous government support and protection, the economy would fail alongside the government. From the framers' viewpoint, history proved that every society eventually decayed. If the delegates to the constitutional convention failed to restructure American government, then the United States would prematurely die—or at least, the delegates feared as much. Early at the constitutional convention, Edmund Randolph emphasized "the difficulty of the crisis, and the necessity of preventing the fulfillment of the prophecies of the American downfall."[30] The nation had reached a crucial juncture.[31]

In April 1787, a month before the constitutional convention would begin in Philadelphia, Madison wrote a memorandum, *Vices of the Political System of the United States*, which explained, point-by-point, the problems that had arisen under the Articles of Confederation, with its weak national government and relatively strong state governments. Over and over again, Madison emphasized what had been "found by experience" or "proved" by "fact and experience" in the operation of the state governments—experiences that he contrasted with the utopian ideals of "Republican Theory." The drafters of the Articles, because of their "inexperience," reliance on civic republican ideals, and "enthusiastic virtue," had mistakenly believed in the "good faith [and] honor" of state legislatures. But through the 1780s, state legislatures had produced "vicious legislation" and "injustice." Too many citizens and elected state officials had pursued "base and selfish measures," even though they often "masked [such measures] by pretexts of public good." Madison, for instance, specifically criticized Rhode Island for printing paper money without considering the ramifications for the nation and the common good.[32]

Madison also largely composed the so-called Virginia Plan, which would provide the initial framework for further discussions at the constitutional convention. When Randolph, a more polished speaker than Madison, introduced the Plan at the outset of the convention, he emphasized the events of the 1780s, particularly how the state constitutions had not adequately protected against the democratic excesses of insufficiently virtuous citizens.[33] Then, throughout the rest of the convention, the delegates repeatedly referred to their experiences in the 1780s. John Dickinson went so far as to proclaim that "[e]xperience must be our only guide," while Elbridge Gerry admitted that "experience" had demonstrated that he had "been too republican heretofore."[34] In other words, the delegates were especially wary, as Dickinson put it, of "those multitudes without property and without principle" who might threaten property rights through the democratic process. To be sure, Benjamin Franklin and Gouverneur Morris recognized that the wealthy as well as the poor could form factions bent on government corruption. "[T]he possession of property increased the desire of more property," Franklin said. "Some of the greatest rogues he was ever acquainted with, were the richest rogues."[35] But the unequivocal weight of the delegates' sentiment was that the poor were the more likely threat.[36]

In sum, the events of the early- to mid-1780s played a crucial role in the constitutional framing. Political leaders, including future delegates to the constitutional convention, were disabused of their idealism. The people were not so uniformly virtuous that they would not seek to use government for their own advantages. At the convention, Hamilton emphasized that utopian conceptions of human nature, depicting people as pristinely virtuous, were dangerous. "We must take man as we find him," Hamilton said. "A reliance on pure patriotism had been the source of many of our errors."[37] Hamilton, Madison, and the other framers had become hardheaded realists, pragmatic about politics. As such, they realized that the constitutional system needed to protect against likely efforts to use the government for corrupt purposes.[38] But while the framers were no longer utopian idealists, they had not become cynics. They did not repudiate the goal of republican government. Madison explained that if the goal of principled government for the common good was jettisoned, if the people and their elected officials could not act virtuously, then "nothing less than the chains of despotism" would be possible.[39]

Consequently, the framers began with a more realistic depiction of human nature—of the citizen-self—and then attempted to build a republican government based on that foundation.

THE NATURE OF THE CITIZEN-SELF

From the perspective of the delegates who gathered in convention in Philadelphia in 1787, the people had demonstrated that they were not as exceptionally virtuous as they had seemed in 1776. Yet, the delegates, in general, did not believe that humanity was completely wicked or selfish. Both Madison and Hamilton, for instance, followed the Scottish philosopher David Hume in characterizing people as partly good and partly bad. Men were not "angels," as Madison phrased it, but neither were they beasts.[40] "As there is a degree of depravity in mankind which requires a certain degree of circumspection and distrust," Madison explained, "so there are other qualities in human nature which justify a certain portion of esteem and confidence."[41] The framers, thus, did not follow any reductionist or utopian model of human nature and behavior. They not only perceived human nature to be richly complex, but also recognized the variability of human reactions in different contexts. In particular, the framers believed that men are more likely to reveal their baser sides when acting in concert rather than alone. A type of mob mentality would frequently emerge: "Regard to reputation has a less active influence," observed Hamilton, "when the infamy of a bad action is to be divided among a number than when it is to fall singly upon one."[42] To be sure, this mob-like tendency rendered republican government more problematic because such government requires group decision making within a political community. Nonetheless, the delegates believed that the American people possessed sufficient virtue to sustain republican government. Despite the problems that had arisen in the states during the 1780s, Madison declared those state-level experiments in republicanism to be partial successes. And those successes could be attributed only to "the virtue and intelligence of the people of America."[43] Indeed, the framers understood that their attempt to construct a republican government at the national level "presupposes the existence" of men's virtue.[44]

The framers attended closely to the motivations of the American citizen-self. From the framers' perspective, a motive resembled a Newtonian force, insofar as it would produce physical action. Thus, although Madison admitted that, to a degree, "the faculties of the mind" remained obscure, the framers repeatedly suggested that three overarching motives drove Americans: passion, interest, and reason.[45] In *Federalist, Number 10*, for instance, Madison explicitly discussed the importance of "passions," "interests," and "opinions" as human motivations, with opinions arising from one's reason. To be sure, while the framers frequently distinguished among these three motives, they did not define them precisely. Moreover, they were not rigorously consistent, as they used the terms in varying senses.[46] Regardless, the framers' general notions of passion, interest, and reason can be gleaned from the historical materials, particularly the convention notes and *The Federalist*. By passion, the framers usually referred to emotions such as ambition, hate, and joy. Hamilton did not mince words when, discussing human motives, he reminds the reader not "to forget that men are ambitious, vindictive, and rapacious."[47] By interest, the framers typically referred to a general and often calm desire for one's own happiness.[48] Interest entails "self-love,"[49] while also denoting "an element of reflection and calculation."[50] Unquestionably, the framers believed that the most common, "durable," and divisive form of interest is economic. "Those who hold and those who are without property," Madison wrote, "have ever formed distinct interests in society." Moreover, the occurrence of diverse economic interests is inevitable. "The diversity in the faculties of men, from which the rights of property originate, is ... an insuperable obstacle to a uniformity of interests. ... From the protection of different and unequal faculties of acquiring property, the possession of different degrees and kinds of property immediately results; and from the influence of these on the sentiments and views of the respective proprietors, ensues a division of the society into different interests and parties."[51]

Reason, as used by the framers, entails a combination of experience (empiricism) and logic (rationalism). Like Enlightenment philosophers, such as Locke, Hume, and Montesquieu, the framers drew extensively from experience—from political history, near and distant. Thus, they not only criticized state governments of the 1780s because of the concrete failings of those experiments in civic republicanism, but they also contemplated earlier republics, including Greece and Rome.[52] Simultaneously, also like Enlightenment philosophers, the framers logically analyzed the successes and failures of those prior republican governments. Looking to the future, the framers firmly believed that reason should control over passion and interest in government affairs. As Madison maintained, "it is the reason, alone, of the public, that ought to control and regulate the government."[53] When citizens and elected officials exercise reason, when they deliberate rationally together, then the government is likely to identify and pursue the common good. But when, instead, passions and interests predominate, then factions form. And a government that acts to appease a faction's passions or to satisfy its interests is corrupt.

For the framers, then, reason was the essence of the citizen-self. Reason was the source of human control over the external world as well as over oneself.[54] Reason was why individuals in a Lockean state of nature would agree to a social contract.[55] Reason was why "We the People" could presume "to form a more perfect Union [to] promote the general Welfare."[56] Reason was why Americans could overcome passion and interest so as to pursue the common good.[57] But, unfortunately, reason sometimes proved weak or "fallible."[58] Experience had shown that, all too often, passion and interest overpower reason, rather than vice versa. As Hamilton lamented, "Has it not ... invariably been found that momentary passions, and immediate interest, have a more active and imperious control over human conduct than general or remote considerations of policy, utility or justice?"[59] Madison agreed. If all Americans had been philosophers (or good philosophers), he stated, then they would have naturally and flawlessly followed reason along the virtuous path to the common good. "But a nation of philosophers," Madison concluded ruefully, "is as little to be expected as the philosophical race of kings wished for by Plato."[60]

Here was the crux of the problem, from the framers' perspective. Too many citizens followed their passions and interests rather than reason. Factions had frequently seized state governments, pursued their own interests (especially economic interests), and thus tyrannized the people. Proclamations of the common good had become pretexts for corruption. While Revolutionary-era Americans had accepted civic republican ideology—believing optimistically that reason and virtue would consistently overcome passion and interest—the framers had grown more pessimistic. Civic republican government, though arising from the sovereign people, could trample on individual rights and liberties as destructively as a monarchy could do. Given these realizations—"the evidence of known facts," as Madison phrased it—the framers shifted their political theory in a Lockean direction.[61]

Locke had maintained that individuals rationally leave a state of nature for civil society, and from there, create a government because they seek to secure their natural rights to life, liberty, and property. To be sure, then, like Locke, and like the Revolutionary-era Americans before them, the framers emphasized that government rested on the sovereignty of the people. But crucially, the state government problems of the 1780s had led the framers to appreciate more fully two additional and interrelated components of Lockean philosophy.[62] First, the framers recognized the benefit of conceptually distinguishing two separate spheres or realms: that of civil society and that of government. The people lived simultaneously in both spheres. If the government sphere was the realm of public affairs, then civil society was the realm of private affairs, such as commercial intercourse and the accumulation of wealth. The framers repeatedly distinguished between the public and the private. Neither sphere could be ignored when framing the Constitution. During the Revolutionary era, attention had been focused on the public sphere. Individuals were contemplated as citizens, first and foremost. And as citizens, they were to display virtue by disregarding private concerns and pursuing the common good. Now, the framers understood that such slighting of private concerns was unrealistic. In writing a Constitution, the framers needed to acknowledge the human motivations that originated and operated primarily in the private sphere. As the 1780s had revealed, if people enjoyed liberty, then they would revel in their passions and interests. The strongest and most enduring interest was economic (property and wealth).[63]

Second, Lockean philosophy suggested to the framers that they needed to devote greater attention to protecting individual rights from government—even republican government. Before the Revolution, Americans understood the need to protect individual rights from the British monarchy. With the repudiation of the monarchy, however, the protection of rights from the government seemed less urgent. After all, in the American (state) republics, the people were the source of government, and the government represented the people. Could the people threaten their own rights? Surprisingly, the experiences of the 1780s had answered that question affirmatively. Thus, now, the framers unequivocally declared that Lockean rights, particularly to liberty and property, must be strongly protected. Even though liberty and property caused factionalism—Madison metaphorically explained that "[l]iberty is to faction what air is to fire"—protecting such individual rights should be, said Madison, "the first object of government." Why create a republican government if it requires the suppression of individual rights and liberties, the framers asked rhetorically.[64]

Still, despite absorbing these Lockean lessons, the framers did not relinquish their civic republican principles. Instead, they imaginatively fused Lockean and republican themes. For this reason, the framers can be said to have occupied a "Machiavellian moment," to use J.G.A. Pocock's famous phrase. They straddled two paradigmatic visions of human nature and government: the civic humanist (civic republican) and the modern (or Enlightenment).[65] Locke had traveled far along the modernist path, and yet like the framers, he retained vestiges of republican convictions or principles. For instance, Locke repeatedly stated that government should pursue the "public good" or the "common good."[66] More so than Locke, though, the framers fought against the modernist tide. To be sure, they recognized the modernist impulses to pursue profit in the commercial or private world and to pursue one's own passions and interests in the public world. They understood that factions would inevitably form and seek to control government. But the framers nonetheless struggled to preserve civic republican principles in government. Like prior civic humanists, the framers still believed that virtue and reason could overcome passion and interest in public affairs.[67]

Ultimately, based on the knowledge accumulated from their experiences, Madison and the other framers sought to construct a republican democratic constitutional system that would provide sufficient protection for property and other individual rights. Simultaneously, though, they still sought to encourage government in pursuit of the common good. Thus, if the constitutional framers had an overarching goal, it was to achieve balance: balance between, on the one hand, government power and, on the other hand, individual rights, especially as related to property and wealth. The key to maintaining such a balance lays in the conceptual separation of the two spheres: that of civil society or the private sphere, and that of government or the public sphere.[68]

REPUBLICAN DEMOCRATIC GOVERNMENT
AND THE PUBLIC SPHERE

The framers conceived of American government as republican democratic.[69] Citizens and elected officials were supposed to be virtuous. In the political realm, they were to pursue the common good or public welfare rather than their own partial or private interests.[70] The Preamble of the Constitution memorialized the government goal of the common good: "We the People" were to "promote the General Welfare." When citizens or officials used government institutions to pursue their own interests, then the government was corrupt. Groups of like-minded citizens who corrupted the government were deemed factions, whether constituted by a majority or a minority of citizens. In *Federalist, Number 10*, James Madison described a faction as "a number of citizens, whether amounting to a majority or a minority of the whole, who are united and actuated by some common impulse of passion, or of interest, adverse to the rights of other citizens, or to the permanent and aggregate interests of the community."[71] But how could a democratic majority constitute a faction? It was possible only because the framers understood the common good to be objective or, in other words, "out there."[72] From the framers' standpoint, the people's "true interests" determined the common good, whether or not the people recognized those interests.[73] Thus, the common good could not be calculated merely by adding together the private interests of the majority of citizens. In a letter to James Monroe, Madison explained that, when a government establishes "the interest of the majority [as] the political standard of right and wrong. ... it is only re-establishing, under another name and a more specious form, force as the measure of right."[74] By definition, then, a government pursuing "partial interests" or "private passions" rather than the common good was corrupt.[75]

The crucial question for the framers, then, was how to structure the Constitution and government institutions to engender government for the common good. To a great degree, the framers found their answer in their conception of the citizen-self. As Alexander Hamilton explained at the constitutional convention: "The science of policy is the knowledge of human nature."[76] The individual citizen-self—the framers' self, so to speak—could reason and act virtuously. Virtue was not inherited through bloodlines; there would be no hereditary aristocracy in America. Instead, virtue could be cultivated and learned. Yet, the framers had concluded, from experience, that in many if not most circumstances, the average person acts in accordance with passion and interest. The framers, moreover, were not only pragmatic realists—in their view of human nature—but they were also unapologetic elitists. Specifically, the framers believed in the existence of a *virtuous* elite—including themselves—who would pursue the common good in the public sphere even while pursuing their own interests in the private sphere. Unsurprisingly, given that most of them were reasonably wealthy, many framers believed the virtuous elite would arise mostly from among the richest men.[77] Alexander Hamilton perceived that many people were disinclined to become involved in public affairs in the first place. Indeed, from the framers' standpoint, they had good reason to be skeptical of the knowledge and education of the average American regarding national political affairs. The typical American newspaper in 1787 was only four pages long, with more than half of that devoted to classified advertising. Because of the limited communication and transportation technologies, the papers printed little national news, and what national news the papers contained was necessarily dated. The average American largely lacked access to extensive information about national politics and issues.[78]

Regardless, the framers insisted that virtue and reason should and could overcome passion and interest in public affairs. Government should and could be conducted in accord with civic republican principles. Given their elitist attitudes, the framers hoped that voters would elect "speculative men" to be the "guardians" for "the mass of the citizens."[79] But the framers did not leave the functioning of the government to mere hope. Rather, they attempted to structure the constitutional system to produce a government most likely to pursue the common good. "The aim of every political constitution is, or ought to be," Madison declared, "first to obtain for rulers men who possess most wisdom to discern, and most virtue to pursue, the common good of the society; and in the next place, to take the most effectual precautions for keeping them virtuous whilst they continue to hold their public trust."[80] Yet, how could the framers insure pursuit of the common good when they refused to limit the primary cause of factionalism, the liberty to pursue one's own passions and interests? The answer, the framers believed, was to structure the government institutions to control the "effects" of factionalism.[81] The constitutional controls over factionalism would operate at three levels.

At the first level, the framers designed the Constitution to promote the election of a virtuous elite as government officials, who would then voluntarily pursue the common good. Consequently, Madison championed a large over a small republic—the nation over the state. In a large republic (the nation), the electorate supposedly would be difficult to fool or trick into electing a self-interested demagogue. As Madison explained, "it will be more difficult for unworthy candidates to practice with success the vicious arts by which elections are too often carried." From this perspective, representative government was better than direct democracy because "the public voice, pronounced by the representatives of the people, will be more consonant to the public good than if pronounced by the people themselves."[82]

Yet, the framers knew that, even in a large republic, sometimes the people would mistakenly elect an official lacking in virtue. Furthermore, even the virtuous would occasionally be tempted by passion or interest to ignore the common good. Thus, at the second level, the framers structured the system to induce elected officials to pursue the common good despite temptations and inclinations to do otherwise. Once again, having a larger republic would help in this regard. With a larger population, the number of "opposite and rival interests" would multiply and would challenge each other. In other words, the framers designed the Constitution to take advantage of human nature, particularly the inclination to pursue passions and interests. At the national level, Madison explained, "[a]mbition [would] be made to counteract ambition." Faction would fight faction. With diverse passions and interests battling against each other, government officials would realize that, often, they could act only for the common good—or not act at all.[83]

Even so, the framers knew that some officials would persist in trying to act for partial or private interests. Thus, at the third level, the framers designed the government institutions to prevent such officials from successfully using their government powers in contravention of the common good. Various structural mechanisms—including federalism, separation of powers, bicameralism, and checks and balances—dispersed power among a multitude of government departments and officials, each of which would have its own interests. "[T]he constant aim is to divide and arrange the several offices in such a manner as that each may be a check on the other—that the private interest of every individual may be a sentinel over the public rights." In other words, the Constitution dispersed power among so many institutions, departments, and officials that the self-interested grasping of one would inevitably be met by the self-interested grasping of another. Government sluggishness was built into the system.[84]

The framers intended these three levels of structural constitutional controls on factionalism *both* to promote the virtuous pursuit of the common good *and* to protect individual rights and liberties. The framers pragmatically designed the Constitution to fit their experience-based conception of the citizen-self, of human nature. Significantly, then, the framers' citizen-self was Janus-faced: one face animated by virtue and reason, but the other face animated by passion and interest, especially economic interest. To a great degree, passion and interest were to enjoy free rein in the private sphere. Yet, in the public sphere, the founders designed the Constitution to produce results in accord with virtue and reason as often as possible. The constitutional design, in other words, would enable the citizen-self to act virtuously in the public sphere while reveling in passions and interests in the private sphere. And even when virtue was in short supply in the public sphere, the Constitution was designed to channel self-interest toward pursuit of the common good.[85]

PROPERTY AND THE PRIVATE SPHERE

If individuals enjoyed liberty and property, according to the framers, then they would inevitably pursue their own passions and interests in the private sphere, with wealth or property being the most important interest. Indeed, the framers recognized that many if not most citizens would be motivated to pursue their own passions and interests not only in the commercial or private world but also in the public world. Factionalism was foreordained. Yet, the framers unequivocally sought to protect liberty and property.

The framers manifested their desire to protect property, in particular, by repeatedly emphasizing that the Constitution needed to limit democratic excesses. To be clear, all of the framers viewed themselves as supporters of republican government, but most of them were simultaneously suspicious of democracy. Almost all delegates to the convention believed that the people should directly elect "the larger branch" of the national legislature.[86] At least one legislative house should arise directly from the people, the ultimate sovereigns. As Madison put it, "the popular election of one branch of the national Legislature [is] essential to every plan of free Government."[87] Beyond that point, however, few framers supported direct democracy. With the notable exception of James Wilson, who wanted both branches and a national executive to be directly elected, most delegates wanted an upper legislative house, as well as an executive, chosen through some other means.[88] "[T]he general object was to provide a cure for the evils under which the U.S. laboured," explained Randolph. "[I]n tracing these evils to their origin every man had found it in the turbulence and follies of democracy: that some check therefore was to be sought for against this tendency of our

Governments: and that a good Senate seemed most likely to answer the purpose."[89] Indeed, Madison argued strenuously that the national government should be able to veto state laws because he distrusted the democratic excesses—the unchecked factionalism—of the state legislatures.[90]

Thus, the framers wanted to prevent factions—even if they were democratic majorities—from using the government to undermine property and other individual rights. To be sure, property rights were enigmatic in their effects. As experience had shown, private property was a given in American society. The ownership or desire to own property could motivate people to act in positive ways in the private sphere. Moreover, for many, ownership of property or other wealth seemed to be necessary for civic virtue. Under all but one of the state constitutions in effect in 1787, private ownership of property or similar economic wealth was a prerequisite to an individual's full participation in the polity. In Maryland, for instance, suffrage was extended only to those "freemen ... having a freehold of fifty acres of land [or] having property in this State above the value of thirty pounds current money."[91] Private ownership of property or other wealth supposedly established one's independence, necessary for the disinterestedness of civic virtue. Moreover, wealth gave one a sufficient "stake in society" or concern for the common good so as to justify the power to vote and to hold office.[92] Yet, simultaneously, the framers realized all too well that desire or greed for property was often the root source of factionalism and corruption.[93]

Crucially, the concept of property was in flux in the late-eighteenth century. In accord with the common law, states defined property as it had developed under feudalism and mercantilism. In the 1760s, William Blackstone had defined property as "that sole and despotic dominion which one man claims and exercises over the external things of the world, in total exclusion of the right of any other individual in the universe."[94] This definition had developed in an agrarian world not conducive to capitalist development. In the founding era, America clearly was not feudal, but it was, at least in part, mercantile. Mercantilism developed from the sixteenth to the eighteenth centuries as nation-states arose. It entailed close ties between the state and merchants. In general, a state would grant a monopoly to a merchant or a company—an early form of corporation—in order to allow the merchant to develop a particular market, often times in a new or incipient colony. The Dutch East India Company, the British East India Company, and the Hudson Bay Company are renowned examples of mercantilist enterprises.

The primary purpose of a mercantilist endeavor was to enhance the treasure (gold and silver) and military power of the mother country. Thus, while mercantilism relied on an economic market, it was not based on a competitive free market. Rather, in a mercantilist system, the state and economy intertwined closely, working together for common purposes through the creation of monopolies and the implementation of protectionist policies. In such a system, property rights were inherently limited. The North American colonies were, for the most part, founded as mercantilist outposts for the benefit of the mother country. They were expected to export only those resources and products not being produced in England, and to serve as an import market for English-produced goods. In the decades before American independence, England was to a great degree still treating the colonies as parts of its mercantilist empire.[95]

For years, though, Americans had been chafing and resisting against their subservient position in the English mercantilist system. And while, from an economic standpoint, the Americans were not in fact faring badly under the system, the American Revolution arose in part from a desire to escape the strictures of English control. Moreover, the Americans were not the only ones to protest against English mercantilism in 1776. In that year, Adam Smith published *The Wealth of Nations*, which advocated that a competitive free-market economy would benefit society more than the mercantilist system. Smith's writings influenced numerous framers, especially Alexander Hamilton, but one must be careful not to overstate Smith's sway. For instance, Publius (the pseudonym of Madison, Hamilton, and John Jay) did not cite Smith even once in *The Federalist*. Smith wrote in part because of his observations of the developing Industrial Revolution in England, but the Industrial Revolution would not fully sweep into the United States for nearly another century.[96] Smith's concept of a competitive free-market system driven by a desire for profit would eventually be known as capitalism, yet he used neither this term nor the term laissez faire. In fact, neither term would enter the English lexicon until the early decades of the nineteenth century. Smith, it should be reiterated, was not describing an already completed transition in England from mercantilism to capitalism; rather he was advocating in favor of this change. Thus, during the founding era, the mercantilist concept of property still controlled; "ownership did not include the absolute right to buy or sell one's property in a free market; that was not a part of the scheme of things in eighteenth-century England and America."[97]

Most important, then, when placed in the proper context of the late-eighteenth century, the framers and other contemporary Americans could not have understood the economy as being truly capitalist, much less laissez faire.[98] Capitalism had not yet fully emerged in England; it had developed even less in the United States. After the Revolution, numerous state governments purposefully created quasi-mercantilist systems that lasted into the early-nineteenth century. Even so, the framers, or at least some of the framers, had a partial vision of a competitive free-market.[99] Indeed, perhaps the most remarkable feat of the framers was their pragmatic (Machiavellian) synthesis of civic republican thought, Lockean philosophy, and Smith's incipient capitalism into a coherent political-economic system. They understood, for instance, that a type of private sphere or social virtue was beginning to emerge in the 1780s. This nascent notion of virtue, distinct from the civic virtue associated with civic republican government yet consistent with Smith's writings, suggested that the individual pursuit of self-interest in the private sphere could itself further the common good, though at that time, such self-interest still had to be tempered by a benevolent and decent Protestant civility.[100] In other words, the experiences of the 1780s had a flip side. The decade had revealed that many Americans, enjoying unprecedented liberty, would pursue their own passions and interests with determined vigor. On the one side, as the Philadelphia delegates emphasized, this self-interest threatened republican government. But on the other side, this same self-interest could generate great personal and social benefits when brought to bear in commercial endeavors. By 1800, a Columbia professor complained, "From one end of the continent to the other, the universal roar is Commerce! Commerce! at all events, Commerce!"[101] But other Americans were celebrating rather than complaining.[102] Thus, despite the persistence of mercantilism, with its close linkage between the state and the economy, the framers had glimpsed the benefits of conceptually separating a private sphere from a public sphere. The public sphere would still be governed by republican democratic principles, while the private sphere would be constituted in part by a still-evolving economic marketplace.

The framers' multiple discussions and ultimate acceptance of slavery as a legal institution illustrated both their desire to protect property and their incomplete adoption of capitalism—as well as their racism.[103] In 1787, slaves constituted approximately 20% of the American population, with the percentage much higher in the southern states. In fact, 90% of the nation's slaves lived in the five states below the Mason–Dixon line.

At that time, South Carolina and Georgia were most dependent on slave labor because their economies were based on the labor-intensive crops of rice and indigo, but even Virginia had one-third of its wealth tied up in slavery. The framers did not anticipate how important slavery would soon become. South Carolinian Charles Pinckney did not even mention cotton when he divided the states into "five distinct commercial interests," but in 1793, Eli Whitney invented the cotton gin and transformed the cotton industry. In short order, cotton became an incredibly profitable crop, highly reliant on slave labor. Slave-supported cotton production would dominate the southern economy, though it also bolstered the northern textile industry. But when the framers met in Philadelphia, nobody knew about the future and King Cotton. Several northern states had already begun moving toward emancipation, and many Americans thought states in the upper South would soon follow in that direction.[104]

Even so, of the 55 delegates who participated during at least part of the convention, 25 owned slaves. The first explicit mention of slavery at the convention arose in the context of legislative representation, particularly in the lower house of Congress. The Virginia Plan had ambivalently proposed that "the rights of suffrage in the National Legislature ought to be proportioned to the Quotas of contribution, or to the number of free inhabitants, as the one or the other rule may seem best in different cases."[105] The delegates turned to this proposal on May 30, 1787, and it immediately proved controversial. Rufus King of Massachusetts pointed out that the calculation of 'quotas of contribution' would be problematic because it would "be continually varying."[106] To be sure, 'quotas of contribution' was an ambiguous concept, but most delegates understood that it suggested state representation would be apportioned in accord with a state's wealth. Yet, the method for determining wealth remained unclear. In particular, would slaves be counted as relevant property for ascertaining quotas of contribution? Given the difficulties surrounding the issue of legislative representation, the delegates postponed discussion for another day.[107]

The convention returned to the problem on June 11. John Rutledge of South Carolina moved that state representation—specifically, "the proportion of [state] suffrage in the first branch"—should be based on "the quotas of contribution." Pierce Butler of South Carolina seconded the motion and added that "money was power." He explained that "States ought to have weight in the Government in proportion to their wealth." Rutledge and Butler unquestionably wanted to protect the interests of southern slaveholding states. King again objected that the determination of state wealth would be problematic. Wilson then moved to delete the reference to quotas of contribution but offered an alternative, which he hoped the southerners would accept as a compromise; indeed, Pinckney seconded Wilson's motion. Wilson proposed that representation be "in proportion to the whole number of white and other free Citizens and inhabitants of every age sex and condition including those bound to servitude for a term of years and three-fifths of all other persons not comprehended in the foregoing description, except Indians not paying taxes, in each State." Gerry, from Massachusetts, immediately protested that, if "property [were] not the rule of representation, why then should the blacks, who were property in the South, be in the rule of representation more than the cattle and horses of the North." Nobody responded to Gerry. Instead, they voted to approve Wilson's motion.[108]

This exchange concerning legislative representation was crucial in multiple ways. The delegates had begun by considering two opposed methods of proportional representation: one based on wealth (quotas of contribution), and one based on population (number of free inhabitants). Significantly, the delegates chose to repudiate representation—and hence, government power—based explicitly on wealth. This decision, in and of itself, suggested the importance of separating the public (government) sphere from the private (economic) sphere. The delegates opted instead to base representation on population, but rather than equating population solely with the number of free inhabitants, they chose to count each slave as three-fifths of a person. This approach would significantly increase southern representation and legislative power. Moreover, this decision emblematized the delegates' attitudes towards slavery. After Gerry protested against the three-fifths clause, nobody declared that slavery was immoral—at least at this point. Nobody declared that slavery should be abolished. Rather, the delegates treated slavery as a political and economic issue in which, for the most part, southerners and northerners had differing interests.[109]

The three-fifths clause still left an ambiguity. Were slaves being counted because they were part of the population—even if not free—or were they being counted as property—thus reintroducing an implicit element of wealth into the calculation of proportional representation? The delegates never completely clarified this murkiness.[110] The three-fifths formula, however, had originated in a failed 1783 Continental Congress proposal for calculating the wealth of particular states.[111] Moreover, the delegates' subsequent statements and actions regarding slavery underscored their commitment to protecting property. When, approximately 1 month later, the delegates revisited the issue of whether slaves should be counted as three-fifths of a person for purposes of proportional representation, Butler argued that three-fifths was not enough. He explained that "equal representation ought to be allowed for [slaves] in a Government which was instituted principally for the protection of property, and was itself to be supported by property."[112] Wilson objected: "[H]e could not agree that property was the sole or the primary object of Government and society. The cultivation and improvement of the human mind was the most noble object."[113] Wilson was an outlier in viewing cultivation of the human mind as the primary goal of the Constitution, though not all delegates agreed with Butler that property was the primary object. When it came to slavery, however, the overwhelming sentiment was that slaves were property. In the words of Charles Cotesworth Pinckney, "property in slaves should not be exposed to danger."[114]

While many delegates worried about protecting the property interests of slave-owners, no delegates protested that slavery would contravene the most fundamental principles of a capitalist economy. Capitalism depends on the drive for profit in a competitive free market. Slavery is the antithesis of a free market; it is coerced labor. Without doubt, slavery enabled slave-owners to accumulate capital in a commercial market economy and thus facilitated the eventual emergence of capitalism. In fact, slavery crucially supported the gradual nineteenth-century development of capitalism in multiple ways. Regardless, throughout the pre-Civil War decades, slavery skewed the natural movement of capital among various productive and profitable market activities. Slavery constrained the marketplace as it constrained human freedom.[115]

George Mason of Virginia came closest to acknowledging a tension between slavery and a free market when he stated, "Slavery discourages arts and manufactures. The poor despise labor when performed by slaves."[116] After Mason's observation, though, nobody elaborated or pursued his concern. Although slavery would contravene a modern competitive free market revolving around contractual agreements, slavery appeared consistent with a premodern economy. At the time of the American founding, England was developing a modern theory of contract based on marketplace values, but this innovation would not be adopted in any American states until the early-nineteenth century, well after ratification of the Constitution. In late-eighteenth-century America, the assignability and enforcement of contracts were limited by notions of fairness and equity. Contract law, in fact, emerged as a separate common law realm in the United States only after the turn into the nineteenth century. Under the American common law of the late-eighteenth and early-nineteenth centuries, duties arose because of established status relationships. The common law, for example, attached a specific duty of care to many occupations. Innkeepers owed a particular duty to protect lodgers, while ferrymen owed a duty of safe transportation to travelers. In civil liability (tort) cases, structured around common law writs or forms of action, such as trespass or trespass on the case, judges (or juries) would be unlikely to conclude that a defendant was negligent, but might conclude that the defendant neglected to fulfill a duty in accord with his distinct status. For example, in the 1786 case of *Purviance v. Angus,* involving the liability of a ship's captain for damaged goods, the court explained the captain's duties: "Reasonable care, attention, prudence, and fidelity, are expected from the master of a ship, and if any misfortune or mischief ensues from the want of them, either in himself or his mariners, he is responsible in a civil action." Slave and master constituted a status relationship within this pre-modern worldview.[117]

A scarce few delegates condemned slavery as immoral. When discussing whether Congress should have power to regulate or prohibit the slave trade, Roger Sherman of Connecticut denounced it as "iniquitous."[118] Luther Martin of Maryland stated that the slave trade "was inconsistent with the principles of the revolution and dishonorable to the American character."[119] Gouverneur Morris uttered perhaps the strongest condemnation of slavery. On August 8, Morris declared: "It was a nefarious institution. It was the curse of heaven on the States where it prevailed. [If the northern states accepted it, they would] sacrifice of every principle of right, of every impulse of humanity." Morris moved to count only "free" inhabitants, not slaves, in determining representation. Jonathan Dayton of New Jersey seconded the motion. Yet Sherman, who had just denounced the iniquity of slavery, explained that he "did not regard the admission of Negroes into the ratio of representation, as liable to such insuperable objections." Charles Pinckney thought "the fisheries and the Western frontier as more burdensome to the U.S. than the slaves." The state delegations then defeated Morris's motion by near-unanimous vote, with only one exception.[120] Almost 2 weeks later, Mason offered the most surprising moral denunciation of slavery, given that he owned 300 slaves. He managed, though, to weave his moral judgment together with pragmatism and racism. "[The existence of slavery] prevent[s] the immigration of Whites, who really enrich and strengthen a Country. [Slaves] produce the most pernicious effect on manners. Every master of slaves is born a petty tyrant. They bring the judgment of heaven on a Country."[121] Such condemnatory statements demonstrate that at least some of the framers understood the immoral ramifications of their ultimate acceptance of slavery. Yet, one cannot but be struck by the usual reactions to these moral denunciations. Silence—or at most, quick dismissal. These statements never provoked any extended debate on the morality of slavery. Rutledge spoke for many delegates when he declared: "Religion and humanity had nothing to do with this question. Interest alone is the governing principle with nations."[122]

While the framers' pragmatism served them well in many ways, it led them to acquiesce far too readily to slavery. Wilson, for instance, puzzled over slavery as a logical conundrum. "Are they admitted as Citizens? Then why are they not admitted on an equality with White Citizens? Are they admitted as property? Then why is not other property admitted into the computation?" Yet, Wilson immediately bypassed this logical problem for practical purposes, "by the necessity of compromise."[123] Unquestionably, one reason for such pragmatic acquiescence to slavery was unabashed racism. Even Gouverneur Morris, who strongly condemned slavery as immoral, objected "against admitting the blacks into the census [for purposes of proportional representation, because] the people of Pennsylvania would revolt at the idea of being put on a footing with slaves. They would reject any plan that was to have such an effect." Wilson agreed that "the tendency of the blending of the blacks with the whites [would] give disgust to the people of Pennsylvania." Neither Morris nor Wilson criticized this racist attitude of their fellow Pennsylvanians. In fact, during this era, racism was so thick that even free blacks were saddled with legal and social disabilities.[124] Meanwhile, the delegates from South Carolina, North Carolina, and Georgia all threatened to abandon the proposed constitution if it did not protect slavery. The northern delegates' desire for a union of all thirteen states, combined with the widespread racism, left little doubt as to the likely result: The northern delegates would readily accept constitutional protections for slavery.

In the end, the Constitution, as ratified, included numerous provisions that either explicitly or implicitly protected slavery; indeed, the northern delegates agreed to several such provisions without securing any southern concessions.[125] One clause, for instance, apportioned congressional representation and direct taxes by counting slaves as three-fifths of a person.[126] Another clause prohibited Congress from banning the slave trade before the year 1808.[127] The Fugitive Slave Clause mandated that an escaped slave did not become free if entering a free state; to the contrary, the escaped slave was to be "delivered up on Claim" of the slave-owner.[128] Some protections of slavery were more subtle but no less significant. For instance, when discussing the possible methods for choosing a chief executive (president), the delegates primarily considered the legislature (Congress), the people (in a direct vote), and a group of electors (an Electoral College). Wilson favored election by the people and "perceived with pleasure that the idea was gaining ground."[129] Madison immediately *agreed* about the merits of the people. "The people at large," Madison stated, "was in his opinion the fittest in itself [to choose the executive]." But Madison nonetheless did not support this method. "There was one difficulty however of a serious nature attending an immediate choice by the people," he explained. "The right of suffrage was much more diffusive in the Northern than the Southern States; and the latter could have no influence in the election on the score of the Negroes. The substitution of electors obviated this difficulty and seemed on the whole to be liable to fewest objections."[130] In other words, because African American slaves could not vote, southern states would not accept a direct vote by the people when choosing the executive. In a direct vote, northern (white) votes would typically outweigh southern (white) votes. But an Electoral College would allow southern states to receive electoral credit for their slaves (based on the three-fifths accounting) without allowing slaves themselves to vote.[131]

Although historians have subsequently disagreed about the extent of protection afforded to slavery, the southern delegates to the constitutional convention were satisfied. Charles Cotesworth Pinckney reported back to the South Carolina legislature: "In short, considering all circumstances, we have made the best terms for the security of this species of property it was in our power to make. We would have made better if we could; but on the whole, I do not think them bad."[132] If anything, Pinckney was being too modest. Early presidential elections were telling. Slave states dominated because of their outsized power in the Electoral College. Of the first seven presidents, from George Washington to Andrew Jackson, from 1789 to 1836, five were slave owners. Not coincidentally, the two non-slave owners, John Adams and his son, John Quincy Adams, were the only single-term presidents during that time. And of course, slave-owning presidents were empowered to nominate federal judges that supported and protected slavery.[133]

BALANCING THE PUBLIC AND PRIVATE

The framers, as a whole, were strongly concerned with the protection of property rights, including property interests in slaves. But most framers did not view the protection of property as the be-all and end-all of the Constitution. Instead, for most framers, both the public and private spheres were important, and as such, they sought to achieve a balance between the two. Madison famously argued in *Federalist, Number 10*, that in a large republic a multiplicity of factions would protect liberty and republican government (in pursuit of the common good). In a properly structured constitutional system, competing factional interests would balance against or offset each other.[134] Likewise, in *Federalist, Number 51*, Madison maintained that a balance among a "multiplicity of sects" would preserve religious liberty.[135] Madison similarly viewed the public and private spheres. If both were vigorous, they would balance against each other and, in doing so, preserve individual liberty and republican government. Neither government nor private (economic) actors would be able to tyrannize the people. In *Federalist, Number 10*, Madison wrote: "To secure the public good *and* private rights against the danger of such a faction, and at the same time to preserve the spirit and the form of popular government, is then the great object to which our inquiries are directed." A constitutional system that unduly favored either the public or the private could not long survive. If the private interests and passions of the people were ignored, the government system would be divorced from reality and would inevitably collapse. Yet, a government that merely catered to the private passions and interests of the people could not truly be called a republic and would spiral soon into oblivion. Ultimately, then, the framers hoped that the constitutional structures would promote the virtuous pursuit of the common good in the public sphere while simultaneously protecting individual rights and liberties in the private sphere. The framers wanted balance, yet they knew it would not be easily achieved. To attain a proper balance, they needed to construct an integrated system consisting of a liberal society—emphasizing individual liberty—and a republican government—pursuing the common good. The government could facilitate economic development but could not succumb to the control of private (economic) interests. If the framers failed to construct such an integrated system, with balance between the public and private spheres, then the entire political-economic society would likely crumble.[136]

Enlightenment thinkers typically conceived of the self (or individual) living in a world divided into dichotomous realms. The spiritual was separate from the material. The mind was separate from the body. Numerous philosophers, from Descartes to Locke to Hume, who died in 1776, to Kant, who was the founders' contemporary, conceptualized a self confronting these characteristic modernist dichotomies.[137] Given such a vision of the self vis-à-vis the world, the framers could not only readily imagine a citizen-self who acted as a virtuous citizen in the public sphere (at least some of the time) but also acted as a self-interested commercial and economic striver in the private sphere.[138]

The existence (or conception) of this dichotomous citizen-self had numerous ramifications. The framers' citizen-self was to remain well balanced, standing with one foot in the public sphere and one foot in the private sphere. As such, the framers' self served as a connection, a bridge, between the two spheres. The citizen-self enjoyed liberty, for instance, in both spheres, though the meaning of liberty differed in each. In the public sphere, liberty denoted individual freedom to participate in republican government. In the private sphere, liberty denoted individual freedom to satisfy one's passions and interests, or at least to try to do so.[139] The self could use reason, too, in both the public and private spheres. In the public sphere, reason could identify substantive content. That is, the citizen-self reasoned—or rationally deliberated with other citizens—to discern the substance of the common good. In the private sphere, however, reason was primarily instrumental. The self sought to use reason to calculate the most advantageous means for satisfying a goal arising from passions and interests. Yet, the framers realized that such calculations were often imprecise. From the framers' standpoint, individuals were swayed as much by their passions and prejudices as by a rational assessment of their own opportunities.[140]

With the citizen-self as a bridge, the public and private spheres were conceptually (or intellectually) separable, but they were not pristine. In practice, they often overlapped or bled into each other. For example, religion (primarily Protestantism) supposedly would be a matter for the private sphere under the national Constitution—implicitly so in the original document and explicitly so after the adoption of the Bill of Rights in 1791. The Free Exercise Clause of the First Amendment protected freedom of conscience, a Protestant prerequisite for individual religious salvation. The Establishment Clause, meanwhile, prohibited the institution of a national church, which would too closely resemble the Church of England. Yet, establishments were allowed to continue at the state level, and did so for several years.[141] Unquestionably, then, in those states that maintained establishments, the people officially recognized religion in the public sphere. With or without such state establishments, however, de facto Protestantism continued unabated throughout the nation. And de facto Protestantism, whether emanating from the private sphere or otherwise, strongly influenced the public sphere: The Protestant self of the private sphere was also a citizen of the public sphere. Unsurprisingly, then, conceptions of virtue and the common good often reflected Protestant values and interests. The first Congress did not hesitate to appoint Protestant chaplains for both houses and to ask the president to declare "a day of Thanksgiving and Prayer."[142]

While the framers sought balance between the public and private, they did not view the two spheres as completely separate or exactly equal. Constitutional provisions such as the Commerce Clause anticipated that the government would sometimes be explicitly involved in private-sphere affairs.[143] More precisely, the framers believed the government could diminish or infringe on individual rights and liberties if the government acted in pursuit of the common good (and otherwise acted consistently with the Constitution). In this sense, the balance was skewed in favor of the public over the private. The Fifth Amendment in the Bill of Rights—"nor shall private property be taken for public use without just compensation"—illustrates this key point. On the one hand, the Constitution unequivocally protected private property, but on the other hand, the government could still take private property for public use—that is, to promote the common good. To be sure, under the Fifth Amendment, the government was required to pay just compensation for a taking. But the government was otherwise permitted to regulate property and the economic marketplace—anything short of an actual taking—without paying compensation, so long as the regulation was for the common good. In *Federalist, Number 10*, Madison stated that the government must have power to regulate individuals with diverse economic interests in the private sphere: "Those who hold and those who are without property have ever formed distinct interests in society. Those who are creditors, and those who are debtors, fall under a like discrimination. A landed interest, a manufacturing interest, a mercantile interest, a moneyed interest, with many lesser interests, grow up of necessity in civilized nations, and divide them into different classes, actuated by different sentiments and views. *The regulation of these various and interfering interests forms the principal task of modern legislation.*"[144] The framers understood that, ultimately, the crucial public–private balance depended on government empowerment to control private interests when they threatened the common good. As Wilson put it, "no government, either single or confederated, can exist, unless private and individual rights are subservient to the public and general happiness of the nation."[145]

The framer with the most well-developed vision of a modern competitive free-market economy bustling with industry and commerce was undoubtedly Hamilton.[146] His understanding of the relationship between the public and private spheres is, therefore, especially illuminating. Hamilton strongly admired the British political-economic system and sought to create an American system that would move in a roughly similar direction.[147] At that time, in the late-eighteenth century, England was deep into its Industrial Revolution and had traveled far along the transitional road from mercantilism to capitalism.

In his position as the first Secretary of the Treasury, in President George Washington's administration, Hamilton attempted to implement his vision of an economic system in accord with the recently ratified Constitution. From Hamilton's perspective, the nation faced financial catastrophe largely because the state and national governments still carried heavy debts from the Revolutionary War. During the 1780s, the ineffective state and national governments could not meet those debts, so public securities lost value and public credit vanished. Consequently, the framers' desire to protect property rights while simultaneously strengthening the national government required that the nation be put on firm financial footing. To achieve these goals, Hamilton conceived a "grand design" for a "utopian financial system." Hamilton laid out this plan in three reports to Congress: *Report on Public Credit* (January 9, 1790), *Report on a National Bank* (December 13, 1790), and *Report on Manufactures* (December 5, 1791).[148]

Hamilton's *Report on Manufactures*, in particular, illuminates his view of the American political-economic system. In this *Report*, Hamilton argued that the national government should actively encourage the development of manufacturing in the United States. He articulated the main objections to such government support and then responded to each objection. For instance, Hamilton acknowledged that some Americans viewed manufacturing in opposition to agriculture. Thus, any support for manufacturing was necessarily antagonistic to agriculture. Moreover, many political leaders thought this conflict between manufacturing and agriculture reflected the regional interests of the North and South, respectively.[149] In fact, though Hamilton did not mention him by name, Jefferson was known to believe that the strength of the nation lay in its agrarianism. Jefferson not only was the primary author of the Declaration of Independence, but he also was the first Secretary of State and owned the Virginia plantation, Monticello, worked by between 100 and 200 slaves. Jefferson, however, participated directly in neither the constitutional convention nor the Virginia ratification debates because he was serving, at the time, as the nation's minister to France.[150]

Even so, because of Jefferson's national prominence, his antagonism to Hamilton's financial plan and Hamilton's response to Jefferson bear elaboration. Two streams of thought, one British and one French, helped shape Jefferson's outlook. In the early-eighteenth century, the British Country (or Opposition) theorists, including Trenchard and Gordon, had argued that the enhanced power of England's central (Court) government, tied to commercial interests, had corrupted the republican British government. Meanwhile, in the latter part of the eighteenth century, the French Physiocrats advocated for minor reforms in an effort to preserve the ancient French regime (which subsequently would collapse in the French Revolution). The Physiocrats opposed industrialization and instead argued that the natural development of an agrarian economy led to prosperity; all moral and economic values were based on the land and agriculture. From Jefferson's perspective, the Country ideology demonstrated that Hamilton's desire to strengthen the national government, in conjunction with commercial development, would corrupt the American republic. Jefferson favored a weaker national and stronger state government, similar to the confederated system that had existed under the Articles of Confederation.[151] Meanwhile, the Physiocrats' writings suggested to Jefferson that the strength of the American political-economic system grew from the existence of independent and self-sufficient agrarian households.[152] Even before the conflict with Hamilton had emerged, Jefferson had written that "[t]hose who labour in the earth are chosen people of God," while manufacturers display "subservience and venality." In case his views were not clear enough, Jefferson added: "The mobs of great [manufacturing] cities add just so much to the support of pure government, as sores do to the strength of the human body."[153] And several years later, soon after he became president, Jefferson wrote to his friend and former Physiocrat, Pierre Samuel du Pont de Nemours, to praise "the agricultural inhabitants" of the United States, whom Jefferson sharply distinguished "from those [residents] of the cities."[154]

Hamilton responded to the Jeffersonian position not by attacking agriculture but by explaining that an opposition between manufacturing and agriculture was false. Government support for manufacturing would inevitably benefit agriculture as well as the national economy as a whole. In other words, Hamilton maintained that support for manufacturing would promote the common good. His contention that manufacturing and agriculture were compatible had an obvious political slant: deflection of southern hostility away from northern manufacturing. And to a degree, all of Hamilton's arguments in his *Report* were politically oriented. He wanted to persuade Congress to enact measures that would promote manufacturing—with manufacturing being but one component of his complex program to put the young nation's finances in order. Naturally, then, his next argument was not only politically pointed, but it also related specifically to the constitutional plan for the public and private spheres. One of the primary objections to Hamilton's proposal for government support of manufacturing was that, quite simply, the government should not intrude on the free operation of the economic marketplace. In other words, the objection was that laissez faire was better than government regulation or interference. Hamilton stated the laissez-faire objection as follows:

> To endeavor by the extraordinary patronage of Government, to accelerate the growth of manufactures, is in fact, to endeavor, by force and art, to transfer the natural current of industry, from a more, to a less beneficial channel. Whatever has such a tendency must necessarily be unwise. Indeed it can hardly ever be wise in a government, to attempt to give a direction to the industry of its citizens. This under the quick-sighted guidance of private interest, will, if left to itself, infallibly find its own way to the most profitable employment; and it is by such employment, that the public prosperity will be most effectually promoted. To leave industry to itself, therefore, is, in almost every case, the soundest as well as the simplest policy.[155]

Hamilton, in this passage, of course did not explicitly use the term, laissez faire, but he unquestionably was articulating the laissez-faire position against government control. He would reiterate it later in the *Report*: "Industry, if left to itself, will naturally find its way to the most useful and profitable employment: whence it is inferred, that manufactures without the aid of government will grow up as soon and as fast, as the natural state of things and the interest of the community may require."[156]

As one would expect from Hamilton, he answered the laissez-faire objection with a sophisticated and powerful argument. He stated, in effect, that the economic marketplace is riddled with imperfections. Any individual who might contemplate the start of a new manufacturing business would be confronted with numerous obstacles, totally apart from supply and demand. Such an individual would be discouraged by "the strong influence of habit and the spirit of imitation—the fear of want of success in untried enterprises—the intrinsic difficulties incident to first essays towards a competition with those who have previously attained to perfection in the business to be attempted—the bounties, premiums, and other artificial encouragements, with which foreign nations second the exertions of their own Citizens in the branches, in which they are to be rivalled." To counter such market imperfections, Hamilton maintained that government "interference and aid ... are indispensable." To be sure, Hamilton acknowledged that the laissez-faire objection was reasonable in the abstract, but abstractness was also the root of its weakness. The laissez-faire position arose from "the pursuit of maxims too widely opposite." In other words, it was an argument based on utopian ideals, but Hamilton, being a pragmatic realist, explained that such ideals rarely applied in their pristine form to the real world. "Most general theories ... admit of numerous exceptions, and there are few, if any, of the political kind, which do not blend a considerable portion of error, with the truths they inculcate." Instead of following utopian ideals, Hamilton recommended a more balanced approach that weighed the various factors in the particular circumstances. Thus, in evaluating the arguments, Congress should evaluate "the considerations, which plead in favour of manufactures, and which appear to recommend the special and positive encouragement of them; in certain cases, and under certain reasonable limitations."[157] Finally, as numerous historians have observed, the ultimate political goal of Hamilton's entire financial plan was clear: He wanted to persuade the wealthy to support—not control—the national government. As Lance Banning put it, Hamilton "never meant for monied men to use the government." In fact, if anything, Hamilton "intended the reverse."[158]

Overall, though, one should be careful not to overstate the clarity of the framers' vision. There were many ambiguities, partly because of the changing contemporaneous notions of government and the market and partly because the Constitution was drafted and ratified in a political crucible. In fact, it is worth mentioning one of the largest ambiguities because some commentators might mistakenly claim that it suggests the constitutionalization of a fully capitalist competitive free market. The Contract Clause states: "No State shall ... pass any ... Law impairing the Obligation of contracts."[159] Toward the end of the convention, Rufus King moved to add a Contract Clause. After a brief discussion, generally negative, the motion was dropped.[160] Even so, the committee of style (consisting of five delegates) subsequently added a Contract Clause on their own, without any authorization from the other delegates.[161] No documentation clarifies the thoughts of the committee members regarding the inclusion or meaning of this clause. During the ratification debates, the Contract Clause was most commonly understood as "simply a catchall extension of the bans on paper money and legal-tender laws."[162] That is, most viewed it as a relatively unimportant reassertion that the state governments would not be able to undermine private debts and disrupt credit and finances. In the Virginia ratification convention, however, Patrick Henry and George Mason worried that the clause would cost the state money by forcing it to redeem old continental debts. Nobody suggested that the clause would protect profit-driven exchanges in a competitive free market—or in other words, capitalism. After all, as I already mentioned, the American common law did not yet identify a separate realm of contract law based on marketplace values.[163]

Keeping in mind the ambiguities of the framers' overall vision as well as more specific ones (such as the Contract Clause), we nonetheless can reasonably conclude that the framers created a political-economic system balancing the public and private spheres. The government was republican democratic, and the economy was a hybrid of a dissipating mercantilism and an incipient capitalism. For the sake of stylistic simplicity, I will refer to the framers' system as democratic capitalist, but the imprecision of this shorthand label should be evident. The government system was not fully democratic. In most states, white Protestant men possessing some degree of wealth could vote, but large swathes of the population, including women, racial minorities, some religious minorities, and the poor, were excluded from directly participating in government. Of course, some of the broad proscriptions against suffrage would eventually be lifted—though to be clear, progress toward full suffrage in the United States has not been steady and uninterrupted.[164] Meanwhile, capitalism would continue to develop during the early-nineteenth century, but the United States could not be accurately described as capitalist until the eradication of slavery. Over time, then, the government would become more democratic, and the economy would become more capitalist.[165]

In any event, under republican democracy, the pursuit of the common good both empowered and limited the government. This was as true at the state and local levels as at the national level. Government could act in almost any manner—even taking property—so long as it was for the common good, but simultaneously, government could not act unless it was for the common good. In fact, throughout much of the nineteenth century, a "well-regulated" or "well-ordered society," including a well-regulated marketplace, was understood to evince a republican democratic government that had achieved the proper public–private balance.[166] During this era, economic marketplaces were local, for the most part. Rudimentary transportation and communication technologies limited the development of a national marketplace until after the Civil War. Thus, municipal and state governments frequently exercised their so-called police powers to regulate the economy, particularly in the antebellum decades. Such regulations could be purely promotional—intended to generate economic activity—or restrictive, or both.[167] Moreover, regulations were rarely, if ever, neutral; instead, some individuals or groups in society would be favored over others.[168]

Given the frequency and effects of economic regulations, individuals sometimes challenged the legality (or constitutionality) of government actions. These judicial challenges often not only invoked state constitution Due Process Clauses or the analogous Law of the Land provisions, but they also sometimes relied on common law or natural law principles.[169] Regardless of the specific legal foundation for the challenge, the key to the typical judicial analysis was the categorization of the government purpose: Was it for the common good—which was permissible—or was it merely for the benefit of one private interest over another—which was impermissible? The law could not be allowed to take wealth from one societal group and transfer it to another group for no reason other than that the favored group controlled the government. Chief Justice Stephen Hosmer of Connecticut phrased this judicial approach in typical terms: "If the legislature should enact a law, without any assignable reason [read: the common good], taking from A. his estate, and giving it to B., the injustice would be flagrant, and the act would produce a sensation of universal insecurity."[170]

Regardless, federal and state courts consistently upheld government actions as being in pursuit of the common good, even when they allegedly infringed on individual rights and liberties, including the right to property. For instance, in an 1845 case, an entrepreneur sought to sell poultry in Boston that he had acquired in New Hampshire. He ran afoul, however, of strict municipal regulations on the marketplace. Specifically, the city required a seller to show "that all the said articles are the produce of his own farm, or of some farm not more than three miles distant from his own dwelling-house." The seller objected, contending that "the by-law is contrary to common right, in restraint of trade, against public policy, unreasonable and void." The court upheld the regulations, with an opinion by Lemuel Shaw. Shaw reasoned that the city necessarily had the power to "control" its "accommodations" for sales so "as best to promote the welfare of all the citizens." Shaw concluded: "[W]e think [the regulations] are well calculated to promote the public and general benefit," notwithstanding the restrictions on the economic marketplace.[171] Chancellor James Kent of New York, in his influential *Commentaries on American Law*, succinctly summarized this fundamental judicial perspective: "[P]rivate interest must be made subservient to the general interest of the community."[172]

FREE SPEECH AND A FREE PRESS

What about free expression?[173] In particular, did the adoption of the First Amendment, with its express protections of free speech and a free press, accord greater protection to liberty of expression than to other liberties? And did the constitutional guarantee of free expression encompass the protection of property rights and other wealth in some direct manner? The overwhelming majority of delegates to the constitutional convention believed a Bill of Rights, which would include explicit protections for expression, was unnecessary. Several times, Charles Pinckney suggested considering a Free Press Clause, but the delegates never followed his lead.[174] Toward the end of the convention, Gerry and Mason sought to add a Bill of Rights, which Mason asserted "might be prepared in a few hours." Gerry's motion, seconded by Mason, failed. Sherman expressed the general sentiment: "It is unnecessary—The power of Congress does not extend to the Press."[175] For the most part, the framers believed that the scheme of enumerated rights in article I would limit congressional power and render a Bill of Rights superfluous.[176] Once the ratification debates had begun, however, the Anti-Federalist opponents of the proposed Constitution seized on the lack of a Bill of Rights as an issue with strong political traction. Given that many of the state constitutions contained a Bill of Rights, why had the framers not included one? Were the framers and the Federalist supporters of ratification seeking to create a centralized national government that would tyrannize the people?[177]

Eventually, under political pressure, Madison and the other Federalists promised to add a Bill of Rights if the states first ratified the Constitution as originally proposed.[178] And in fact, after ratification, Madison was elected to serve in the first House of Representatives, where he promptly introduced a draft Bill of Rights, on June 8, 1789. Madison viewed the proposed amendments as fulfilling his political promise but as otherwise being relatively unimportant. When presenting his draft amendments, he explained that the addition of a Bill of Rights would be "neither improper nor altogether useless." He asked that Congress "devote but one day to this subject, so far as to satisfy the public that we do not disregard their wishes." The rest of the Federalist-controlled House apparently thought a Bill of Rights so insignificant that they did not want to devote even a day to it, at least at that point. After all, from their perspective, the Constitution did not grant Congress power to infringe on individual liberties such as the freedoms of speech and of the press. Thus, James Jackson of Georgia first stated that he thought a Bill of Rights was unnecessary, but added that "if gentlemen should think it a subject deserving of attention, they will surely not neglect ... more important business.... I am against taking up the subject at present." South Carolinian Aedanus Burke agreed that until "other important subjects are determined, he was against taking this up." Madison himself explained that he did not wish, at present, "to enter into a full and minute discussion of every part of the subject, but merely to bring it before the House, that our constituents may see we pay a proper attention to a subject they have much at heart."[179]

Congress finally considered the Bill of Rights on July 21, 1789, 6 weeks after Madison had introduced the proposed amendments. As the future Bill of Rights wound its way through the congressional process, the most striking aspect of the discussions was the paucity of debate about the substantive meanings of the proposed rights, including free speech and a free press. The bulk of the congressional deliberations revolved instead around the form or felicity of phrasing in the various amendments. Gerry, who had wanted a Bill of Rights in the original document and was also now a member of the House, expressed disgust with his congressional colleagues. He was angry because they were saying "it is necessary to finish the subject [merely] in order to reconcile a number of our fellow-citizens to the government."[180] Thus, if one wants to understand the content or substantive meaning of free speech or a free press, one will not find it within the congressional debates. Furthermore, the ratification debates in the various states were inadequately documented and therefore do not elucidate the meaning of the First Amendment. It is clear, however, that Congress had included the freedoms of speech and press in the *third* of the proposed articles or amendments sent to the states for ratification. The states rejected the first two proposed amendments, and thus the third article moved up ordinally, almost by happenstance, to become the First Amendment.[181] The ultimate position of free expression in the First Amendment, consequently, should not be construed to suggest that Congress thought that the freedoms of speech and press were more important than other liberties.

At that time, state constitutions typically had Free Press Clauses but only two had explicit Free Speech Clauses.[182] In the states, the constitutional concept of free expression (primarily a free press) largely echoed the common law. The government could not impose a prior restraint—such as requiring a license or permit before publishing—but government could impose subsequent punishment on criminal statements, particularly seditious libel (criticisms of government officials or policies). In a Pennsylvania state case decided in 1788, Chief Justice Thomas McKean reasoned that prior restraints are prohibited, but that criminal punishment after publication is consistent with "true liberty" if the writing was intended to "delude and defame" rather than to advance the "public good."[183] Approximately a decade later, in 1797, McKean still understood free expression in similar terms: "The liberty of the press is, indeed, essential to the nature of a free State, but this consists in laying no previous restraints upon public actions, and not in freedom from censure for criminal matter, when published. Every freeman has an undoubted right to lay what sentiments he pleases before the public; to forbid this, is to destroy the freedom of the press; but if he publishes what is improper, mischievous or illegal, he must take the consequences of his temerity."[184]

Ambiguity in the American law of free expression centered on the degree to which states should follow Zengerian reforms, modifications of the common law implicitly followed in the 1735 trial of John Peter Zenger.[185] Zengerian reforms were twofold. First, juries rather than judges should decide whether the disputed speech was libelous. Second, truth should be a defense to a charge of seditious libel (under the English common law of the eighteenth century, not only was truth not a defense, but it was also grounds for aggravation of the crime). In 1790 and 1791, while the states were debating ratification of the proposed Bill of Rights, James Wilson delivered at the College of Philadelphia (University of Pennsylvania) the seminal lectures on American constitutional law. When he came to free expression, Wilson stated: "The citizen under a free government has a right to think, to speak, to write, to print, and to publish freely, but with decency and truth, concerning public men, public bodies, and public measures." Therefore, he reasoned that the law of seditious libel is "wise and salutary when administered properly, and by the proper persons." What constitutes wise and salutary administration of seditious libel, according to Wilson? Although not all Americans would have agreed, Wilson insisted that Zengerian reforms must be followed in full: Truth should always be a defense, and juries should always decide whether the disputed speech was libelous.[186]

Thus, the meaning of the First-Amendment protection of free speech and a free press was murky, to say the least. Unquestionably, Americans highly valued free expression; a cultural tradition of dissent or speaking one's mind reached back to colonial times and the Revolution.[187] Many Americans had declared, for example, that free expression was the grand palladium, the bulwark of liberties, echoing the British Country theorists, Trenchard and Gordon, who had written in 1720 that "Freedom of Speech is the great Bulwark of Liberty; they prosper and die together."[188] The Virginia *Bill of Rights*, adopted nearly 1 month before the Declaration of Independence, proclaimed: "That the freedom of the press is one of the great bulwarks of liberty, and can never be restrained but by despotic governments."[189] During the ratification debates, Anti-Federalists repeatedly declared that freedom of the press was the grand or sacred palladium of freedom.[190] In fact, Madison's first draft of the article that would eventually be ratified as the First Amendment read: "The people shall not be deprived or abridged of their right to speak, to write, or to publish their sentiments; and the freedom of the press, as one of the great bulwarks of liberty, shall be inviolable."[191] Regardless of the precise meaning (or inherent ambiguity) of the First Amendment and any subsequent developments in free-expression doctrine, many Americans believed in and experienced a robust de facto liberty of speech and writing.

Yet, alongside this cultural tradition of dissent, one must acknowledge a countervailing tradition of suppression. While Americans have reasonably expected to speak their minds, without penalty, many (and often the same) Americans simultaneously have been quick to suppress social and cultural outsiders, whether based on race, religion, or otherwise. Suppression has often operated through unofficial but nonetheless effective mechanisms. Mob violence, tar-and-feathering, and chasing outsiders from town have been common and widely accepted means of suppressing those who seem to diverge too far from the mainstream. In fact, as is true with the tradition of dissent, the tradition of suppression reaches back to before the constitutional framing. While many Revolutionary-era Patriots enjoyed a full sense of free expression, those same patriotic Americans often suppressed Tories who wanted to voice their support for the British. For instance, at the direction of the Continental Congress, numerous towns created Committees of Observation or Inspection that monitored the output of suspected Tory printers, frequently scaring the Tories into silence.[192]

Thus, the general meaning of free speech and a free press in America was inherently enigmatic, and the law of free expression in the states was even more ambiguous partly because of the uncertain Zengerian reforms. The congressional debates and subsequent state ratifications of the First Amendment did nothing to clarify the obscurities of free speech and a free press. Nobody, it should be added, ever suggested that free speech or a free press directly protected the expenditure of wealth whether in relation to politics or otherwise. In any event, the indeterminacy of the First Amendment would contribute to controversy during the 1790s. The Federalists, recently unified in support of constitutional ratification, split into two opposed "proto-parties," the Republicans (led by Jefferson and Madison) and the Federalists (led by Hamilton).[193] Jefferson and the Republicans' opposition to Hamilton's financial plan for the nation was but one of several contentious issues, albeit an explosive one. Through the decade, the conflict between the Republicans and Federalists grew increasingly bitter. In the midst of John Adams's term as president, the Federalists still controlled both houses of Congress as well as the executive branch, but they then made a monumental political miscalculation. They enacted the Sedition Act of 1798 and began prosecuting Republican printers and politicians for seditious libel. Free expression suddenly became a concrete and combustive political issue.[194]

From the Federalist perspective, Congress had power to enact the Sedition Act despite the First Amendment. True, Congress could not abridge free speech or a free press, but in the 1790s, one could have reasonably concluded that seditious libel was not within the realm or category of free expression. In other words, the First Amendment precluded Congress from restricting only certain types of speech and writing, and seditious libel was not among the protected types. Freedoms of speech and of the press were, from this perspective, beside the point: Congress could criminally punish criticisms of public officials and policies. In fact, the Federalists believed they had enacted the most liberal seditious libel statute imaginable because the Sedition Act fully incorporated Zengerian reforms.[195]

In terms of the contemporaneous meaning of the First Amendment, the Republicans' initial response was significant. They articulated a jurisdictional or federalism-based argument: The states but not the national government were empowered to punish seditious libel.[196] Congress's enumerated powers, the Republicans emphasized, did not include a power to punish seditious libel. The First Amendment merely reinforced this congressional impotency. Most important, then, the Republicans did not claim that government punishment of seditious libel contravened the meaning of free speech or a free press. To the contrary, they argued that if punishment was merited because of the publishing of libels, then state governments could impose the punishment, regardless of state constitutional guarantees of free expression.[197] Thus, for instance, 1 month after the first Sedition Act prosecution, Kentucky protested the Federalist actions by issuing a legislative resolution that articulated the jurisdictional argument (Jefferson actually wrote the first draft of the resolution). If the national government attempted to act beyond its enumerated powers, the resolution stated, its actions were "unauthoritative, void, and of no force." The resolution then focused on free expression: "[N]o power over the … freedom of speech, or freedom of the press, being delegated to the United States by the Constitution, nor prohibited by it to the states, all lawful powers respecting the same did of right remain, and were reserved to the states, or to the people." By this reasoning, the Sedition Act was invalid, though the states themselves retained "the right of judging how far the licentiousness of speech, and of the press, may be abridged without lessening their useful freedom."[198]

Because of ambiguity in the First Amendment, both the Federalists and the Republicans were able to articulate reasonable though opposed arguments. Interestingly, they agreed on one point: The criminal punishment of seditious libel is consistent with republican democratic government. They disagreed on whether both the states and the national government—the Federalist position—or only the states—the Republican position—could impose the punishment. Politically, the end result of the Sedition Act crisis was that the Republicans swept the elections of 1800. Jefferson became president, and the Republicans gained control of both houses of Congress.[199] With regard to free speech and a free press, the crisis eventually spurred Republican politicians and writers to develop more sophisticated and protective theories of free expression.[200] Nevertheless, when courts articulated the legal doctrine of free expression in the nineteenth century, these expansive theories were largely ignored or forgotten. Courts treated legal rights to free speech and a free press similarly to other individual rights under republican democracy. To be sure, state constitutions, as well as the national Constitution, protected citizens' rights to free expression, but government could always limit such rights if in pursuit of the common good. As it was often phrased, individuals enjoyed rights to speech and press but were nonetheless responsible for abuses of those freedoms.[201] Liberty was not equivalent to license.[202]

The lower courts, consequently, developed free-expression doctrine consistent with these republican democratic principles, recognizing government power to punish speech or writing if such punishment would further the common good. This republican democratic approach engendered the bad tendency test to delineate the scope of free expression: The government could not impose prior restraints on expression, but it could impose criminal penalties for speech or writing that had bad tendencies or likely harmful consequences. Many courts added that the criminal defendant, to be convicted, must also have intended harmful consequences. Even so, under the doctrine of constructive intent, the courts typically reasoned that a defendant was presumed to have intended the natural and probable consequences of his or her statements. If a defendant's expression was found to have bad tendencies, then the defendant's criminal intent would be inferred.[203]

NOTES

1. Michael J. Klarman, The Framers' Coup: The Making of the United States Constitution 88–92 (2016); George R. Minot, The History of the Insurrections, In Massachusetts 83–86 (1788); Richard Beeman, Plain, Honest Men 16 (2009); Forrest McDonald, Novus Ordo Seclorum 176–77 (1985); Leonard L. Richards, Shays's Rebellion 1–2, 6 (2002); David P. Szatmary, Shays' Rebellion 66 (1980). Additional sources on the founding cited in this chapter include: Bernard Bailyn, The Ideological Origins of the American Revolution (1967); Sanford Levinson, Framed: America's 51 Constitutions and the Crisis of Governance (2012); Pauline Maier, Ratification (2010); Jennifer Nedelsky, Private Property and the Limits of American Constitutionalism (1990); J.G.A. Pocock, The Machiavellian Moment (1975); The Federal and State Constitutions, Colonial Charters, and other Organic Laws of the United States (Ben Perley Poore ed., 2d ed. 1878) [hereinafter Poore]; Gerald Stourzh, Alexander Hamilton and the Idea of Republican Government (1970); Gordon S. Wood, The Creation of the American Republic, 1776–1787 (1969); Gordon S. Wood, The Radicalism of the American Revolution (1991) [hereinafter Radicalism]; Sonia Mittal et al., The Constitutional Choices of 1787 and Their Consequences, in Founding Choices: American Economic Policy in the 1790s 25 (Douglas A. Irwin and Richard Sylla eds., 2011). For the most complete record of the constitutional convention, see The Records of the Federal Convention of 1787 (Max Farrand ed., 1966 reprint of 1937 rev. ed.) [hereinafter Farrand].

   I rely heavily on Madison's notes from the constitutional convention, though I modify some quoted passages for stylistic purposes. For instance, I spell out Madison's abbreviations.

   All citations to The Federalist are to the Project Gutenberg Etext of The Federalist Papers.

2. Knox Letter to Washington (Oct. 23, 1786).

3. Beeman, supra note 1, at 16–18; Szatmary, supra note 1, at 98–106; Howard Zinn, A People's History of the United States 93–94 (1980).

4. Jay Letter to Washington (June 27, 1786); Wood, supra note 1, at 412–413.

5. Washington Letter to Jay (Aug. 1, 1786).

6. Madison Letter to Edmund Pendleton (Feb. 24, 1787), *reprinted in* James Madison: Writings 61, 62 (Library of America, 1999).
7. Mittal, supra note 1, at 33. On conceptions of the self, see Philip Cushman, Constructing the Self, Constructing America (1995); Charles Taylor, Sources of the Self (1989).
8. *Political Problems*, Essex Journal, Dec. 27, 1786, at 3 (characterizing Shays' Rebellion as a "political problem"). Sources discussing economic development cited in this chapter include: John Kenneth Galbraith, A History of Economics (1987); Robert Heilbroner and William Milberg, The Making of Economic Society (10th ed. 1998); Robert Heilbroner and Aaron Singer, The Economic Transformation of America (1999); Ronald E. Seavoy, An Economic History of the United States From 1607 to the Present (2006); Herbert Hovenkamp, *Inventing the Classical Constitution*, 101 Iowa L. Rev. 1 (2015). Sources discussing the legal development of corporations include: Lawrence M. Friedman, A History of American Law (2d ed. 1985); Kermit L. Hall, The Magic Mirror (1989); Morton J. Horwitz, The Transformation of American Law, 1780–1860 (1977); Pauline Maier, *The Revolutionary Origins of the American Corporation*, 50 William and Mary Q. 51 (1993).
9. Klarman, supra note 1, at 239.
10. Beeman, supra note 1, at 66–67, 180, 359–368.
11. The Declaration of Independence, *reprinted in* 2 Great Issues in American History 70, 92–93 (Richard Hofstadter ed., 1958) [hereinafter Great Issues]; The English Libertarian Heritage (David L. Jacobson ed., 1994 ed.) [hereinafter English] (writings of Trenchard and Gordon); Bailyn, supra note 1, at 1–21, 34–35, 94–103; Pocock, supra note 1, at 406–408, 486–487 (Court and Country ideologies); Quentin Skinner, 1 The Foundations of Modern Political Thought: The Renaissance (1978) (history of early civic humanist thought); Wood, supra note 1, at 46–90.
12. Wood, supra note 1, at 3.
13. Declaration of Independence, supra note 11, at 71; Morton White, The Philosophy of the American Revolution (1978).
14. Mr. Barlow's Oration (July 4, 1787), *in* Hezekiah Niles, Principles and Acts of the Revolution in America 384, 389 (1822); Declaration of Independence, supra note 11, at 72–74; Bailyn, supra note 11, at vi-vii (American Revolution as an ideological struggle); Edmund S. Morgan, The Birth of the Republic, 1763–1789, at 7 (rev. ed. 1977); Wood, supra note 1, at 100.
15. Sydney E. Ahlstrom, A Religious History of the American People 124 and n.1 (1972); Radicalism, supra note 1, at 329; Ellis Sandoz, A Government of Laws: Political Theory, Religion, and the American

Founding 99–101, 110–113, 134–136 (1990) (importance of religion to Revolution); William G. McLoughlin, *'Enthusiasm for Liberty': The Great Awakening as the Key to the Revolution,* 87 Proceedings of the Am. Antiquarian Soc. 69, 70–73, 77–78, 93–94 (1977).

16. Ahlstrom, supra note 4, at 149 (quoting Urian Oakes, New England Pleaded With 49 (1673)).
17. Wood, supra note 1, at 118 (quoting Adams).
18. Id. at 117.
19. Constitution of Massachusetts (1780), *reprinted in* 1 Poore, supra note 1, at 956, 958; Constitution of New Hamsphire (1784), *reprinted in* 2 Poore, supra note 1, at 1280, 1281.
20. Wood, supra note 1, at 59; Mittal, supra note 1, at 33 (discussing Revolutionary-era emphasis on virtue).
21. Virginia Bill of Rights (1776), *reprinted in* 2 Poore, supra note 1, at 1908, 1909; Constitution of Maryland (1776), *reprinted in* 1 Poore, supra note 1, at 817, 818.
22. Beeman, supra note 1, at 8, 346–347; Willi Paul Adams, The First American Constitutions (2001); Wood, supra note 1, at 125–256, 356–357.
23. John Locke, The Second Treatise of Government 4–5, 70–74, 119, 139 (Thomas P. Peardon ed., 1952).
24. Constitution of North Carolina (1776), *reprinted in* 2 Poore, supra note 1, at 1409, 1409; Constitution of Massachusetts (1780), *reprinted in* 1 Poore, supra note 1, at 958.
25. Cushman, supra note 7, at 30–31; Taylor, supra note 7, at 174.
26. ~1Virginia Bill of Rights (1776), *reprinted in* 2 Poore, supra note 1, at 1909; *see* Constitution of New York (1777), *reprinted in* 2 Poore, supra note 1, at 1328, 1338 (protecting "liberty of conscience"). On liberty of conscience, see Jean Calvin, Institutes of the Christian Religion, at bk. 3, ch. XI, § 19; bk. 3, ch. XIII, § 5; bk. 3, ch. XVII, § 1; bk. 3, ch. XVIII, § 9; bk. 4, ch. X, § 3 (Ford Lewis Battles trans., John T. McNeill ed., 1960) (1st published 1536); Ralph C. Hancock, Calvin and the Foundations of Modern Politics 128–129, 132 (1989). For a more extensive discussion of religion during the Revolution and the 1780s, see Stephen M. Feldman, Please Don't Wish Me a Merry Christmas: A Critical History of the Separation of Church and State 145–174 (1997) [hereinafter Critical History].
27. Mark DeWolfe Howe, The Garden and the Wilderness 11 (1965); Martin E. Marty, Protestantism in the United States: Righteous Empire 22 (2d ed. 1986).

28. Constitution of Pennsylvania (1776), *reprinted in* 2 Poore, supra note 1, at 1540, 1543; Morton Borden, Jews, Turks, and Infidels 11–15 (1984). States that maintained some type of establishment included South Carolina, Maryland, Georgia, Massachusetts, Connecticut, Virginia, and New Hampshire. Jon Butler, Awash in a Sea of Faith: Christianizing the American People 258–261 (1990); Thomas J. Curry, The First Freedoms: Church and State in America to the Passage of the First Amendment 134–192 (1986).

29. Letter from John Jay to George Washington (June 27, 1786); James Wilson, *In the Pennsylvania Convention* (Nov. 24, 1787), *in* 3 Farrand, supra note 1, at 138, 141–142, appendix A (lamenting licentiousness of citizens and government problems); Beeman, supra note 1, at 16–18; Wood, supra note 1, at 409–413.

30. 1 Farrand, supra note 1, at 18 (May 29, 1787); Federalist No. 44 (Madison) (tying limits on state government powers to economic concerns); Nedelsky, supra note 1, at 30, 125–126; McDonald, supra note 1, at 94–96, 138–142, 177–179; Wood, supra note 1, at 403–425. For statements about the dangers emanating from state governments, see 1 Farrand, supra note 1, at 153 (June 7, 1787) (Wilson); id. at 356 (June 21, 1787) (Wilson); id. at 356 (June 21, 1787) (Madison).

31. 1 Farrand, supra note 1, at 255 (June 16, 1787) (Randolph); id. at 282–283, 291 (June 18, 1787) (Hamilton); Beeman, supra note 1, at 3–21; Stourzh, supra note 1, at 38; Wood, supra note 1, at 413–425; Mittal, supra note 1, at 26–28 (defects of the Articles and policy concerns that arose during the 1780s); *see* Stephen M. Feldman, American Legal Thought From Premodernism to Postmodernism: An Intellectual Voyage 61–65 (2000) (discussing framers' premodern or cyclical view of history).

32. James Madison, *Vices of the Political System of the United States, reprinted in* James Madison: Writings 69, 71–72, 75–77 (Library of America, 1999); Beeman, supra note 1, at 27–29.

33. 1 Farrand, supra note 1, at 27 (May 29, 1787); James Madison, *The Virginia Plan, reprinted in* James Madison: Writings 89 (Library of America, 1999); Beeman, supra note, at 86–92. Gouverneur Morris stated: "Every man of observation had seen in the democratic branches of the State Legislatures, precipitation," or in other words, rash or impetuous action. 1 Farrand, supra note 1, at 512 (July 2, 1787).

34. 2 Farrand, supra note 1, at 278 (Aug. 13, 1787) (Dickinson); 1 Farrand, supra note 1, at 48 (May 31, 1787) (Gerry); id. at 101 (June 4, 1787) (Mason).

35. 2 Farrand, supra note 1, at 202 (Aug. 7, 1787) (Dickinson); id. at 249 (Aug. 10, 1787) (Franklin); id. at 248 (Aug. 10, 1787) (Pinckney); 1 Farrand, supra note 1, at 512 (July 2, 1787) (Morris).

36. *E.g.*, 1 Farrand, supra note 1, at 153–155 (June 7, 1787) (discussing protection of property in relation to the election of legislators); Beeman, supra note 1, at 281.

37. 1 Farrand, supra note 1, at 376 (June 22, 1787).

38. 1 Farrand, supra note 1, at 125 (June 5, 1787) (Pierce Butler) (arguing that delegates should not devise the best possible government, but the best the people would receive); Levinson, supra note 1, at 131.

39. Federalist No. 55 (Madison); Peter Gay, 2 The Enlightenment: An Interpretation 170, 566 (1969); McDonald, supra note 1, at 70–77; *see* Levinson, supra note 1, at 80 (emphasizing Madison's belief in the public good).

40. Federalist No. 51 (Madison); Morton White, Philosophy, The Federalist, and the Constitution 97, 127 (1987) (tying to Hume). Hamilton believed a citizen could cooperate in pursuit of the "public good, notwithstanding his insatiable avarice and ambition." Adams, supra note 22, at 225 (quoting Hamilton, who was quoting Hume).

41. Federalist No. 55 (Madison); Stephen Holmes, *The Secret History of Self-Interest, in* Beyond Self-Interest 267, 286 (Jane Mansbridge ed., 1990).

42. Federalist No. 15 (Hamilton). An individual's opinion would "depend much on the number which he supposes to have entertained the same opinion." Federalist No. 49 (Madison).

43. Federalist No. 49 (Madison).

44. Federalist No. 55 (Madison).

45. Federalist No. 37 (Madison); 1 Farrand, supra note 1, at 82 (June 2, 1787) (Benjamin Franklin); id. at 285 (June 18, 1787) (Hamilton); id. at 491 (June 30, 1787) (Gunning Bedford); Federalist No. 1 (Hamilton); Federalist No. 2 (Jay); *see* Albert O. Hirschman, The Passions and the Interests (1997 ed.); White, supra note 40, at 102–112; Gordon S. Wood, *The Fundamentalists and the Constitution*, N.Y. Rev. Books, Feb. 18, 1988, at 33 (comparing reason, passion, and interest in ancient and modern philosophy).

46. Federalist No. 10 (Madison); White, supra note 40, at 102–128 (puzzling through Publius's uses of reason, passion, and interest). Publius was not merely being sloppy. Rather, in western thought, this was a transitional period in the understanding of the concepts of passion, interest, and reason—and the transition was far from linear. Hirschman, supra note 45, at 33–48.

47. Federalist No. 6 (Hamilton); 1 Farrand, supra note 1, at 285 (June 18, 1787) (Hamilton); Federalist No. 72 (Hamilton) (discussing potential influence of avarice, vanity, and ambition on president); White, supra note 40, at 106.

48. *E.g.*, Federalist No. 10 (Madison); *see* White, supra note 40, at 108–109 (distinguishing passions and interests). In 1776, Adam Smith defined economic interest—"the desire of bettering our condition"—as "generally calm and dispassionate." Adam Smith, The Wealth of Nations, bk. II, ch. 3, p. 453 (1776).

49. Federalist No. 10 (Madison) (distinguishing between "reason" and "self-love"). Smith argued that one must appeal to another's "own interest" or "self-love." Smith, supra note 48, at bk. I, ch. 2, p. 30.

50. Hirschman, supra note 45, at 32.

51. Federalist No. 10 (Madison); 1 Farrand, supra note 1, at 49 (May 31, 1787) (George Mason); 1 Farrand, supra note 1, at 581 (July 11, 1787) (Pierce Butler emphasizing protection of property).

52. Federalist No. 6 (Hamilton); 2 Farrand, supra note 1, at 278 (Aug. 13, 1787) (Dickinson arguing experience is more important than reason); Gay, supra note 39, at 563 (calling *The Federalist* "a classic work of the Enlightenment"); White, supra note 40, at 86–87.

53. Federalist No. 49 (Madison); Cushman, supra note 7, at 31 (explaining Enlightenment philosophers as relying on empiricism and logic). Pangle and White both emphasize Locke's rationality, but Locke is typically characterized as an empiricist. Thomas L. Pangle, The Spirit of Modern Republicanism 134–135 (1988); White, supra note 1, at 86–87. Cushman writes that "[t]he self of the early modern era .... was capable of building the order of the universe from sense impressions and inner logic." Cushman, supra note 7, at 381.

54. Taylor, supra note 7, at 167–171. Kant declared that "[t]he motto of enlightenment is ... Have courage to use your *own* understanding!" Immanuel Kant, *An Answer To The Question: What Is Enlightenment?* (1784), *reprinted in* Kant's Political Writings 54, 54 (Hans Reiss ed., H.B. Nisbet trans., 1970). Kant was but one of several writers to respond to the question, 'What is Enlightenment?' For a collection of the various responses, see *What Is Enlightenment? Eighteenth-Century Answers and Twentieth-Century Questions* (James Schmidt ed., 1996).

55. Pangle, supra note 53, at 244–246, 266–272; Taylor, supra note 7, at 172. Locke equated the "personal identity" of a "self" with "a thinking intelligent being, that has reason and reflection." John Locke, *An Essay Concerning Human Understanding, reprinted in* The English Philosophers From Bacon to Mill 238, 315 (Edwin A. Burtt ed., 1939).

56. U.S. Const. pmbl.
57. *E.g.*, Federalist No. 49 (Madison). Publius, here, disagreed with Hume, who argued that reason cannot overcome passion so as to produce virtuous action. David Hume, Treatise of Human Nature (1739–1740), at book II, part 3, § 3; Hirschman, supra note 45, at 20–31.
58. Federalist No. 10 (Madison).
59. Federalist No. 6 (Hamilton).
60. Federalist No. 49 (Madison).
61. Federalist No. 10 (Madison); Federalist No. 6 (Hamilton); Pangle, supra note 53, at 47, 129–275; Pocock, supra note 1, at 516–517; Wood, supra note 1, at 391–564.
62. U.S. Const. pmbl. ("We the People"); Federalist No. 39 (Madison); Locke, supra note 23, at 71–74; *see* Frank Tariello, Jr., The Reconstruction of American Political Ideology, 1865–1917, at 6–7, 11–14 (1982) (emphasizing Lockean premises of American republicanism). Louis Hartz famously argued that American government was grounded solely on Lockean liberalism, Louis Hartz, The Liberal Tradition in America (1955), but his thesis was undermined by the likes of Bailyn, supra note 1; Pocock, supra note 1; and Wood, supra note 1. Some commentators, however, still argue the framers were influenced more by Locke than by civic republicanism. David F. Prindle, The Paradox of Democratic Capitalism 2–5 (2006).
63. Federalist No. 10 (Madison) (distinguishing between "public and private faith" as well as "public and personal liberty"); Federalist No. 14 (Madison) (emphasizing government would be "in favor of private rights and public happiness"); 1 Farrand, supra note 1, at 166 (June 8, 1787) (Wilson); 1 Farrand, supra note 1, at 288–290 (June 18, 1787) (Hamilton); *see* Taylor, supra note 7, at 20 (distinguishing between public life of a citizen or warrior and private life aimed at "peace and economic well-being").
64. Federalist No. 10 (Madison); 1 Farrand, supra note 1, at 581 (July 11, 1787) (Butler emphasizing protection of property); Federalist No. 48 (Madison) (emphasizing the need to protect the people from even their own legislature).
65. Pocock, supra note 1 at 466 (discussing two paradigms); id. at 506–552 (focusing on America). For Pocock's definition of the Machiavellian moment, see id. at vii–viii; *cf.*, Gay, supra note 39, at 563–564 (emphasizing Publius contributed to the Enlightenment by fusing philosophical themes into a practical framework for government).
66. Locke, supra note 23, at 73, 82.
67. Pocock, supra note 45, at 466; Wood, supra note 1.

68. "Madison's political thought was characterized by an often agonized effort to find a working balance between the rights of property and republican principles." Nedelsky, supra note 1, at 12; id. at 22, 203–204; Richard C. Sinopoli, The Foundations of American Citizenship 4–7 (1992) (emphasizing balance).

69. McDonald, supra note 1, at 189–209; Nedelsky, supra note 1, at 37; Pocock, supra note 1, at 513–526; Wood, supra note 1, at 391–468. The founders themselves did not agree on a precise definition of republican government. Stourzh, supra note 1, at 44–45. My definition of republican democracy overlaps but is not identical with some technical definitions of civic republicanism. Sinopoli, supra note 68, at 9–12.

70. Virginia Bill of Rights (1776), reprinted in 2 Poore, supra note 1, at 1908; Wood, supra note 1, at 59.

71. Federalist No. 10 (Madison); James Madison, In Virginia Convention, June 5, 1788, reprinted in The Complete Madison: His Basic Writings 46, 46 (Saul K. Padover ed., 1953) (majority factions have produced unjust laws) [hereinafter Complete].

72. White, supra note 40, at 120.

73. 1 Farrand, supra note 1, at 422 (June 26, 1787) (Madison); Federalist No. 1 (Hamilton); Federalist No. 2 (Jay); Federalist No. 6 (Hamilton); Federalist No. 10 (Madison).

74. Madison Letter to Monroe (Oct. 5, 1786), reprinted in Complete, supra note 71, at 45, 45.

75. Federalist No. 37 (Madison); Federalist No. 6 (Hamilton).

76. 1 Farrand, supra note 1, at 378 (June 22, 1787).

77. U.S. Const., Art. I, § 8, cl. 8 ("No title of Nobility shall be granted"); Federalist No. 39 (Madison); Federalist No. 36 (Hamilton) ("strong minds" could come from "every walk of life"). On the virtuous elite, see 1 Farrand, supra note 1, at 154 (June 7, 1787) (Wilson); id. at 422 (June 26, 1787) (Madison); White, supra note 1, at 125–127; see Nedelsky, supra note 1, at 158 (even virtuous elite could not be expected to rise constantly "above self-interest"). On wealth and the framers, see Beeman, supra note 1, at 67; id. at 114, 280–281; Nedelsky, supra note 1, at 142–144.

78. Beeman, supra note 1, at 130–131; Stourzh, supra note 1, at 82–83.

79. Federalist No. 17 (Hamilton); Federalist No. 71 (Hamilton).

80. Federalist No. 57 (Madison).

81. Federalist No. 10 (Madison).

82. Id.; Federalist No. 3 (Jay) (the "best men" would be elected to national offices because the people would have "the widest field for choice"). Publius, here, was influenced by Hume, who argued that factionalism was more likely in smaller republics. David Hume, *Of Parties in General, in* Essays: Moral, Political and Literary 54, 56 (Oxford University Press ed. 1963).

83. Federalist No. 51 (Madison).

84. Id.

85. Federalist No. 10 (Madison); Federalist No. 14 (Madison); *see* Harold J. Berman, *The Impact of the Enlightenment on American Constitutional Law*, 4 Yale J. L. and Human. 311, 321–329 (1992) (arguing American revolution and Constitution had two faces).

86. 1 Farrand, supra note 1, at 48 (May 31, 1787) (Mason); Beeman, supra note 1, at 122–123.

87. Id. at 49 (May 31, 1787).

88. Id. at 52 (May 31, 1787); id. at 68 (June 1, 1787) (statements of Wilson).

89. Id. at 51 (May 31, 1787).

90. Id. at 164–165 (June 8, 1787); Beeman, supra note 1, at 228. Joyce Appleby argued the Constitution weakened the state governments yet constrained the national government, and in doing so, it enhanced the protection of the private realm of liberty and property. Joyce Appleby, *The American Heritage: The Heirs and the Disinherited*, 74 J. Amn. Hist. 798, 804 (1987).

91. Constitution of Maryland (1776), *reprinted in* 1 Poore, supra note 1, at 817, 821; Adams, supra note 22, at 315–127; Alexander Keyssar, The Right to Vote 8–24, 340–341 (2000).

92. Keyssar, supra note 91, at 5, 9; G. Edward White, *The Political Economy of the Original Constitution*, 35 Harv. J. L. and Pub. Pol'y 61, 83 (2011).

93. Several years after the framing, James Sullivan perfectly captured the dual nature—the costs and benefits—of property. "This propensity [to acquire wealth], has a manifest tendency to the advancement of the public interest; and will produce the prosperity of the community, where it is exerted; unless the publick mind is so corrupted, as to embrace wealth, in preference to virtue, by making property a qualification to the publick confidence, superior to those of integrity, industry, learning, and ability." James Sullivan, The Path to Riches 3 (1809).

94. William Blackstone, 2 Commentaries on the Laws of England 2 (1st ed. 1765–1769); Horwitz, supra note 8, at 32.

95. Galbraith, supra note 8, at 39–42; Heilbroner and Singer, supra note 8, at 26–27, 48–49.

96. Smith, supra note 48; Galbraith, supra note 8, at 31; Heilbroner and Singer, supra note 8, at 26, 70–71; McDonald, supra note 1, at 97–98, 108–142; Hovenkamp, supra note 1, at 8 and n.33 (on Smith's influence on Madison); *see* Heilbroner and Milberg, supra note 8, at 60–69 (England's Industrial Revolution).

97. McDonald, supra note 1, at 14; Online Oxford English Dictionary (showing English use of laissez faire in 1825 and capitalism in 1833); Karl Polanyi, The Great Transformation 143 (2001 ed.) (laissez-faire ideology emerged in 1830s).

98. "The United States Constitution was written at an important transitional time in the history of western political and economic thought. To the extent the Constitution reflects a theory of economics and government intervention, it came mainly from the predecessors of classical economic thought." Hovenkamp, supra note 8, at 9.

99. Heilbroner and Milberg, supra note 8, at 55; Horwitz, supra note 8, at xiii–xiv, 33; McDonald, supra note 1, at 18, 101–06. Hamilton, Wilson, and Gouverneur Morris hoped the American economy would develop similarly to that of England. McDonald, supra note 1, at 115, though in 1787, "the concept of an 'economy' as an entity having a life of its own was just emerging." Id. at 4.

100. Joyce Appleby, Capitalism and a New Social Order 14–15 (1984); Radicalism, supra note 1, at 215–219, 230; *see* Lawrence D. Brown and Lawrence R. Jacobs, The Private Abuse of the Public Interest 8–9 (2008) (Adam Smith and David Hume were also pragmatic realists, not market ideologues); Sean Wilentz, Chants Democratic 14–15 (2004) (discussing struggles over the meaning of virtue and the common good); Isaac Kramnick, *Republican Revisionism Revisited*, 87 Am. Historical Rev. 629, 662 (1982) (emphasizing changing notion of virtue).

101. Wood, supra note 1, at 326 (quoting Samuel Mitchill).

102. *E.g.*, Samuel Blodget, Economica 12 (1806) (emphasizing social cohesion engendered by commerce); *see* Wood, supra note 1, at 325–347 (describing emerging celebration of commerce).

103. Mittal, supra note 1, at 38 ("slavery was the real, material, palpable interest that had to be accommodated if a lasting, intersectional Union was to be created, and with it the benefits of economic integration the Constitution was intended to promote"); Klarman, supra note 1, at 257–304. Helpful sources focusing on slavery include the following: Derrick Bell, Race, Racism, and American Law (2d ed. 1980); Paul Finkelman, Slavery and the Founders (3d ed. 2014); Staughton Lynd, *Slavery and the Founding Fathers, in* Black History: A Reappraisal 115 (Melvin Drimmer ed., 1968).

104. 2 Farrand, supra note 1, at 449 (Aug. 29, 1787) (Pinckney); Gordon S. Wood, Empire of Liberty: A History of the Early Republic, 1789–1815, at 164–165, 519–524 (2009) [hereinafter Empire]; Beeman, supra note 1, at 310–315; Hall, supra note 8, at 130; Seavoy, supra note 8, at 111; *see* Sven Beckert, The Empire of Cotton 140 (2014) (on the development of cotton mills in northern and border states); id. at 98–109 (on the expansion of the cotton industry); Bell, supra note 103, at 8 (listing years in which northern states abolished slavery); Finkelman, supra note 103, at ix (detailing when states eliminated slavery).

105. 1 Farrand, supra note 1, at 20 (May 29, 1787).

106. Id. at 36 (May 30, 1787).

107. Beeman, supra note 1, at 106–107, 309–311.

108. 1 Farrand, supra note 1, at 196–197, 201 (June 11, 1787); Beeman, supra note 1, at 152–153.

109. Bell, supra note 103, at 22; Finkelman, supra note 103, at 34.

110. Beeman, supra note 1, at 153–155. Madison subsequently acknowledged this ambiguity. Federalist No. 54 (Madison).

111. 1 Farrand, supra note 1, at 201 (June 11, 1787); Beeman, supra note 1, at 154.

112. 1 Farrand, supra note 1, at 580–581 (July 11, 1787).

113. Id. at 605 (July 13, 1787).

114. 1 Farrand, supra note 103, at 594 (July 12, 1787); Beeman, supra note 1, at 334; Finkelman, supra note 1, at 3–36; Lynd, supra note 103, at 130–131; McDonald, supra note 1, at 3–4, 268.

115. David Brion Davis, The Problem of Slavery in the Age of Revolution, 1770–1823, at 346–354 (1975); Eugene D. Genovese, Roll, Jordan, Roll: The World the Slaves Made 44–45, 291–292 (1974); Heilbroner and Singer, supra note 8, at 9–12, 132; Eric Williams, Capitalism and Slavery vii, 210 (1961). On the crucial role played by slavery in the development of capitalism, see Beckert, supra note 104, at 98–135; Sven Beckert and Seth Rockman, *Slavery's Capitalism, in* Slavery's Capitalism: A New History of American Economic Development 1 (2016).

116. 2 Farrand, supra note 1, at 370 (Aug. 22, 1787).

117. 1 U.S. 180, 185 (Pa. Err. and App. 1786); Alan Calnan, A Revisionist History of Tort Law 235, 279 (2005); Friedman, supra note 8, at 225–226; Hall, supra note 8, at 119–223, 131; Horwitz, supra note 8, at 180–181; McDonald, supra note 1, at 113–114; G. Edward White, *The Intellectual Origins of Torts in America*, 86 Yale L.J. 671, 685 (1977).

118. 2 Farrand, supra note 1, at 220 (Aug. 8, 1787).

119. Id. at 364 (Aug. 21, 1787).

120. Id. at 221–223 (Aug. 8, 1787).

121. Id. at 370 (Aug. 22, 1787); Beeman, supra note 1, at 321–322.
122. 2 Farrand, supra note 1, at 364 (Aug. 21, 1787).
123. 1 Farrand, supra note 1, at 587 (July 11, 1787); Bell, supra note 103, at 11 (explaining "analytical contortions" common within the law of slavery); Lynd, supra note 103, at 131.
124. 1 Farrand, supra note 1, at 583, 587 (July 11, 1787); Bell, supra note 103, at 9–10; Lynd, supra note 103, at 129.
125. Beeman, supra note 103, at 332–333; Finkelman, supra note 1, at 34–35. Even the provisions explicitly protecting slavery did not use the words 'slave' or 'slavery.' Beeman, supra note 1, at 335–336; Finkelman, supra note 1, at 6. See 2 Farrand, supra note 103, at 364 (Aug. 21, 1787) (Charles Pinckney stating "South Carolina can never receive the plan if it prohibits the slave trade").
126. U.S. Const. art. I, § 2, cl. 3.
127. U.S. Const. art. I, § 9, cl. 1.
128. U.S. Const. art. 4, § 2, cl. 3. For more complete lists of the constitutional provisions, see Bell, supra note 103, at 22–23; Finkelman, supra note 103, at 6–9.
129. 2 Farrand, supra note 1, at 56 (July 19, 1787).
130. Id. at 56–57.
131. Akhil Reed Amar, *The Troubling Reason the Electoral College Exists*, Time Magazine (Nov. 8, 2016).
132. Finkelman, supra note 103, at 103 (quoting Pinckney); id. at 9–10 (southern attitudes toward protection of slavery); Klarman, supra note 1, at 297–303 (same). During ratification debates in the northern states, the proposed constitutional protections of slavery generated contentious debate. Finkelman, supra note 103, at 35–36; Maier, supra note 1, at 175–176, 351–352.
133. Erik W. Austin, Political Facts of the United States Since 1789, at 94–95 (1986) (Table 3.1, National Electoral and Popular Vote Cast for President, 1789–1984).
134. Federalist No. 10 (Madison).
135. Federalist No. 51 (Madison); Critical History, supra note 26, at 160.
136. Federalist No. 10 (Madison) (emphasis added); Federalist No. 14 (Madison) (the new government would be "in favor of private rights and public happiness"); Maier, supra note 8, at 81–82; Nedelsky, supra note 1, at 174; Mittal, supra note 1, at 36–37. The Constitution successfully created "a common market" that developed over the next decades. Mittal, supra note 1, at 40–41.
137. Cushman, supra note 7, at 381. Much of modern philosophy has been devoted to attempting to bridge various gaps in this dichotomous world. Richard J. Bernstein, Beyond Objectivism and Relativism (1983); Richard Rorty, Philosophy and the Mirror of Nature (1979).

138. Brown and Jacobs, supra note 100, at 10 (Adam Smith and David Hume argued for both strong markets and strong government).

139. Wood, supra note 1, at 24, 410–411, 609; McDonald, supra note 1, at 4, 9–55 (ambiguity of terms such as liberty).

140. Alexander Hamilton, *Letter to Robert Morris* (1780), *in* 3 The Works of Alexander Hamilton (Henry Cabot Lodge ed., 1904) (do not to overestimate the ability of individuals to calculate rationally); Federalist No. 1 (Hamilton) (calling on Americans "to deliberate" about the merits of the proposed Constitution); Nedelsky, supra note 1, at 76 (Gouverneur Morris questioning individual rationality); Pocock, supra note 1, at 464–465, 522–523 (discussing public and private rationalities).

141. U.S. Const. amend. I; Federalist No. 51 (Madison) ("multiplicity of sects" would protect "religious rights"); Critical History, supra note 1, at 148–149, 155; Isaac Kramnick and R. Laurence Moore, The Godless Constitution 118 (2005) (Massachusetts eliminated the final state establishment in 1833); Noah Feldman, *From Liberty to Equality: the Transformation of the Establishment Clause*, 90 Cal. L. Rev. 673, 690 (2002).

142. Annals of Congress (Sept. 25, 1789), *reprinted in* Anson Phelps Stokes, 1 Church and State in the United States 486 (1950); Critical History, supra note 26, at 158–168; Curry, supra note 28, at 218; Sandoz, supra note 15, at 130–131, 151–162.

143. U.S. Const. art. I, § 8, cl. 3.

144. Federalist No. 10 (Madison) (emphasis added). The Constitution did not embody a "free market" approach to economic activity. White, supra note 92, at 84.

145. James Wilson, *In the Pennsylvania Convention* (Nov. 24, 1787), *in* 3 Farrand, supra note 1, at 141, appendix A; *see* William J. Novak, The People's Welfare 9–11 (1996) (emphasizing the superiority of the public over the private sphere continued at least through the nineteenth century).

146. Stanley Elkins and Eric McKitrick, The Age of Federalism 93, 113–116 (1993); Heilbroner and Singer, supra note 8, at 85 (Hamilton was ahead of his times); James Roger Sharp, American Politics in the Early Republic 33–43 (1993); Empire, supra note 104, at 98.

147. 1 Farrand, supra note 1, at 288–289 (June 18, 1787); McDonald, supra note 1, at 115; Sharp, supra note 146, at 33, 43.

148. Elkins and McKitrick, supra note 1, at 93; McDonald, supra note 146, at 94–96, 138–142; Nedelsky, supra note 1, at 125–126; Empire, supra note 104, at 95–139.

149. Alexander Hamilton, *Report on Manufactures* (Communicated to the House of Representatives, December 5, 1791), 2 Annals of Congress 971, 1005 (1791–1793).

150. Thomas Jefferson, *Notes on the State of Virginia* (1787), *reprinted in* Thomas Jefferson: Writings 123 (Library of America, 1984); Finkelman, supra note 103, at 193–194; Seavoy, supra note 8, at 84–85; Henry Wiencek, Master of the Mountain 13 (2012).
151. Thomas Jefferson, *First Inaugural Address* (March 4, 1801); Elkins and McKitrick, supra note 146, at 13–19; Empire, supra note 104, at 287–301. On the Country ideology, see English, supra note 11; Bailyn, supra note 1, at 34–35; Pocock, supra note 1, at 406–408, 486–487.
152. Lance Banning, The Jeffersonian Persuasion 187–191 (1978); Elkins and McKittrick, supra note 146, at 199–200; Galbraith, supra note 8, at 46–56; Heilbroner and Singer, supra note 8, at 79–81; Lawrence S. Kaplan, Thomas Jefferson: Westward the Course of Empire 51–52 (1999); McDonald, supra note 1, at 98, 106–108.
153. Jefferson, supra note 150, at 290–291.
154. Thomas Jefferson, *To P.S. Dupont de Nemours* (Jan. 18, 1802), *reprinted in* Thomas Jefferson: Writings 1099 (Library of America, 1984).
155. Hamilton, supra note 149, at 972–973, 1006; Elkins and McKitrick, supra note 146, at 92–114.
156. Hamilton, supra note 149, at 988.
157. Id. at 973, 988–989. In other contexts, Madison repeatedly argued the government could assist a particular business enterprise if doing so would further the common good. James Madison, *In First Congress* (April 9, 1789), *reprinted in* Complete, supra note 71, at 276; James Madison, *In First Congress* (1789), *reprinted in* Complete, supra note 71, at 272; James Madison, *Letter to Clarkson Crolius* (Dec. 1819), *reprinted in* Complete, supra note 71, at 270; James Madison, *Letter to D. Lynch, Jr. (June 27, 1817), reprinted in* Complete, supra note 71, at 271.
158. Banning, supra note 152, at 139; Richard Hofstadter, *Federalists and Republicans, in* 2 Great Issues, supra note 11, at 141; Prindle, supra note 62, at 32; Empire, supra note 104, at 97.
159. U.S. Const. art. I, § 10, cl. 1.
160. 2 Farrand, supra note 1, at 439–440 (Aug. 28, 1787).
161. Id. at 597 (Report of the Committee of Style).
162. McDonald, supra note 1, at 270–274.
163. Maier, supra note 8, at 285; Horwitz, supra note 8, at 180–181; McDonald, supra note 1, at 113–114, 274.
164. Keyssar, supra note 91, at xxi–xxiv, 340–341(state suffrage requirements through 1790); U.S. Const. amend. XV (prohibiting denial of vote based on race; 1870); U.S. Const. amend. XIX (prohibiting denial of vote based on sex; 1920).
165. Beckert, supra note 104, at 117 (on the transition from a "mercantilist logic" to a more free flowing capitalist market).

166. Novak, supra note 145, at 1–2; Commonwealth v. Alger, 61 Mass. 53, 7 Cush. 53, 85–86 (1851) ("well ordered governments"); Robert A. Dahl, A Preface to Economic Democracy 1 (1985) ("a well-ordered society" required "political equality, political liberty, and economic liberty").

167. Stephen M. Feldman, Free Expression and Democracy in America: A History 167–169 (2008); Heilbroner and Milberg, supra note 8, at 87–88; Novak, supra note 145, at 10, 86, 237 (emphasizing local control); White, supra note 92, at 84; John Joseph Wallis, *The Other Foundings: Federalism and the Constitutional Structure of American Government, in* Founding Choices: American Economic Policy in the 1790s 177 (Douglas A. Irwin and Richard Sylla eds., 2011) (emphasizing the significance of state government policies for antebellum economic development). A growing emphasis on individualism was not equivalent to laissez faire. Walter Light, Industrializing America: The Nineteenth Century 191 (1995).

168. Hall, supra note 8, at 88; Horwitz, supra note 8, at xiv-xv; William J. Novak, *The Myth of the "Weak" American State*, 113 Am. Hist. Rev. 752, 754, 769–771 (2008) (government exercise of infrastructural power influenced distribution of wealth); *see* Jerry L. Mashaw, Creating the Administrative Constitution 3–12, 18–25 (2012) (there was far more regulation of the economy, even at the federal level, than is ordinarily acknowledged).

169. Calder v. Bull, 3 U.S. (3 Dall.) 386, 388 (1798) (Chase, J.) (natural law); Vanzant v. Waddel, 10 Tenn. 260 (1829) (state law of the land provision).

170. Goshen v. Stonington, 4 Conn. 209, 221 (1822). For additional examples, see *State Bank v. Cooper*, 10 Tenn. 599 (1831);*Eakin v. Raub*, 12 Serg. and Rawle 330 (Pa. 1825); *Calder v. Bull*, 3 U.S. (3 Dall.) 386, 388 (1798) (Chase, J.); *VanHorne's Lessee v. Dorrance*, 28 F.Cas. 1012 (C.C. Pa. 1795).

171. Commonwealth v. Rice, 9 Metcalf 253, 50 Mass. 253, 256, 259 (1845); Novak, supra note 145, at 51–233 (cataloguing examples of government regulations and restrictions upheld as promoting the common good or the people's welfare). For similar cases, see *Thorpe v. Rutland and Burlington Railroad Co.*, 27 Vt. 140 (1855); *Vandine's Case*, 23 Mass. 187 (1828); *Vanderbilt v. Adams*, 7 Cow. 349, 351–352 (N.Y. 1827).

172. James Kent, 2 Commentaries on American Law 276 (1827; Legal Classics Library Reprint). Although courts readily upheld numerous government actions, the republican concept of limited government was not specious. State Bank v. Cooper, 10 Tenn. 599 (1831) (invalidating law creating special court for Bank of Tennessee); Pingrey v. Washburn, 1 Aik. 264, 15 Am.Dec. 676 (1826) (invalidating turnpike toll law).

173. For extensive discussions of free expression in the early years of nationhood, including the Sedition Act crisis, see Feldman, supra note 167, at 46–100; Leonard W. Levy, Emergence of a Free Press (1985); David A. Anderson, *The Origins of the Press Clause*, 30 U.C.L.A. L. Rev. 455 (1983). Helpful sources on the adoption of the Bill of Rights can be found in the following collections: The Complete Bill of Rights: The Drafts, Debates, Sources, and Origins (Neil H. Cogan ed., 1997) [hereinafter Cogan]; The Founders' Constitution (Philip B. Kurland and Ralph Lerner eds., 1987) [hereinafter Founders]; The Bill of Rights: A Documentary History (Bernard Schwartz ed., 1971) [hereinafter Schwartz, Documentary].

174. 3 Farrand, supra note 1, at 599 (Appendix D. The Pinckney Plan); 2 Farrand, supra note 1, at 334, 341 (Aug. 20, 1787); id. at 617 (Sept. 14, 1787).

175. 2 Farrand, supra note 1, at 587–588 (Sept. 12, 1787); id. at 618 (Sept. 14, 1787).

176. James Wilson, Speech at a Meeting in Philadelphia (Oct. 6, 1787), *reprinted in* Cogan, supra note 173, at 102 (Congress without power over freedom of the press).

177. Herbert J. Storing, What the Anti-Federalists Were For (1981). For examples of Anti-Federalists questioning the lack of protection for freedom of the press, see Centinel, No. 1 (Oct. 1787), *reprinted in* 5 Founders, supra note 173, at 13, 19–20; Federal Farmer, No. 4 (Oct. 12, 1787), *reprinted in* 5 Founders, supra note 173, at 54, 59; Centinel, No. 2 (Oct. 24, 1787), *reprinted in* Cogan, supra note 173, at 103, 103–104; Federal Farmer, No. 16 (Jan. 20, 1788), *reprinted in* 5 Founders, supra note 173, at 79, 85–86.

178. Letter from James Madison to Alexander Hamilton (June 22, 1788), *reprinted in* Schwartz, Documentary, supra note 173, at 848; *see* James Madison, Speech in the Virginia Ratifying Convention on Ratification and Amendments (June 24, 1788), *reprinted in* James Madison: Writings 401, 406–407 (Library of America 1999).

179. Proposal by Madison in House (June 8, 1789), *reprinted in* Cogan, supra note 173, at 83; House of Representatives, Amendments to the Constitution (June 8, 1789) (from The Annals of Congress), *reprinted in* 5 Founders, supra note 173, at 20–22, 26.

180. House of Representatives, Amendments to the Constitution (Aug. 15, 1789) (from The Annals of Congress), *reprinted in* 5 Founders, supra note 173, at 204; Schwartz, Documentary, supra note 173, at 1050; Anderson, supra note 173, at 478.

181. Senate Journal (Sept. 1789), *reprinted in* Schwartz, Documentary, supra note 173, at 1163–1165.

182. Feldman, supra note 167, at 64.
183. Respublica v. Oswald, 1 Dall. 319 (Pa. 1788), *reprinted in* 5 Founders, supra note 173, at 124, 127.
184. Levy, supra note 173, at 213 (quoting Thomas McKean).
185. Id. at 37–45.
186. James Wilson, 2 The Works of James Wilson 287, 395–397 (James DeWitt Andrews ed., 1895 ed.)
187. Feldman, supra note 167, at 3–13, 46–60.
188. *Of Freedom of Speech: That the same is inseparable from Publick Liberty* (Feb. 4, 1720), *reprinted in* English, supra note 11, at 38, 42 (signed by Thomas Gordon). Samuel Adams emphasized "the bulwark of the People's Liberties." Levy, supra note 173, at 67 (quoting *Boston Gazette*, March 14, 1768).
189. Virginia Bill of Rights (1776), *reprinted in* 2 Poore, supra note 173, at 1908, 1909.
190. John Dawson at Virginia Ratification Convention (June 24, 1788), *reprinted in* Cogan, supra note 173, at 101; Patrick Henry at Virginia Ratification Convention (June 14, 1788), *reprinted in* Schwartz, Documentary, supra note 173, at 800; Cincinnatus, No. 2, to James Wilson (Nov. 8, 1787), *reprinted in* 5 Founders, supra note 173, at 122; Centinel, No. 2 (Oct. 24, 1787), *reprinted in* Cogan, supra note 173, at 103.
191. Proposal by Madison in House (June 8, 1789), *reprinted in* Cogan, supra note 173, at 83.
192. Wilbur H. Siebert, The Loyalists of Pennsylvania (1920) (describing treatment of Philadelphia Tories in 1775); Claude H. Van Tyne, The Loyalists in the American Revolution 62–65 (1902) (discussing the formation of various committees). Many of the most important nine-teenth-century struggles over free expression, particularly those involving abolition and slavery, took place outside the courts—sometimes in Congress but sometimes in less formal settings—and thus revolved more around the traditions of dissent and suppression than around the legal doctrine of free expression. Feldman, supra note 167, at 118–152; Michael Kent Curtis, Free Speech, "The People's Darling Privilege:" Struggles for Freedom of Expression in American History 3 (2000). On the relationship between the traditions and doctrine, see Feldman, supra note 167, at 4, 222, 470–471.
193. Sharp, supra note 146, at 8–9.
194. *See* Feldman, supra note 167, at 70–100 (discussing Sedition Act crisis).

195. The Sedition Act of 1798, 1 U.S. Statutes at Large 597, § 3, 5th Congress, 2d sess. (July 14, 1798); *see* The Legislature of Rhode Island on the Virginia Resolutions (Feb. 1799), *in* 2 Great Issues, supra note 11, at 184–186 (arguing Congress acted within its power to promote the general welfare).

196. *E.g.*, Annals of Congress of the United States, 1797–1799, 5th Congress, 2d sess. 2139 (July 1798) (statement of Virginia Representative John Nicholas).

197. Id. at 2153 (statement of New York Representative Edward Livingston).

198. Kentucky Resolutions (Nov. 10, 1798; Nov. 14, 1799), *reprinted in* 5 Founders, supra note 173, at 131–132; Sharp, supra note 146, at 196–197.

199. Elkins and McKittrick, supra note 146, at 746–750; Sharp, supra note 146, at 226–275.

200. *E.g.*, James Madison, *Report on the Alien and Sedition Acts* (Jan. 7, 1800), *reprinted in* James Madison: Writings 608 (Library of America 1999); George Hay, An Essay on the Liberty of the Press (1799), *reprinted in* Two Essays on the Liberty of the Press (1803; 1970 reprint ed.).

201. Constitution of Pennsylvania (1838), *reprinted in* 2 Poore, supra note 1, at 1557, 1564; Constitution of Arkansas (1836), *reprinted in* 1 Poore, supra note 1, at 101, 102.

202. State v. Van Wye, 136 Mo. 227, 37 S.W. 938, 939 (1896).

203. The bad tendency test first emerged as a truth-conditional standard. As articulated by Judge James Kent in *People v. Croswell*, 3 Johns. Cas. 337 (N.Y. Sup. Ct. 1804), truth was a defense to a charge of criminal libel but only if the defendant published for good motives and justifiable ends. If the published material was either false, or true but with bad tendencies, then it was criminally punishable. *E.g.*, Castle v. Houston, 19 Kan. 417 (1877); Perkins v. Mitchell, 31 Barb. 461 (N.Y. Sup. 1860); Commonwealth v. Morris, 3 Va. 176 (1811).

PART II

The Transformation of the Constitutional System

CHAPTER 3

Republican Democracy Evolves: Corporations and Laissez Faire

Despite the problems that had arisen during the 1780s—state government corruption and national economic straits—many Americans continued to believe they were well-suited for republican democratic government.[1] An agrarian economy in which a majority of white men owned property produced a rough material equality, unknown elsewhere in the world. At the constitutional convention, Gouverneur Morris estimated that "nine-tenths of the people are at present freeholders."[2] Even if Morris overstated land ownership, the existing material equality engendered, in turn, a culture of political equality. Charles Pinckney declared that, because of widespread property ownership, "equality is... the leading feature of the U.S." Relative material equality facilitated the public–private balance, the simultaneous flourishing of republican democratic government, dependent on political equality, and private property rights. To Pinckney, "the people of the United States are more equal in their circumstances than the people of any other Country."[3] In comparison, in 1790 England, a mere 400 families owned one-fifth of all the farmland. Shortly after the convention, Thomas Jefferson wrote: "I think our governments will remain virtuous for many centuries; as long as they are chiefly agricultural; and this will be as long as there shall be vacant lands in any part of America."[4] Of course, the ostensibly vacant lands would often be forcibly taken from Native American tribes.[5] In any event, with an overwhelming number of Americans committed to Protestantism and tracing their ancestral roots to Western or Northern Europe, the people seemed sufficiently homogeneous to join together in the pursuit of the common good.[6]

© The Author(s) 2017
S.M. Feldman, *The New Roberts Court, Donald Trump, and Our Failing Constitution*, DOI 10.1007/978-3-319-56451-7_3

Not all Americans, though, were Protestant Anglo-Saxon male property owners. Nevertheless, exclusion preserved at least a surface homogeneity. According to republican democratic theory, non-virtuous
individuals (or non-virtuous societal groups) would be unwilling to
forgo the pursuit of their own private interests. Instead, they would
form factions bent on corrupting republican democratic government.
Significantly, then, an alleged lack of civic virtue could supposedly justify the forced exclusion of a group from the polity. On this pretext,
African Americans, Irish-Catholic immigrants, women, and other peripheral groups were precluded from participating in republican democracy
for much of American history. To take one instance, when large numbers of Catholic immigrants began coming to the United States in the
mid-nineteenth century, Protestant nativists condemned the immigrants
as unqualified for citizenship. "Protestantism favors Republicanism,"
declared Samuel Morse, "whereas 'Popery' supports 'Monarchical
power.'"[7] Thus, although the concepts of virtue and the common good
typically remained nebulous in the abstract, they closely mirrored mainstream white, male, Protestant values and interests in concrete political
(and judicial) contexts.

With these premises in place—that is, widespread land ownership
among white Protestant males, and exclusion of many others from the
polity—the basic principles of republican democracy predominated
throughout the nineteenth century. Yet, the specific understandings of
virtue and the common good changed during that time. For example,
whereas many framers believed that virtue was concentrated in an elite
segment of American society, a growing number of Americans began to
believe during the early-nineteenth century that virtue was shared equally
by all common people (particularly by white Protestant men).[8] Similarly,
from the Revolution until the 1820s, political parties were understood to
corrupt republican democratic government. Political parties were viewed
as factional interest groups that pursued private and partial interests
rather than the common good. Yet, in the 1820s and 1830s, the perception of political parties changed with a growing recognition that parties
could be useful means for facilitating more widespread political participation and thus should be an acceptable republican democratic institution.[9]

An important change in the American understanding of the common good revolved around corporations and commerce.[10] During the
early decades of nationhood, corporations could be formed only when
legislatures specially chartered them—general incorporation laws did

not exist—and legislatures rarely granted such special state charters. The ratification of the Constitution had prompted a modest burst of incorporation in the 1790s, but even so, by 1800, only 300–350 corporations existed in the United States. Legislatures almost never granted corporate charters to businesses that focused solely on profit-making. Instead, in a manifestation of the lingering mercantilist outlook, states would charter corporations that promoted the common good by performing a function useful to the public. For example, corporate charters were frequently granted for the building of infrastructure, including roads, bridges, and canals, as well as for the operation of ferries, banks, and insurance companies.[11]

Numerous arguments were voiced in opposition to charters of incorporation, with most arguments rooted in the nature of republican democracy. Many Americans viewed a legislative grant of a corporate charter as the granting of special privileges, the opposite of a law for the common good. In 1809, Judge Spencer Roane of Virginia explained: "With respect to acts of incorporation, they ought never to be passed, but in consideration of services to be rendered to the public... It may be often *convenient* for a set of associated individuals, to have the privileges of a corporation bestowed upon them; but if their object is merely *private* or selfish; if it is detrimental to, or not promotive of, the public good, they have no adequate claim upon the legislature for the privilege."[12] In a similar vein, others maintained that a corporate charter resonated too closely with hereditary aristocracies, contrary to republican government, because certain individuals were being separated from the body of the people. Indeed, some critics of incorporation insisted that when a state granted a corporate charter, the state sacrificed the people's sovereignty. Charles Jared Ingersoll commented at a Pennsylvania state constitutional convention in the 1830s that "whatever power is given to a corporation, is just so much power taken from the State, in derogation of the original power of the mass of the community."[13] Many Americans denounced corporations as "soulless," while others explicitly worried that corporate wealth corrupted politics.[14] When President Andrew Jackson vetoed the re-incorporation of the Second National Bank, he reasoned that Bank officers and stockholders, especially foreign stockholders, might unduly "influence elections" and thus undermine their "purity."[15]

Yet, during those early decades of the nineteenth century, America grew increasingly commercial. "We are no longer to remain plain and simple republics of farmers, like New-England colonists, or the Dutch settlements on the Hudson," declared James Kent at the 1821 New York state constitutional convention. "We are fast becoming a great nation, with great commerce, manufactures, population, wealth, and luxuries."[16] In the 1830s, Tocqueville observed that even American farmers typically "combine some trade with agriculture; most of them make agriculture itself a trade."[17] In fact, the gross national product per capita more than doubled over the first six decades of the nineteenth century. For certain commercial enterprises, the corporate form offered potential advantages such as the aggregation of capital from a multitude of people. Even so, in the Jacksonian era, opposition to the legislative granting of special corporate privileges remained strong and widespread. In his Bank veto, Jackson attacked not only the National Bank's favored status but all such government-granted privileges: "Every monopoly and all exclusive privileges are granted at the expense of the public...."[18] But during this period, the process of incorporation democratized. Jacksonian-era Americans objected to special charters and privileges granted to the few—to "the rich and powerful," in Jackson's words. These same Americans, however, readily accepted government actions that appeared to apply to all equally. "If [government] would confine itself to equal protection," Jackson explained, "and, as Heaven does its rains, shower its favors alike on the high and the low, the rich and the poor, it would be an unqualified blessing."[19]

In other words, corporations no longer appeared to be inherently problematic. Rather, only specially chartered corporations, favoring a select few, seemed abhorrent. Since, in this commercial age, government facilitation of commerce appeared to promote the common good, states found a solution to the incorporation problem: They enacted general incorporation laws, which created simple processes for forming corporations without special legislative charters. The first state to do so was Connecticut, in 1837, with other states following suit over the next 20 years. Despite the passage of general incorporation laws, many businesses preferred a special charter, and frequently, state legislatures would accommodate these requests. Even so, New York in 1846 became the first state to adopt a constitutional provision prohibiting the legislative granting of special corporate charters; subsequently, all corporate charters had to be pursuant to the general incorporation law. Again, other states followed suit, so that by the 1880s, almost all new corporations were created under state general incorporation laws. Incorporation itself, supposedly available to all equally, now seemed to further the common good, promoting commerce and progress.[20]

Two Supreme Court decisions from the first half of the nineteenth century illustrate the changing American attitudes toward commerce and corporations. *Dartmouth College v. Woodward*,[21] decided in 1819, arose when the New Hampshire legislature amended the charter incorporating the College. Chief Justice John Marshall's opinion for the Court categorized the initial corporate charter as a contract protected under the Contract Clause of the Constitution. The attempted legislative amendment, Marshall reasoned, materially changed and therefore unconstitutionally impaired the charter. To a great degree, *Dartmouth College* protected traditional property rights. The decision resonated with a quasi-mercantilism where the state issues and preserves corporate charters, often monopolistic in nature, while corporations act for the common good. By 1837, when the Court decided *Charles River Bridge v. Warren Bridge Company*,[22] the justices' conception of property had shifted in a capitalist direction. Massachusetts in 1785 had enacted a corporate charter for the building and operation of a toll bridge across the Charles River. In 1828, the state legislature chartered a new corporation, the Warren Bridge Company, to build and operate a second bridge across the Charles River. Because of this second bridge, the Charles River Bridge Company lost much of its expected traffic and toll income. Citing *Dartmouth College*, the Company argued that its original charter had created a vested property right protected by the Contract Clause. The Court, now under Chief Justice Roger B. Taney, rejected this argument. Taney's majority opinion focused more on economic competition in the private sphere than on the protection of traditional property rights. From the Court's vantage, legislatures could now encourage such competition, even in the building of infrastructure such as bridges, because doing so promoted the public good. Taney wrote: "[I]n a country like ours, free, active and enterprising, continually advancing in numbers and wealth, new channels of communication are daily found necessary, both for travel and trade, and are essential to the comfort, convenience and prosperity of the people." After *Charles River Bridge*, corporations needed to compete rather than claim exclusive or monopolistic privileges.[23]

Sparked by the general incorporation laws, new corporations multiplied like stars in a clear evening sky. And many of these corporations participated in and generated tremendous changes in American society after the Civil War, as increasing industrialization, immigration, and urbanization strained the republican democratic system. In 1870, nearly twice as many Americans worked in agriculture as in manufacturing, construction, and related jobs, but by 1900, agricultural workers constituted only one-third of the workforce. The steel industry, buoyed by the Bessemer process, supplied material for the construction (or improvement) of railroads, subways, and (suddenly possible) skyscrapers, as well as products ranging from bridge beams to boiler plates to wires, pipes, and needles.[24] Steel production jumped from 19,643 tons in 1867, to 198,796 tons in 1873, to over 10 million tons in 1900, and to over 20 million in 1905. And as the economy shifted from agriculture to manufacturing, Americans moved from rural areas to cities, particularly those of the Northeast and Midwest. Before the Civil War, the rural population was more than quadruple the size of the urban, with approximately 25 million in rural territories and 6 million in cities. By 1900, the overall population had increased considerably, and the percentage in cities had done likewise, with approximately 46 million in rural territories and 30 million in cities. Many of these new city dwellers (and factory workers) were immigrants. From 1882 to 1902, more than 400 thousand new Americans arrived per annum 13 times; industrialists supported this massive immigration because it supplied surplus labor for the factories. Significantly, the countries of origin for most of these immigrants differed from those of previous immigrants, who had come primarily from Western Europe. As late as 1882, out of the total of almost 800 thousand immigrants to arrive in that year, only 50 thousand (approximately) came from Southern and Eastern Europe. But by 1902, merely 22% of immigrants came from Western Europe, while 78% arrived from Southern and Eastern Europe.[25]

During the postbellum decades, money was to be made, and at least some Americans were making it. The Gross National Product (GNP) approximately tripled from the period, 1869–1873, to the period, 1889–1893. Corporations and their shareholders were accumulating much of the wealth (immigrant factory workers usually were not becoming rich). Railroads, in particular, became models for large corporations while also facilitating the growth of other large businesses, including corporations. The miles of railroad track being laid exploded after the Civil War. In 1871, the amount of track built, 6660 miles, was more than quadruple the amount from just before the war began, and thousands of miles of additional track were laid every year until the early-twentieth century. The railroads needed massive inputs of capital to finance the construction of tracks as well as the purchasing of locomotives, railroad cars, and other necessities of business. The corporate form empowered the railroads to raise the needed capital, especially as an increasing number of states developed the concept of limited shareholder liability, so investors would not be at risk for corporate debts. The corporate bureaucracy also proved effective for managing large business organizations.[26]

In an 1886 decision, *Santa Clara v. Southern Pacific Railroad,* which involved both the Southern Pacific and Central Pacific Railroads, the Supreme Court established, without explanation, that corporations were persons within the meaning of the Fourteenth Amendment.[27] This constitutional status would be a long-term economic boon for corporations. The spreading reach of the railroad corporations and their tracks fused the multitude of regional economic markets into a national marketplace that, in turn, engendered the growth of other large business corporations. Businesses could ship their products to any and all points, so long as they were within the railroad-track tentacles. Consequently, economies of scale encouraged the growth of ever-larger corporations. From 1890 to 1904, so many businesses merged that approximately fifty corporations controlled the bulk of American industry. In 1901, J. P. Morgan merged 158 companies, including the already massive Carnegie Steel, into a single corporation, United States Steel, which produced two-thirds of the nation's steel in 156 factories, employed a quarter of a million people, and was vertically integrated from the mining of ore to the production of steel products.[28]

During the post-Civil War decades, a growing number of individuals began to infuse the concept of the common good with a stronger emphasis on laissez-faire economic thinking. In the pre-Civil War era, as discussed, state and local governments extensively regulated economic marketplaces, with numerous courts recognizing "the subserviency of private rights to public security," in the words of Vermont Supreme Court Justice Isaac Redfield.[29] Even so, commerce boomed during these antebellum years without laissez-faire demands for less regulation. To the contrary, law was viewed as an instrument for "the release of [creative and economic] energy."[30] But in the late-nineteenth century, many Americans, particularly corporate leaders—and no small number of government officials—insisted that a laissez-faire system would produce more wealth and thus allow individuals—at least, certain individuals—to make even more money. From this perspective, government regulations of the marketplace inevitably dampened economic incentive and stifled initiative.[31] President Grover Cleveland declared in 1887 that "though the people support the Government, the Government should not support the people."[32] Unsurprisingly, postbellum congressional debates over a graduated income tax produced vociferous laissez-faire proclamations. Differential taxation, declared Vermont Representative Justin S. Morrill, could "only be defended on the same ground as the highwayman defends his acts."[33] To be sure, the nation never moved to a pure laissez-faire system. Indeed, government persistently bolstered business. For instance, to nurture the development of the railroads, the national government gave them immense tracts of public land—including 128 million acres during the years 1862–1871. Yet, advocates of laissez faire conveniently ignored such government intrusions into commercial affairs, so long as they directly benefitted business. Throughout the late-nineteenth and early-twentieth centuries, the utopian dream of an unregulated economic marketplace continued to motivate many Americans. These laissez-faire ideologues insisted that any government regulation shifting money or property from A to B or otherwise interfering with the operation of the marketplace necessarily transgressed the common good.[34]

The sources of American laissez-faire thought were diverse and complex. Unquestionably, economic self-interest motivated many American supporters: They believed they could make more money if governments stopped regulating the marketplace. But more forces than economic interest were in play. For several decades already, British thinkers such as James Mill and David Ricardo had been advocating for unregulated economic markets.[35] And in a perverse twist, slavery also contributed prominently to the elaboration of American laissez faire.

Before the Civil War, the emerging Republican party of Abraham Lincoln had advanced a free labor, free soil ideology.[36] The crux of this ideology was to contrast free labor with slave labor. As Republican journalist and politician Horace Greeley wrote in the 1850s: "Enslave a man and you destroy his ambition, his enterprise, his capacity." But free labor, Greeley explained, was consonant with "the constitution of human nature, the desire of bettering one's condition [as] the mainspring of effort."[37] The free labor, free soil ideology closely integrated the private and public spheres in the context of a still-agrarian and rural nation. The farmer working his own land (or the independent artisan in his shop) promoted commercial progress and the republican common good. During the 1860 presidential campaign, a Republican newspaper declared: "We say to the government, give us protection to our labor that we may advance the national prosperity by developing the unbounded resources of our country."[38] Whereas slave labor degraded "free and honest industry," free labor produced "hardy, industrious, intelligent and free citizens." In the words of Lincoln, "Men, with their families... work for themselves on their farms, in their houses, and in their shops, taking the whole product to themselves, and asking no favors of capital on the one hand nor of hired laborers or slaves on the other."[39]

Thus, free labor on free soil supposedly assured that each individual possessed the autonomy to contract freely, to own property, and to support himself and his family. And from the northern standpoint, the Union victory in the Civil War marked, according to Greeley, "the triumph of republicanism and free labor." Congressional Republicans consequently sought to translate their free labor principles into enforceable statutory and constitutional rights, especially for the freedmen or former slaves.[40] For instance, the 1866 Civil Rights Act included protections "to make and enforce contracts, to sue, be parties, and give evidence, to inherit, purchase, lease, sell, hold, and convey real and personal property." This statute, explained Pennsylvania Representative Martin Thayer, would prevent states from enacting "laws which declare [that freedmen] shall not have the privilege of purchasing a home for themselves and their families; laws which impair their ability to make contracts for labor in such manner as virtually to deprive them of the power of making such contracts, and which then declare them vagrants because they have no homes and because they have no employment."[41] In short, Reconstruction-era Republicans sought to enforce the fundamental economic rights that had distinguished free labor from slave labor.[42]

Yet, as Republicans continued to press their free labor, free soil principles, postbellum industrialization and urbanization started a tidal-wave break over the rural agrarianism of antebellum America. During the years of Reconstruction, many Americans were slow to recognize the new rifts developing in their society, particularly those between labor and capital. Free labor ideology presumed that the ideal republican democratic citizen was the independent farmer or artisan. Where free labor and free soil existed, any wage laborer could work to eventually attain the independence and liberty of the farmer (or artisan). And even if the laborer was not dreaming of a farm in the countryside, the laborer could nonetheless become a capitalist, or at least many Americans believed as much.

In 1867, Edwin L. Godkin wrote in *The North American Review*: "Most successful employers of labor have begun by being laborers themselves; most laborers hope, and may reasonably hope, to become employers."[43] Labor and capital, it seemed, functioned in a seamless unity. Before long, however, northern factory workers were questioning this supposed harmony between capital and labor and, more generally, doubting the relevance of the free labor ideology. Immigrant factory workers in New York, Boston, or other growing metropolises knew nothing of the bucolic existence of the farmer or small-town artisan. The American labor movement emerged in this context of social and economic transformation. In a remarkable statement, the 1873 *Declaration of Principles* of the International Labor Union of America denounced the "despotism" of the "wage-system," and proclaimed that "there can be no government of the people, by the people, and for the people, where the many are dependent upon the few for an existence."[44]

Even while factory workers were questioning antebellum ideals, free labor ideology was beginning an alchemical transmutation into laissez faire. An early signal of the coming change appeared in an 1873 Supreme Court case, *The Slaughterhouse Cases*. The Louisiana state legislature had enacted a statute granting a monopoly to one slaughterhouse for the butchering of cattle within an area including New Orleans. A group of local butchers challenged the law as violating the Thirteenth and Fourteenth Amendments, but the Court upheld the constitutionality of the statute in a five-to-four decision. The majority opinion, written by Justice Samuel Miller, emphasized local sovereignty and showed great deference to the state legislature. According to Miller, the regulation of animal slaughtering was a typical exercise of the police power. To a great degree, Miller's opinion read like an antebellum judicial opinion upholding a state or local police power regulation. In fact, Miller quoted one of James Kent's descriptions of the well-ordered republican society. "'Unwholesome trades, slaughter-houses, operations offensive to the senses, the deposit of powder, the application of steam power to propel cars, the building with combustible materials, and the burial of the dead, may all,' says Chancellor Kent, 'be interdicted by law, in the midst of dense masses of population, on the general and rational principle, that every person ought so to use his property as not to injure his neighbors; and that private interests must be made subservient to the general interests of the community.'"[45]

The alchemy thus crystallized not in Miller's majority opinion, but in Justice Stephen J. Field's dissent, joined by three other justices. Like Miller, Field reasoned that the case raised an issue related to the scope of the state's police power, but Field argued that the Reconstruction (Thirteenth and Fourteenth) Amendments precluded deference to the state legislature. Significantly, Field then interpreted the police power and the common good consistently with free labor ideology. The statute, Field maintained, violated "the right of free labor, one of the most sacred and imprescriptible rights of man." Even more important (for the future), Field then elaborated free labor in a footnote that quoted Adam Smith.

"The property which every man has in his own labor," says Adam Smith, as it is the original foundation of all other property, so it is the most sacred and inviolable. The patrimony of the poor man lies in the strength and dexterity of his own hands; and to hinder him from employing this strength and dexterity in what manner he thinks proper, without injury to his neighbor, is a plain violation of this most sacred property. It is a manifest encroachment upon the just liberty both of the workman and of those who might be disposed to employ him. As it hinders the one from working at what he thinks proper, so it hinders the others from employing whom they think proper.[46]

Antebellum Republicans had articulated free labor in opposition to slave labor. In their agrarian world, each man could achieve economic independence by owning and farming his own land. Field, now, bent free labor in a radically different direction. Smith had written in protest against mercantilism and in support of the incipient capitalism of the English Industrial Revolution. In Field's hands, free labor was being molded into the freedom "of an employee contracting with his employer, ... something more like 'free contract.'"[47] As the United States was careening into its own Industrial Revolution, Field had planted a seed that would bloom several years later: Free labor would mutate and grow into laissez faire.

In subsequent years, laissez-faire thinking intertwined with Social Darwinism, as inspired by Herbert Spencer, and its celebration of natural selection in society. Unregulated competition in the economic marketplace supposedly led to the survival of the fittest, which corresponded with the republican democratic common good—or at least it was so claimed. In an 1883 book, Yale professor William Graham Sumner lauded the accumulation of vast fortunes and denounced social welfare legislation. "Society needs first of all to be freed from these meddlers—that is, to be let alone," he wrote. "Here we are, then, once more back at the old doctrine—laissez faire. Let us translate it into blunt English, and it will read, Mind your own business. It is nothing but the doctrine of liberty."[48] From the perspective of Social Darwinists, economic inequality was legitimated as a positive good for society. Andrew Carnegie explained that the law of competition not only was inevitable, but also was "best for the race, because it insures the survival of the fittest in every department. We accept and welcome therefore, as conditions to which we must accommodate ourselves, great inequality of environment, the concentration of business, industrial and commercial, in the hands of a few, and the law of competition between these, as being not only beneficial, but essential for the future progress of the race."[49]

In the late-nineteenth and early-twentieth centuries, laissez-faire ideology continued to spread in Europe as well as in the United States.[50] Indeed, while the concept of globalization was not yet in vogue, many laissez-faire thinkers extended the commitment to an open unregulated marketplace beyond national boundaries. The gold standard, in particular, was intended to facilitate the operation of an international marketplace. Numerous countries followed Great Britain's lead by switching to gold; the United States adopted it in 1879. When a country adopted the gold standard, the country committed to a set rate of exchange between its currency and gold, thus linking its currency to all others likewise tied to gold. The gold standard created, in effect, a single international currency. With such financial predictability in place, "the gold standard facilitated world trade, lending, investment, migration, and payments."[51] American business leaders, in particular, expected that the nation's move to gold would assure foreign investors of the country's economic stability. And as the Americans hoped, foreign investors responded by funneling capital into American enterprises, especially railroads. Even in times of economic crises, such as the 1893 depression, many American business and government leaders remained committed to gold as "a standard of value the world over," in the words of a Wisconsin congressional representative.[52] In fact, international trade and economic interaction in the early-twentieth century, before the onset of war in 1914, was more extensive than during any prior point in history. British economist John Maynard Keynes would comment that "internationalization…

was nearly complete in practice."[53] Given the worldwide appeal of laissez faire—in its manifestation as an unregulated international market—and its ostensible success in generating wealth, the strength of the ideology in the United States was unsurprising, even when Progressivism emerged as a powerful political force and successfully pushed for at least some social welfare legislation in the early-twentieth century.[54]

Justice Field had dissented in *The Slaughterhouse Cases*, but other jurists and scholars were soon following his lead, as laissez-faire ideology burrowed deeply into American constitutional jurisprudence. A leading constitutional scholar, Christopher G. Tiedeman, published his *Treatise on the Limitations of Police Power in the United States* in 1886. He unequivocally explained his purpose: to support "laissez-faire doctrine, which denies to government the power to do more than to provide for the public order and personal security by the prevention and punishment of crimes and trespasses." Tiedeman opposed any form of social welfare legislation and argued that courts should interpret constitutional provisions to limit state police powers. To be sure, Tiedeman acknowledged that republican democratic governments could legitimately enact regulations if they truly promoted the common good, but from his perspective, such legitimate regulations were rare.[55] More important, perhaps, state and federal courts shifted toward a laissez-faire tinged interpretation of the republican democratic common good. Lawyers representing corporations and other wealthy business interests encouraged this judicial shift. These lawyers would explicitly speak the language of constitutional principles and doctrines, but they were implicitly advocating for laissez faire, which would supposedly allow businesses to maximize profits.[56] Courts proved receptive to these arguments. For example, in 1886, the Illinois Supreme Court struck down a law intended to prevent coal companies from cheating their miners when weighing the quantity mined. The court reasoned the legislation was not a "general public law, binding upon all the members of the community, under all circumstances;" rather, it was a "partial or private [law] affecting the rights of private individuals, or classes of individuals."[57]

The United States Supreme Court sympathized strongly with business in the late-nineteenth and early-twentieth centuries. Justices often were culled from the ranks of corporate law firms, especially those representing railroads. Unsurprisingly, then, these justices frequently agreed with the laissez-faire arguments of corporate lawyers. In *Allgeyer v. Louisiana*, decided in 1897, the Court held that a state law restricting insurance contracts violated due process. Writing for a unanimous Court, Justice Rufus Peckham acknowledged that the state could exercise its police power to pursue the common good, but the Court construed the common good narrowly by emphasizing that due process liberty protects marketplace transactions—or, in other words, due process protects "liberty to contract." Although earlier in the nineteenth century, courts regularly had held that economic regulations furthered the common good, the *Allgeyer* Court was especially skeptical of such government actions. Due process liberty, wrote Peckham, embraces the following rights: "the right of the citizen to be free in the enjoyment of all his faculties; to be free to use them in all lawful ways; to live and work where he will; to earn his livelihood by any lawful calling; to pursue any livelihood or avocation; and for that purpose to enter into all contracts which may be proper, necessary, and essential to his carrying out to a successful conclusion the purposes above mentioned."[58]

In the early-twentieth century, the tension between laissez-faire constitutionalism and Progressive politics became manifest in several Supreme Court decisions. *Lochner v. New York*, decided in 1905, perfectly illustrates this tension, and eventually, *Lochner* would become emblematic of this Supreme Court era. The state of New York exercised its police power to enact a prototypical Progressive statute, restricting the number of hours employees could work in bakeries (10 per day and 60 per week). In a five-to-four decision, the Court invalidated the law as violating due process. Peckham again wrote the opinion, which largely followed the *Allgeyer* line of reasoning. After acknowledging the state's police power, the Court examined the state's asserted justifications for the statute: as a regulation of labor relations and as a regulation for health purposes. In the context of this case, Peckham concluded, neither of these purported justifications equated with the common good. "It seems to us that the real [legislative] object and purpose were simply to regulate the hours of labor between the master and his employees (all being men, *sui juris* [or competent]), in a private business, not dangerous in any degree to morals, or in any real and substantial degree to the health of the employees." Put in different words, the statute intruded into the economic marketplace without sufficient justification. Justice Oliver Wendell Holmes's dissent criticized the majority's definition of the common good as being shaped by Social Darwinist or laissez-faire ideology. "The Fourteenth Amendment," Holmes wrote, "does not enact Mr. Herbert Spencer's Social Statics."[59]

The shift toward a laissez-faire tinged common good did not substantially affect the judicial doctrine of free expression. The United States Supreme Court first began to consider free-expression issues in the late-nineteenth and early-twentieth centuries, and like other courts, the Court interpreted free speech and a free press pursuant to republican democratic principles. The Court consistently allowed the government to punish speech or writing that engendered bad tendencies because such expression undermined virtue and contravened the common good.[60] For example, in *Halter v. Nebraska*, which upheld a conviction under a state flag desecration statute, the Court reasoned: "It is familiar law that even the privileges of citizenship and the rights inhering in personal liberty are subject, in their enjoyment, to such reasonable restraints as may be required for the general good." Consequently, because the flag was an important "symbol of [the] country's power and prestige," a statute restricting the display of the flag did not violate "any right of personal liberty."[61] Similarly, in several World War I Espionage Act cases, the Court upheld convictions of defendants for protesting against the draft and the war. In one such case, *Debs v. United States*, the Court explicitly approved jury instructions that tracked the bad tendency doctrine: "[T]he jury were most carefully instructed that they could not find the defendant guilty for advocacy of any of his opinions unless the words used had as their natural tendency and reasonably probable effect to obstruct the recruiting service, &c."[62]

Interestingly, the Court did not expand free expression guarantees even when they might have encompassed and protected economic activities. For instance, the flag desecration statute in *Halter* specifically prohibited displaying the flag in commercial advertisements, yet the Court upheld the convictions. Another example arose when states began regulating the new technology of motion pictures early in the twentieth century. The state of Ohio required that a censorship board pre-approve any movies before they could be shown to the public. In a case decided in 1915, Mutual Film Corporation argued, among other things, that this licensing requirement amounted to a prior restraint contravening the state constitution. The Court rejected this free-speech claim, reasoning "that the exhibition of moving pictures is a business, pure and simple, originated and conducted for profit." As such, the censorship statute constituted a reasonable regulation on personal liberty—that is, economic liberty—because it was "in the interest of the public morals and welfare." While many films might be "educational or entertaining," some might be "used for evil," insidiously corrupting adults and children.[63]

NOTES

1. Helpful sources cited in this chapter focusing on the relationship between government and the economy include Karl Polanyi, The Great Transformation: The Political and Economic Origins of Our Time (2001 ed.); Joseph E. Stiglitz, The Price of Inequality (2013 ed.); Sean Wilentz, Chants Democratic: New York City and the Rise of the American Working Class, 1788–1850 (2004).
2. The Records of the Federal Convention of 1787, at 203 (Max Farrand ed., 1966 reprint of 1937 rev. ed.) [hereinafter Farrand] (Aug. 7, 1787); Gordon S. Wood, The Creation of the American Republic, 1776–1787, at 100 (1969).
3. Farrand, supra note 2, at 400–401 (June 25, 1787).
4. Letter from Jefferson to James Madison (Dec. 20, 1787), reprinted in 2 Great Issues in American History 112, 115 (Richard Hofstadter ed., 1958); Michael J. Thompson, The Politics of Inequality 4 (2007); G. Edward White, 1 Law in American History 86 (2012).
5. Sven Beckert, The Empire of Cotton 105–108 (2014); Patricia Nelson Limerick, The Legacy of Conquest (1987).
6. Federalist No. 2 (John Jay) (emphasizing the homogeneity of the American people); Thomas J. Curry, The First Freedoms: Church and State in America to the Passage of the First Amendment 219 (1986); Stephen M. Feldman, Please Don't Wish Me a Merry Christmas: A Critical History of the Separation of Church and State 161–168 (1997).
7. Rogers M. Smith, Civic Ideals 209 (1997) (quoting Morse from 1830s); John Higham, Strangers in the Land: Patterns of American Nativism, 1860–1925, at 6 (1992 ed.); Stephen M. Feldman, The Theory and Politics of First-Amendment Protections: Why Does the Supreme Court Favor Free Expression Over Religious Freedom?, 8 U. Pa. J. Const. L. 431, 434–435 (2006).
8. E.g., Tunis Wortman, A Treatise Concerning Political Enquiry, and the Liberty of the Press 49 (1800; 1970 reprint ed.); see Richard Hofstadter, Anti-Intellectualism in American Life (1962) (development of American anti-elitism); Smith, supra note 7, at 201 ("anti-elitist rhetoric" of Jacksonian years).
9. Edward Pessen, Jacksonian America 197–232 (rev. ed. 1985); Harry L. Watson, Liberty and Power 171–174 (1990).
10. Sources cited in this chapter discussing the development of corporations and laissez-faire ideology include: Joel Bakan, The Corporation (2004);

Richard F. Bensel, The Political Economy of American Industrialization, 1877–1900 (2000); Barry Eichengreen, Golden Fetters: The Gold Standard and the Great Depression, 1919–1939 (1992); Jeffry A. Frieden, Global Capitalism (2006); Lawrence M. Friedman, A History of American Law (2d ed. 1985); Kermit L. Hall, The Magic Mirror (1989); Morton J. Horwitz, The Transformation of American Law, 1780–1860 (1977); Herbert Hovenkamp, Enterprise and American Law, 1836–1937 (1991); James Willard Hurst, The Legitimacy of the Business Corporation (1970); John Micklethwait and Adrian Wooldridge, The Company: A Short History of a Revolutionary Idea (2003); Benjamin R. Twiss, Lawyers and the Constitution: How Laissez Faire Came to the Supreme Court (1962); Oscar Handlin and Mary F. Handlin, *Origins of the American Business Corporation*, 5 J. Econ. Hist. 1 (1945); Herbert Hovenkamp, *The Classical Corporation in American Legal Thought*, 76 Geo. L.J. 1593 (1988) [hereinafter Classical]; Pauline Maier, *The Revolutionary Origins of the American Corporation*, 50 William and Mary Q. 51 (1993); Charles W. McCurdy, *American Law and the Marketing Structure of the Large Corporation, 1875–1890*, 38 J. Economic Hist. 631 (1978).

Sources cited that discuss economic development in general (or in the United States) include: John Kenneth Galbraith, A History of Economics (1987); Robert Heilbroner and Aaron Singer, The Economic Transformation of America (1999); Walter Light, Industrializing America: The Nineteenth Century (1995); Ronald E. Seavoy, An Economic History of the United States From 1607 to the Present (2006).

11. Friedman, supra note 10, at 179–181; Horwitz, supra note 10, at 33, 112; Hurst, supra note 10, at 14–17; Micklethwait and Adrian Wooldridge, supra note 10, at 44; Handlin and Handlin, supra note 10, at 22; Maier, supra note 10, at 51–55, 84; see Hurst, supra note 10, at 17 (less than 4% of early corporate charters were for "general business corporations"); Robert E. Wright, *Rise of the Corporation Nation*, *in* Founding Choices: American Economic Policy in the 1790s 217 (Douglas A. Irwin and Richard Sylla eds., 2011) (emphasizing incorporation in the 1790s). Many of the earliest corporations were for municipalities. Friedman, supra note 10, at 188; Horwitz, supra note 10, at 112.

12. Currie's Administrators v. Mutual Assurance Society, 14 Va. 315, 4 Hen. and M. 315, 347–348 (1809) (emphasis in original); Hovenkamp, supra note 10, at 36–38; Maier, supra note 10, at 62–69; Hurst, supra note 10, at 30–31.

13. Maier, supra note 10, at 68 (quoting Ingersoll); id. at 62–69.

14. Friedman, supra note 10, at 194; Maier, supra note 10, at 71–72.

15. Andrew Jackson, *President Jackson's Veto Message Regarding the Bank of the United States* (July 10, 1832).

16. Douglas T. Miller, The Birth of Modern America 1820–1850, at 21 (1970) (quoting Kent); Wilentz, supra note 1, at 4–6; Wood, supra note 2, at 308–347; Sonia Mittal et al., *The Constitutional Choices of 1787 and Their Consequences, in* Founding Choices: American Economic Policy in the 1790s 25, 40–41 (Douglas A. Irwin and Richard Sylla eds., 2011) (emphasizing that the Constitution created a common market that facilitated commerce).

17. Alexis de Tocqueville, Democracy in America 157 (Henry Reeve text, revised by Francis Bowen, edited by Phillips Bradley; Vintage Books ed. 1990).

18. Jackson, supra note 15; Stephan Thernstrom, 1 A History of the American People 251–253 (2d ed. 1989).

19. Jackson, supra note 15; Hurst, supra note 10, at 32–33; Classical, supra note 10, at 1634–1635.

20. Liggett v. Lee, 288 U.S. 517, 549 and n.4 (1933) (Brandeis, J., dissenting in part); Hall, supra note 10, at 98–99, 194; Hovenkamp, supra note 10, at 38–39; Hurst, supra note 10, at 32–33; Micklethwait and Wooldridge, supra note 10, at 46; Maier, supra note 10, at 76; see Stephen M. Feldman, American Legal Thought From Premodernism to Postmodernism: An Intellectual Voyage 74–82 (2000) [hereinafter Voyage] (discussing developing notion of progress during the early-nineteenth century).

21. 17 U.S. (4 Wheat.) 518 (1819).

22. 36 U.S. (11 Pet.) 420 (1837).

23. Id. at 547–548; James Willard Hurst, Law and the Conditions of Freedom in the Nineteenth-century United States 27–28 (1956).

24. Heilbroner and Singer, supra note 10, at 174; Seavoy, supra note 10, at 248–250; John A. Garraty, The New Commonwealth 90–91 (1968).

25. The Statistical History of the United States from Colonial Times to the Present 14 (1965) (Table: Population in Urban and Rural Territory) [hereinafter Statistical History]; id. at 56–57 (Table: Immigrants by Country); id. at 74 (Table: Industrial Distribution of Gainful Workers: 1820–1940); id. at 415 (Table: Physical Output of Selected Manufactured Commodities); Erik W. Austin, Political Facts of the United States Since 1789, at 470 (1986) (Table 7.4, Total Number of Immigrants Arriving Annually in the United States, 1820–1980); United States Immigration Commission (Chair: Senator William P. Dillingham), *Dictionary of Races or Peoples* 33 (Dec. 5, 1910) (printed 1911); Bensel, supra note 10, at 207–208; Stephen Steinberg, The Ethnic Myth 36–38 (1989 ed.).

26. Statistical History, supra note 25, at 139 (Table: Gross National Product, Total and Per Capita, in Current and 1929 Prices); id. at 428 (Table: Railroad Mileage, Equipment, and Passenger Traffic and Revenue); Bakan, supra note 10, at 10–13; Melvyn Dubofsky, The State and Labor in Modern America 2 (1994); Hall, supra note 10, at 110; Heilbroner and Singer, supra note 10, at 157–166, 183–191. For discussions of the advantages of incorporation, see Micklethwait and Wooldridge, supra note 10, at xx–xxi; Handlin and Handlin, supra note 10, at 2; Classical, supra note 10, at 1595.

27. 118 U.S. 394, 396 (1886).

28. Heilbroner and Singer, supra note 10, at 200–202; Micklethwait and Wooldridge, supra note 10, at 70; id. at 60–63, 66; Bensel, supra note 10, at 314–315. Railroads also integrated their networks by adopting a standard gauge so that railroad cars would be compatible with tracks anywhere in the nation. Bensel, supra note 10, at 295–297.

29. Thorpe v. Rutland And Burlington Railroad Company, 27 Vt. 140, 156 n.a1 (1855); Commonwealth v. Alger, 61 Mass. 53, 7 Cush. 53, 85–86 (1851) (identifying numerous permissible regulations).

30. Hurst, supra note 23, at 21.

31. Light, supra note 10, at 88; Twiss, supra note 10, at 254–257.

32. Hall, supra note 10, at 190 (quoting Cleveland).

33. Cong. Globe, 39th Cong., 1st Sess. 2783 (May 23, 1866).

34. Garraty, supra note 24, at 9; Stiglitz, supra note 1, at 45–48; see Beckert, supra note 5, at 173 (industrial capitalism arose from combination of state power and capital).

35. James Mill, Elements of Political Economy (1821); David Ricardo, Principles of Political Economy and Taxation (1817).

36. Eric Foner, Free Soil, Free Labor, Free Men (1970).

37. Mitchell Snay, Horace Greeley and the Politics of Reform in Nineteenth-century America 118 (2011) (quoting Greeley); James M. McPherson, Ordeal By Fire 44 (1982) (quoting Greeley). Additional sources cited in this chapter on slavery, abolition, the Civil War, and Reconstruction include: Eric Foner, Reconstruction, 1863–1877 (1988); Pamela Brandwein, *Slavery as an Interpretive Issue in the Reconstruction Congresses*, 34 Law and Soc'y Rev. 315 (2000); Manuel Cachán, *Justice Stephen Field and "Free Soil, Free Labor Constitutionalism": Reconsidering Revisionism*, 20 Law and Hist. Rev. 541 (2002).

38. Richard H. Sewell, Ballots for Freedom 305–306 (1976) (quoting Pennsylvania Weekly Telegraph (June 20, 1860)).

39. *How Shall We Vote*, NY. Daily Times, Oct. 21, 1856, at 2; Foner, supra note 37, at 29 (quoting Lincoln).

40. Foner, supra note 37, at 234 (quoting Horace Greeley); Brandwein, supra note 37, at 342.
41. The Civil Rights Act (April 9, 1866), § 1, 14 Stat. 27; Cong. Globe, 39th Cong., 1st Sess. 1151 (March 2, 1866).
42. Brandwein, supra note 37, at 342; Herbert Hovenkamp, *The Political Economy of Substantive Due Process*, 40 Stan. L. Rev. 379, 395 (1988).
43. Edwin L. Godkin, *The Labor Crisis*, 105 N. Am. Rev. 177, 178 (July 1867).
44. George E. McNeill, *Progress of the Movement From 1861 to 1886, in* The Labor Movement: The Problem of Today 124, 161 (George E. McNeill ed., 1887; 1971 reprint); David Montgomery, Beyond Equality 30 (1967).
45. 83 U.S. (16 Wall.) 36, 62 (1873).
46. Id. at 87, 101, 110 and n.* (Field, J., dissenting) (quoting Adam Smith, The Wealth of Nations (1776), at bk. I, ch. 10, part 2.); Michael Les Benedict, *Laissez-Faire and Liberty: A Re-evaluation of the Meaning and Origins of Laissez-Faire Constitutionalism*, 3 Law and Hist. Rev. 293, 318–319 (1985); Brandwein, supra note 37, at 356; c.f., Cachán, supra note 37, at 550–552, 564 (stressing Field's ambivalence toward free soil and Locofoco democracy).
47. Cachán, supra note 37, at 569.
48. William Graham Sumner, What the Social Classes Owe To Each Other 47, 103–104 (1883; 1966 ed.); Herbert Spencer, Social Statics (1850); see Edward Hallett Carr, The Twenty Years' Crisis, 1919–1939, at 46–50 (1962) (evolving meaning of laissez faire); Richard Hofstadter, Social Darwinism in American Thought 45 (1992) (John D. Rockefeller's views).
49. Andrew Carnegie, *Wealth*, 148 North American Rev. 653 (June 1889); Galbraith, supra note 10, at 122.
50. James Mill, Elements of Political Economy (1821); David Ricardo, Principles of Political Economy and Taxation (1817); Polanyi, supra note 1, at 141–170; *e.g.*, Ludwig von Mises, Socialism: An Economic and Sociological Analysis (1981 ed.; 1st English ed. 1936; 1st German ed. 1922); see Julian Jackson, The Politics of Depression in France, 1932–1936, at 14 (2002) (laissez-faire ideology in France during late-nineteenth and early-twentieth centuries); Barbara W. Tuchman, The Proud Tower 4–5 (resistance to new economic regulation in England in late-nineteenth century).
51. Frieden, supra note 10, at 6–7; Carr, supra note 48, at 43–46; Eichengreen, supra note 10, at 3; Polanyi, supra note 1, at 3–4, 144.
52. Ray Ginger, Age of Excess 168 (1975) (quoting representative); Bensel, supra note 10, at xix, 5–10; Seavoy, supra note 10, at 199–200

(emphasizing railroads). The Populists' free silver campaign challenged the gold standard in the 1890s, but the movement collapsed when their candidate for president, William Jennings Bryan, lost in 1896. Stephen M. Feldman, Free Expression and Democracy in America: A History 189 (2008); Michael Kazin, The Populist Persuasion 30–32 (1995).

53. Frieden, supra note 10, at 29 (quoting Keynes); id. at 16; Margaret MacMillan, The War that Ended Peace xxxii (2013).

54. For discussions of Progressivism, see Feldman, supra note 52, at 190–197; Richard Hofstadter, The Age of Reform (1955); Arthur S. Link and Richard L. McCormick, Progressivism (1983). For an emphasis on the reaction against laissez faire, see Harold U. Faulkner, The Decline of Laissez Faire, 1897–1917 (1951).

55. Christopher G. Tiedeman, A Treatise on the Limitations of Police Power in the United States vi–viii, 4–5 (1886; Da Capo Press ed. 1971); Michael Les Benedict, *Laissez-Faire and Liberty: A Re-evaluation of the Meaning and Origins of Laissez-Faire Constitutionalism*, 3 Law and Hist. Rev. 293 (1985). Laissez-faire ideology also shaped the jurisprudence of Thomas Cooley—a more influential constitutional scholar—though he did not advocate for laissez faire as strongly as did Tiedeman. Thomas M. Cooley, A Treatise on the Constitutional Limitations Which Rest Upon the Legislative Power of the States of the American Union (1868).

56. Godcharles v. Wigeman, 113 Pa. 431 (1886); In re Jacobs, 98 N.Y. 98 (1885); Twiss, supra note 10, at 3–4, 254; McCurdy, supra note 10, at 632–633.

57. Millett v. People, 117 Ill. 294, 301 (1886).

58. 165 U.S. 578, 589, 591 (1897); David J. Brewer, *Protection to Private Property From Public Attack*, Commencement Address, Yale Law School (June 23, 1891) (advocating for laissez faire); Howard Gillman, *How Political Parties Can Use the Courts to Advance Their Agendas: Federal Courts in the United States, 1875–1891*, 96 Am. Pol. Sci. Rev. 511, 517–518 (2002); see David E. Bernstein, Rehabilitating *Lochner* 19–20 (2011) (development of "liberty of contract" language).

59. 198 U.S. 45, 56–59, 64 (1905); id. at 75 (Holmes, J., dissenting). The Court cited *Allgeyer* more often than it cited *Lochner*. Voyage, supra note 20, at 104; see Bernstein, supra note 58, at 116–120 (explaining development of term, "*Lochner* era"). I disagree with Paul Moreno's argument that the dissenters missed the point of the case. Paul D. Moreno, The American State From the Civil War to the New Deal 98–102 (2013). The dissenters and the majority largely agreed about the analysis of the case but differed about the definition of the common good.

60. Fox v. Washington, 236 U.S. 273, 276–277 (1915); Patterson v. Colorado *ex rel.* Attorney General, 205 U.S. 454, 462 (1907);

Feldman, supra note 52, at 101–152, 241–290; Howard Gillman, The Constitution Besieged: The Rise and Demise of *Lochner* Era Police Powers Jurisprudence 19–60 (1993).

61. 205 U.S. 34, 42 (1907).
62. 249 U.S. 211, 216 (1919). As was commonly done, the Court added that the government must prove the defendant had specific intent, but this requirement could be satisfied by constructive intent (which followed from proof of bad tendencies). Id.
63. Mutual Film Corp. v. Ohio Industrial Commission, 236 U.S. 230, 242, 244 (1915); *Halter*, 205 U.S. 34 (1907).

CHAPTER 4

Pluralist Democracy Saves the United States and Invigorates Free Expression

By the early-twentieth century, multiple pressures threatened democracy not only in the United States but also in Europe.[1] In the United States, continuing industrialization, immigration, and urbanization further strained the republican democratic system.[2] From 1910 through 1914, approximately one million immigrants arrived annually. During the years of World War I, immigration diminished, but then resumed its high rate after the war, with over 800,000 in 1921 and over 700,000 in 1924. Meanwhile, in 1920, the urban population for the first time surpassed the rural, with approximately 54 million urban residents and 51 million rural.[3]

Cracks in the republican democratic edifice started to show in the 1920s. Many old-stock Americans had grown disgruntled with the changing makeup of the nation. They now sought to strike back by suppressing or excluding racial, ethnic, and religious outsiders. Many of these old-stock Americans viewed Southern and Eastern European immigrants as racially inferior and as incapable of virtuous citizenship. In this vein, President Calvin Coolidge declared that the "ability for self-government is arrived at only through an extensive training and education. In our own case it required many generations."[4] Prohibition, adopted in 1919, manifested an attempt to save traditional America. Although the temperance movement had existed for decades, the nation finally ratified Prohibition as a blow against the ostensibly foreign immigrant cultures. Even the Ku Klux Klan reemerged, open only to white and American-born Protestants.[5] Its membership surged as many old-stock Americans, disregarding the organization's vigilante outbursts, viewed the Klan as a

© The Author(s) 2017
S.M. Feldman, *The New Roberts Court, Donald Trump, and Our Failing Constitution*, DOI 10.1007/978-3-319-56451-7_4

fraternal order. In truth, though, the Klan aimed to be a "militant wing of Protestantism" enforcing "100 percent Americanism," particularly "the Protestant moral code."[6] In 1921, a new immigration law imposed a quota system, which would be tightened in 1924. The unequivocal purpose of these quotas was to slash immigration from Southern and Eastern Europe while still allowing it from Northwestern Europe. The House Committee Report for the 1924 legislation explicitly declared that the quota manifested "an effort to preserve, as nearly as possible, the racial status quo in the United States. It is hoped to guarantee, as best we can at this late date, racial homogeneity."[7]

AMERICAN DEMOCRACY TRANSFORMS: RECONCILING THE PUBLIC AND PRIVATE

Whatever the wary old-stock Americans had hoped to accomplish, other forces for change were at work, apparent when one places the United States within the wider context of western industrialized nations. All these nations, including the United States, suffered through World War I—indeed, the European nations were at war for more than 4 years. And these same nations would soon be swept into a vortex of additional tragedies: the Great Depression, World War II, and the Holocaust. Of course, no single cause can explain all of these cascading catastrophes. Each was a complex event with multiple intertwined causes. Nevertheless, the widespread laissez-faire ideology stands as a persistent and significant causal link among these disasters.[8] More specifically, laissez-faire ideology contributed in two primary ways to social and economic instability in the domestic and international realms. First, domestically, laissez-faire thinking provokes many individuals and groups to oppose any type of social welfare laws, no matter how important or necessary such laws otherwise appear to be. And frequently, social welfare laws are desperately needed to help offset the economic inequities that naturally develop in capitalist societies. Yet, laissez-faire ideologues simply cannot square social welfare legislation and other economic interventions with their desire for a completely free and self-regulating marketplace. Second, internationally, laissez-faire ideology leads nations to link themselves together with devices such as the gold standard in order to engender and protect an international marketplace. But if economic or social disaster strikes one nation, then its reverberations will likely shake many other nations as well.[9]

Laissez-faire thinking unquestionably remained strong in America throughout the 1920s as true believers incessantly criticized government regulations. Business boomed through most of the decade. From 1911 to 1919, the GNP had more than doubled, and from 1919 to 1929, it grew by more than another 33%. Of course, most of this wealth accrued to those individuals who were already the wealthiest; the rich got richer. Yet, all the while, numerous American leaders, including elected officials, denigrated the government in multiple ways. President Warren Harding asked Congress to repeal "unproductive and ... artificial and burdensome" taxes. Coolidge appointed a chair to the Federal Trade Commission who had previously been hostile to the Commission's existence. Coolidge famously proclaimed that "[t]he chief business of the American people is business," while Harding maintained that he "meant to have less of government in business as well as more business in government."[10] And both the Harding and Coolidge administrations cut federal expenditures so brutally that, by 1927, federal spending was less than one-sixth its 1919 levels.[11]

In many instances, Americans translated this general discontent with government into criticisms of specific democratic practices. For decades, old-stock Americans had complained that spreading the vote had undermined republican democratic government. Tiedeman had lamented that the spread of "universal suffrage" allowed "the great army of discontents" to oppress the rights of the minority through social welfare legislation.[12] In the early-twentieth century, electoral reforms purposefully diminished voter participation, especially in poor and immigrant urban communities. These reforms were often justified as eliminating corruption or producing "a more competent electorate," yet they typically tightened voting requirements. Measures "included the introduction of literacy tests, lengthening residency periods, abolishing provisions that permitted noncitizen aliens to vote, restricting municipal elections to property owners or taxpayers, and the creation of complex, cumbersome registration procedures."[13] In 1923, for example, New York State implemented a "scientifically devised" examination that, in theory, screened new voters for intelligence and literacy, but in practice, blocked thousands of would-be voters.[14] And in the South, mechanisms such as poll taxes and literacy tests successfully disenfranchised most African Americans. In presidential elections, voter turnout after the Civil War sometimes had reached above 80%, but in 1920 and 1924, it fell below 50%. Even so, William B. Munro, former president of the

American Political Science Association, advocated to limit suffrage in 1928. "About twenty percent of those who get on the voters' list have no business to be there," he declared. "Taking the country as a whole, the total number of these interlopers must run into the millions."[15] Walter Lippmann, too, had grown disenchanted with democracy. "[T]he number of mice and monkeys known to have been deceived in laboratories is surpassed only by the hopeful citizens of a democracy," Lippmann lamented. "Man's reflexes are, as the psychologists say, conditioned. And, therefore, he responds quite readily to a glass egg, a decoy duck, a stuff shirt or a political platform."[16]

Criticisms of democratic government go hand-in-hand with laissez faire. Quite simply, laissez faire assumes that the best government is minimal or even non-existent (many laissez-faire ideologues admit that a minimal state is necessary to enforce contract and property rights).[17] One cannot maintain an unregulated economic marketplace unless the government stops regulating. Thus, the less government, the better— whether government is democratic or otherwise.[18] Indeed, one can reasonably argue that a competitive free market economy will inevitably lead many individuals to dream of a laissez-faire utopia with minimal government. When a free market economy emerges in society, when a private sphere of capitalist economics is separated from a public sphere of government, then the two spheres often appear to be in tension, in opposition to each other. In a free market economy, individuals, corporations, and other profit-making enterprises necessarily seek profit. Without profit, an enterprise dies. To remain competitive, an enterprise constantly seeks to introduce change, to develop new products, to expand markets, to open new markets, and ultimately, to increase profits.[19] Capitalism is driven by an "expansionary logic," an inherent desire to grow and to multiply profits. The very notion of government appears to contravene that expansionary logic; democratic law making, it would appear, imposes (or threatens to impose) limits that can constrain economic development and profit.[20]

Indeed, the mere study of economic action intensifies the desire to separate the private sphere of economic transactions and the public sphere of government action. Economic theory, in general, and the academic discipline of economics, in particular, seek to separate economic actions and relations from the rest of society, including government. The nature of any discipline is to identify and isolate certain actions and events and then to describe and analyze them pursuant to particular and arcane methods. It is then, perhaps, not coincidental that economics crystallized as a discipline in the late-nineteenth and early-twentieth centuries, when laissez-faire ideology grew stronger. Because economists seek to explain and predict economic actions, governmental and other societal actions represent obstacles to objective study. From the perspective of the science of economics, that is, government actions appear to obscure or interfere with natural market transactions. Democratic politics is messy, and economists—especially those dreaming of laissez faire—want to escape the mess. Minimal government appears best. To be sure, some economists manage to overcome this disciplinary reductionism, but many do not.[21]

Thus, rational economic action and thinking—the pursuit of profit accompanied by laissez-faire ideology—can have unexpected and disastrous consequences: the undermining and even destruction of democratic government (and in turn, the destruction of the capitalist economy). Historical evidence of this inverse relationship—economic rationalism and laissez-faire ideology weakening democratic government—is all too prevalent during the first half of the twentieth century. As explained by the economic historian, Karl Polanyi, the connection between laissez faire and government collapse is complex; the inverse relationship is neither simple nor direct.[22] In democracies, efforts to impose a laissez-faire system frequently generate a backlash of social welfare laws intended to ameliorate the harsh realities of an industrial marketplace. For example, in the United States, Progressivism emerged as laissez-faire ideology rose to new heights in the early-twentieth century. But the tension between laissez faire and social welfare can stretch society like an "elastic band," and in some circumstances, the band snaps, destabilizing the entire democratic-capitalist system.[23]

From this perspective, the rapid onset of World War I in 1914 was understandable. Early in the twentieth century, the unregulated international market glimmered beneath a veneer of wealth, but it nonetheless engendered economic winners *and* losers. Neither all nations nor all people within specific nations benefitted, yet gross inequalities typically went unremedied. Consequently, the world, including Europe, was not as peaceably stable as it appeared. "The period was not a Golden Age or *Belle Epoque* except to a thin crust of the privileged class."[24] To take one example, from 1866 to 1914, the amount of wheat exported from the United States increased 15 times over, with much of it going to Europe—which was good for American farmers, or at least for the corporate shippers of farm products—but European farmers suffered extensive losses competing against the inexpensive American grain.[25] Meanwhile, overall unemployment grew in England as well as in the United States. England was "the richest country in the world," but one-third of its people lived "in chronic poverty, unable to satisfy the primal needs of animal life."[26] Yet, before World War I, nations that were committed to an unregulated international market often disregarded such serious domestic economic problems. Indeed, many insisted that unemployment arose because of the moral failings of individuals—they were lazy, idle, and so on—rather than because of economic trends and policies. Even when some individuals and groups (such as the Progressives in America) pushed for social welfare programs that might help alleviate poverty and unemployment, critics insisted such programs contravened laissez-faire ideology. Thus, domestic economic and social ills were politically subordinated to maintaining the gold standard and the nation's place in the international market.[27]

Even so, the effectiveness of the international market in the early-twentieth century was due more to certain peacetime attitudes than to laissez faire, the gold standard, or other economic policies. More specifically, the public generally believed in the gold standard and its relation to the international marketplace. Much of the public found these policies to be credible, and those who might question the policies—such as the poor and unemployed—typically lacked political power. Plus, the leading economic nations cooperated to maintain the world market. Crises, when they arose, would be met by cooperative actions among, for instance, Britain, France, and Germany—nations anxious to retain their dominant market positions. But in the lead-up and outbreak to World War I, the public credibility and multinational cooperation necessary for smooth international trade unraveled and then completely disintegrated. Laissez-faire dreams of an unregulated world marketplace and the concomitant resistance to social welfare laws were beside the point. If anything, laissez-faire policies produced deep fissures in national economies while obscuring the true bases for international trade. Thus, the "entire edifice" for the peaceful and thriving international economy collapsed in a matter of months.[28]

Nevertheless, after the war, European nations and the United States still believed that long-lasting peace depended on the resurrection of a world economy grounded on an unregulated international marketplace. The third of Woodrow Wilson's fourteen-point peace plan explicitly advocated for free trade and a laissez-faire market. It recommended "[t]he removal, so far as possible, of all economic barriers and the establishment of an equality of trade conditions among all the nations consenting to the peace." Europe aimed to rebuild its international economy in accordance with this point by, most important, restoring the gold standard.[29] And although the United States Senate would reject Wilson's overall plan, this rejection did not manifest a repudiation of laissez faire. To the contrary, laissez-faire ideology predominated in 1920s America. The Republican presidents, Harding and Coolidge, were followed by the pro-business Herbert Hoover, a former Secretary of Commerce under both his predecessors. Unsurprisingly, then, the United States, too, adhered to the gold standard, consistent with laissez-faire thinking. In fact, by the mid- to late-1920s, many European economies attained pre-World War I levels, with the main difference being that the predominant national economy now belonged to the United States rather than Great Britain. During this interwar period, many corporations flourished and changed, becoming larger and more vertically and horizontally integrated, especially in the United States. Many of the large American corporations went multinational for the first time. And significantly, buoyed by this widespread international prosperity, 26 democracies emerged in Europe during these years.[30]

But the economic foundations for this interwar burst of prosperity and democracy were fundamentally weak. As was true before World War I, wealth was not shared equally. In many European nations, economic developments crushed the middle class of farmers and small businessmen. In the United States, through most of the 1920s, the wealthiest 5% of Americans received more than 25% of the total annual income, and the wealthiest 1% usually received around 14% of the income. By the end of the decade, in 1929, the difference in wages between skilled and unskilled American workers had reached record proportions. Inflation had crept into the American economy, though few paid attention. Because many factory laborers were unable to buy the products they helped manufacture, overproduction and underconsumption threatened the nation's economic stability. Meanwhile, stock market prices skyrocketed to stratospheric highs, fueled partly by the nation's stubborn adherence to the gold standard. These overinflated stock market prices were chimerical, unrelated to the actual stock values. Eventually, the weaknesses in the American economy proved too great to withstand, the stock market crashed, and the Great Depression hit the United States.[31]

When the American stock market crashed, the gold standard was a rigid metal bar that transmitted destructive tremors from the United

States to other nations around the world. "The gold standard magnified that initial destabilizing shock. It was the principal obstacle to offsetting action," explains Barry Eichengreen. "It was the binding constraint preventing policymakers from averting the failure of banks and containing the spread of financial panic."[32] Nations believed that the world economy, based on the gold standard, would naturally self-adjust so long as governments stayed out of the way. Even as economies collapsed and unemployment spiraled out of control, governments insisted that the prudent course remained "free trade, balanced budgets, and the gold standard."[33] The pull of the laissez-faire dream was too strong to escape: A dual commitment to laissez faire, in both domestic and international marketplaces, prevented governments in the United States and other nations from taking actions that might have alleviated mounting economic problems. President Hoover, displaying his blind faith in the market, explained the numerous unemployed individuals who struggled to survive by selling fruit on the street: "Many persons left their jobs for the more profitable one of selling apples."[34] By the time some European countries became desperate enough to go off the gold standard—for instance, Germany in the summer of 1931 and Britain in the fall of that year—it was too late to slow the downward spiral. Economic collapse then led to the downfall of numerous democracies. Indeed, once the Depression hit, they fell like dominoes: "Yugoslavia in 1929, Romania in 1930, Austria in 1932, Germany in 1933, Latvia, Estonia, and Bulgaria in 1934, Greece in 1936." Of the 26 interwar European democracies, only 12 remained by 1938, and seven of those became dictatorships in the next 2 years. As fascism ascended and authoritarian governments took control in Europe, dreams of laissez-faire utopias dissolved into nightmares of suppression and violence.[35]

In the United States, American democracy ultimately proved more resilient than most European types. Yet, as the republican democratic regime teetered, a remarkable number of Americans suggested that fascism or communism might provide a workable alternative. Many worried that democratic government was too sluggishly ineffective to respond to the economic crisis of the Depression. Walter J. Shepard, president of the American Political Science Association, questioned the democratic concept of "the People" because, in his view, individuals are too irrational and manipulable. He therefore sketched a "beginning" for a "new ideology" of government, which, he admitted, included "a large element of fascist doctrine."[36] In a similar vein, another leading political scientist of the time, Charles Merriam, focused less on democracy and more on "what role political power plays in the process of social control."[37] Such views were not limited to intellectuals. A 1934 *Fortune* magazine article explicitly defended fascism: "The good journalist must recognize in Fascism certain ancient virtues of the race, whether or not they happen to be momentarily fashionable in his own country." And at the most concrete level, in 1933–1934, a group of American businessmen offered to finance a former Marine General in a coup d'état, with the General becoming a fascist dictator.[38] Meanwhile, John Dewey praised the Russian Communists for releasing "human powers on such an unprecedented scale that it is of incalculable significance not only for that country, but for the world." Membership in the Communist Party of the United States increased during the 1930s, reaching 30,000 in 1935, and climbing close to 100,000 in 1939.[39]

Thus, Americans witnessed and sometimes admired the ascension of totalitarianism in Europe, but they eventually recognized, by the mid- to late-1930s, that a serious threat loomed over democracy. Instead of renouncing democratic government, they redoubled their commitment. John E. Mulder, a University of Pennsylvania law professor, proclaimed that Americans must "prove democracy the master of totalitarianism."[40] Americans would defend democracy, even as it necessarily transformed. The rural, agrarian, and relatively homogeneous American society that had sustained republican democracy throughout much of the nineteenth century no longer existed. "The Jeffersonian yeoman farmer was a figure from a landscape long gone."[41] America was now urban, industrial, and heterogeneous. And in this new America, new democratic practices and institutions took hold: A pluralist democracy supplanted the moribund republican democratic regime. Mainstream and old-stock Protestant values, long the foundation for the republican democratic principles of virtue and the common good, were now to be balanced with the values of other Americans who constituted the demographically diverse population. No single set of cultural values was authoritative. Ethical relativism took hold as a political reality: All values and all interests—or at least a plurality of values and interests—mattered to Franklin Roosevelt (FDR) and the New Dealers. Democracy now revolved around the assertion of interests and values by sundry individuals and groups. The pursuit of self-interest no longer amounted to corruption; rather it defined the nature of (pluralist) democracy. Diverse voluntary organizations and interest groups openly sought to press their claims through the democratic process—given the chance, they thrust through the doors to political action. In cities, for instance, one might find a Polish Democratic Club or a Lithuanian Democratic League as well as organizations representing business and labor. Lobbying became open, aggressive, and institutionalized.[42]

Significantly, from this perspective, the framers' concept of the citizen-self had eroded. Recall, the framers' citizen-self was Janus-faced: One face was animated by virtue and reason, while the other face was animated by passion and interest. The framers believed that passion and interest should have free rein in the private sphere to a great degree. In the public sphere, however, the framers designed the Constitution to produce results in accord with virtue and reason as often as possible. But in the 1930s, under the emerging pluralist democracy, one face of the founders' self—the civic humanist or virtuous self—had turned into the shadows. Citizens were no longer to deliberate virtuously with others in pursuit of the common good. Only one face remained visible: the self-motivated by passion and interest. To be sure, this conception of the self was still a citizen. It remained engaged in the public sphere. In other words, the pluralist democratic citizen-self actively, even enthusiastically, participated in politics, but it no longer aimed to be disinterested and virtuous. As numerous political scientists, psychologists, social theorists, and historians observed, the American self now focused on its own personal satisfaction.[43]

Moreover, the new pluralist democratic regime, manifested in the New Deal, repudiated laissez faire, at least temporarily. FDR recognized that if a capitalist system approached a laissez-faire reality, it became self-destructive. As the constitutional framers had posited, the public and private spheres need to remain in a relative balance in order for a democratic-capitalist system to be sustained. The dream of a pristine private sphere and shrunken public sphere becomes dangerous if implemented. As Edward Hallett Carr explained, in an idyllic pre-industrial society, where production has not sharply differentiated societal groups based on their respective economic interests, laissez faire might theoretically work because a relative harmony of interests would exist among most of the people. The market, in theory, could operate smoothly enough that an individual's private returns from economic transactions might closely correspond with societal returns or benefits—which is how Adam Smith conceived of an efficient marketplace. But as soon as a society industrializes, harmony transforms into dissonance. Typically, factory owners and workers do not share the same interests. Imagine a town with very few autos, Carr suggested. In such a town, government traffic control might be unnecessary. The drivers cooperate adequately, avoiding accidents, as they travel to their destinations. But when the number of cars reaches a critical point, when the roads become too congested, then accidents and conflict will become common. At that stage, government traffic control, imposing rules of the road, will allow drivers to coexist peacefully while still reaching their destinations. Utopianism, then, can be dangerous. Pretending that the town does not need government traffic control will lead to many injuries and deaths.[44] From this perspective, in America of the 1930s, the government needed to structure, to nurture, the democratic-capitalist system in order to protect capitalism from its own natural impulses and dangerous proclivities. Without such government action, many people would continue to suffer. Democratic and capitalist institutions needed to be blended or "embedded" together, as Keynes suggested. Otherwise, economic transactions might benefit certain individuals and corporations while harming society as a whole. Private returns would not necessarily correspond with societal benefits, or in other words, the market would not produce efficiency.[45]

Thus, to save the American democratic-capitalist system, the national government in the 1930s expanded and centralized power. Under pluralist democracy, the government opened to multiple interests and values, so when those interests aligned properly, the government could reach deeply into the realms of economy and society—without constitutional question. In other words, the supposedly preexisting and objective substantive goal of the common good no longer limited the government. Rather, government goals and limits were established through the pluralist democratic process itself. As a result, Congress passed sweeping statutes that were then administered by agencies staffed with experts. From 1930 to 1936, the percentage of the gross national product consumed by the national government more than doubled, from 4 to 9%. Politically popular statutes such as the National Labor Relations Act (NLRA) and the Social Security Act dramatically reshaped the legal landscape. In 1936, the Works Progress Administration employed 7% of the nation's workforce building or improving hospitals, schools, airports, and playgrounds. By the end of the 1930s, most Americans accepted "the right of the government to pay the farmer millions in subsidies not to grow crops, to enter plants to conduct union elections, to regulate business enterprises from utility companies to airlines, or even to compete directly with business by generating and distributing hydroelectric power."[46]

To be sure, conservatives reacted inconsistently as pluralist democracy and the New Deal unfolded. Some protested when the United States went off the gold standard early in FDR's first term, on June 5, 1933. No less than the Budget Director Lewis Douglas, a Roosevelt appointee, pronounced, "This is the end of Western civilization."[47] Yet, some conservatives eventually accepted the New Deal's reconciliation of the public and private spheres. The earliest neoliberals, emphasizing individual liberty and human dignity, acknowledged the need for government action to preserve the economic marketplace. In the classic neoliberal text, *The Road to Serfdom*, published in 1944, Friedrich Hayek explained that the competitive free market operates efficiently only under certain conditions: when "the owner benefits from all the useful services rendered by his property and suffers for all the damages caused to others by its use." When those conditions do not hold—for example, when a factory emits pollution—then the government must act as a "substitute for the regulation by the price mechanism." Indeed, Hayek acknowledged a further role for the state: "[T]here can be no doubt that some minimum of food, shelter, and clothing, sufficient to preserve health and the capacity to work, can be assured to everybody." Even Milton Friedman, who would become a post-World War II neoliberal icon in the United States, initially renounced the nineteenth-century conception of laissez faire.[48]

Nevertheless, for much of the 1930s, conservative Supreme Court justices resisted the transition to pluralist democracy and attempted to continue enforcing republican democratic principles, including a laissez faire tinged common good. For example, in 1935, *Railroad Retirement Board v. Alton Railroad Company* invalidated a federal statute, the Railroad Retirement Act of 1934, as beyond Congress's power under the Commerce Clause. The Court split five-to-four, with the five-justice conservative majority reasoning that the statute contravened the common good because it infringed on the freedom of employers and employees to negotiate and enter contracts. Congress, according to the Court, had attempted "to impose by sheer fiat noncontractual incidents upon the relation of employer and employee ... as a means of assuring a particular class of employees against old age dependency."[49] One year later, *Morehead v. New York ex rel. Tipaldo* invalidated a state law mandating a minimum wage for women, with the justices again splitting along the same conservative-liberal lines. Although the Court decided this case under the Due Process Clause of the Fourteenth Amendment, the conservative justices reasoned similarly: The legislature had impermissibly intruded into the contractual liberty central to the economic marketplace.[50]

This judicial resistance to New Deal and related social welfare laws provoked Roosevelt's court-packing proposal, a blatant political gesture intended to compel the justices to accept the New Deal and (implicitly) pluralist democracy. By the end of the decade, though—the turning point is usually deemed to be 1937—the Court had accepted the transition and stopped attempting to uphold the republican democratic principles of virtue and the common good.[51] *West Coast Hotel Company v. Parrish*, decided in 1937, repudiated the reasoning of *Morehead* and upheld another state law setting minimum wages for women. With the moderately conservative justice, Owen Roberts, switching his vote and joining the more progressive justices, the Court questioned laissez faire and justified government regulation of the marketplace. "The exploitation of a class of workers who are in an unequal position with respect to bargaining power and are thus relatively defenseless against the denial of a living wage is not only detrimental to their health and well-being, but casts a direct burden for their support upon the community. What these workers lose in wages the taxpayers are called upon to pay. The bare cost of living must be met."[52] The justices divided along the same five-to-four lines in *NLRB v. Jones and Laughlin Steel Corporation* decided only 2 weeks after *West Coast Hotel*. *Jones and Laughlin* upheld the constitutionality of the National Labor Relations Act, a key New Deal statute that facilitated union organizing and changed employer–employee relations. The Court, recognizing the systemic connection of the public and private spheres, reasoned that the democratic process should determine whether government regulation of the economic marketplace was appropriate. "Employees have as clear a right to organize and select their representatives for lawful purposes as the [manufacturer-employer] has to organize its business and select its own officers and agents." Thus, while a manufacturer had a "right to conduct its business in an orderly manner," it could no longer claim that the Constitution shielded it from legislative regulations of a sacrosanct laissez-faire marketplace. Just as manufacturers could organize into corporations, employees also had a "correlative right to organize for the purpose of securing the redress of grievances and to promote agreements with employers relating to rates of pay and conditions of work."[53]

Around this same time, political theorists began to explicate the new practices and institutions of democracy. The foundation for the incipient democratic theory was the scholarly embrace of relativism. While authoritarian governments, such as in Nazi Germany, claimed knowledge of objective values and forcefully imposed those values and concomitant goals on their peoples, democratic governments allowed their citizens to express diverse values and goals. The key to democracy lay not in the specification of supposedly objective goals, such as the common good, but rather in the following of processes that allowed all citizens to voice their particular values and interests within a free and open democratic arena. Dewey zeroed in on the crucial difference between fascism and democracy when, in 1939, he contrasted authoritarian methods with the "plural, partial, and experimental methods" of democracy.[54]

PLURALIST DEMOCRATIC THEORY: FREE EXPRESSION BECOMES A CONSTITUTIONAL LODESTAR

During and after World War II, numerous political and constitutional theorists celebrated pluralist democracy as the best means for accommodating "our multigroup society." These theorists viewed the explanation and justification of pluralist democracy as a necessary defense of American democracy, first in opposition to the Nazis and other fascist regimes and then in opposition to the Soviets and its Cold-War totalitarian allies. As the theorists explained, the only way to determine public values and goals is "through the free competition of interest groups." By "composing or compromising" their different values and interests, the "competing groups [would] coordinate their aims in programs they can all support." Legislative decisions therefore turned on negotiation, persuasion, and the exertion of pressure through the normal channels of the democratic process.[55] But with individuals and groups all pursuing their own respective interests, what would prevent the society from splintering into embattled segments, each invigorated with growing enmity of others? Numerous theorists agreed that only a democratic culture could sustain the inevitable interest-group conflicts of pluralist democracy.[56] Engendered by widespread middle-class economic attitudes and the lack of entrenched aristocratic and proletariat classes, American culture instilled citizens with the "rules of the game" for the "democratic mold."[57] In the 1950s, Daniel Boorstin argued that the "genius" of American politics lay not in any philosophy but in a "genuine community of our values," a "common faith" in the negotiations and compromises of pluralist democracy. Indeed, faith in democracy—the democratic culture—might have helped save American democracy in the 1930s. When other democracies degenerated into authoritarian regimes, American democracy underwent a significant institutional transformation but nonetheless managed to survive.[58]

In the Cold-War period, no one articulated pluralist democratic theory more comprehensively than Robert A. Dahl. Because pluralist (or polyarchal) democracy accepted the inevitable pursuit of self-interest—rather than the pursuit of an objective substantive goal (the common good)—pluralist democracy required the institutionalization of a "process" that would allow the people to determine which interests would be at least temporarily enshrined as communal goals. A communal goal was legitimate only if the conditions for democracy were satisfied—if the proper process was followed. Thus, Dahl identified the conditions, such as the identical weighing of each vote, which were requisite to the operation of a democratic process. The legitimation of self-interest in pluralist democracy, it should be emphasized, has deeply egalitarian implications. A skeptical knife deflates pretensions to elitism. Claims to higher virtue or greater knowledge of objective values, which might merit elite status, are defeated by the universality of self-interest. Virtues and values are merely interests by another name. Unsurprisingly, then, the most important component of the democratic process, according to Dahl, is "effective participation": Citizens must have "adequate" and "equal" opportunities "for expressing their preferences ... for placing questions on the agenda and for expressing reasons for endorsing one outcome rather than another." If these free-expression rights are absent, Dahl insisted, then "the democratic process does not exist." Dahl, it should be pointed out, was neither the first nor the last political (or constitutional) theorist to accentuate the importance of free expression within the pluralist democratic regime. To the contrary, a long line of scholars and justices committed to this self-governance rationale for protecting free speech and writing.[59]

Pursuant to the self-governance rationale, no liberty or right—not even voting—is more crucial to the pluralist democratic process than free expression. Free speech and writing allow diverse groups and individuals to contribute their views in the pluralist political arena. If government officials interfere with the pluralist process, if they dictate or control public debates, then they skew the democratic outcomes and undermine the consent of the governed. In his book, *Free Speech and Its Relation to Self-Government*, Alexander Meiklejohn emphasized that the need to protect political expression "springs from the necessities of the program of self-government," or in other words, from "the structure and functioning of our political system as a whole."[60] Under pluralist democracy, free expression became a constitutional "lodestar."[61] In a stark about-face from the Court's consistent repudiation of First-Amendment claims during the republican democratic era, the justices began to uphold one free-speech claim after another.[62] Justice Robert Jackson wrote for the Court: "If there is any fixed star in our constitutional constellation, it is that no official, high or petty, can prescribe what shall be orthodox in politics, nationalism, religion, or other matters of opinion or force citizens to confess by word or act their faith therein."[63]

NOTES

1. Helpful sources on the relationship between democracy and capitalism cited in this chapter include: Fred Block and Margaret R. Somers, The Power of Market Fundamentalism (2014); Samuel Bowles and Herbert Gintis, Democracy and Capitalism (1986); Paul Krugman, The Conscience of a Liberal (2007); Timothy K. Kuhner, Capitalism v. Democracy (2014); Thomas Piketty, Capital in the Twenty-first Century (Arthur Goldhammer trans. 2014); Karl Polanyi, The Great Transformation: The Political and Economic Origins of Our Time (2001 ed.); David F. Prindle, The Paradox of Democratic Capitalism (2006); Dani Rodrik, The Globalization Paradox (2011); Sidney A. Shapiro and Joseph P. Tomain, Achieving Democracy (2014); Joseph E. Stiglitz, The Price of Inequality (2013 ed.).

2. Robert A. Dahl, A Preface to Economic Democracy 3–4, 72–73 (1985) (the rise of corporate capitalism threatened political equality and democracy). Additional sources discussing economic developments in this chapter include: Joel Bakan, The Corporation (2004); Barry Eichengreen, Golden Fetters: The Gold Standard and the Great Depression, 1919–1939 (1992); Jeffry A. Frieden, Global Capitalism (2006); John Kenneth Galbraith, A History of Economics (1987); Robert Heilbroner and William Milberg, The Making of Economic Society (10th ed. 1998); Robert Heilbroner and Aaron Singer, The Economic Transformation of America (1999); John Micklethwait and Adrian Wooldridge, The Company: A Short History of a Revolutionary Idea (2003); Ronald E. Seavoy, An Economic History of the United States From 1607 to the Present (2006); Benjamin R. Twiss, Lawyers and the Constitution: How Laissez Faire Came to the Supreme Court (1962).

3. The Statistical History of the United States from Colonial Times to the Present 14 (1965) (Table: Population in Urban and Rural Territory) [hereinafter Statistical History]; Erik W. Austin, Political Facts of the United States Since 1789, at 470 (1986) (Table 7.4, Total Number of Immigrants Arriving Annually in the United States, 1820–1980).
4. John Gerring, Party Ideologies in America, 1828–1996, at 86 (1998); *Dictionary of Races or Peoples* (Dec. 5, 1910) (printed 1911) (classifying immigrants as racial groups); Matthew Frye Jacobson, Whiteness of a Different Color 8–9 (1998) (changing concept of whiteness).
5. U.S. Const. amend. XVIII; Lizabeth Cohen, Making a New Deal 211 (1990); William E. Leuchtenburg, The Perils of Prosperity, 1914–1932, at 209 (1958).
6. Lynn Dumenil, The Modern Temper 235–238 (1995); Leuchtenburg, supra note 5, at 209.
7. E. P. Hutchinson, Legislative History of American Immigration Policy, 1798–1965, at 484–485 (1981) (quoting House Committee Report, Act of May 26, 1924); *Immigration Act of 1924, reprinted in* 2 Documents of American History 372 (Henry Steele Commager ed., 3d ed. 1947) [hereinafter Commager]; Jacobson, supra note 4, at 81–87.
8. Polanyi, supra note 1, at 3–5. Much historical scholarship has attempted to explain each of these events, and much scholarship is still being produced. With regard to World War I, alone, three new books have recently appeared: Christopher Clark, The Sleepwalkers: How Europe Went to War in 1914 (2012); Michael S. Neiberg, Dance of the Furies: Europe and the Outbreak of World War I (2013); Margaret MacMillan, The War that Ended Peace (2013).
9. Rodrik, supra note 1, at 121–122 (discussing market failures); Stiglitz, supra note 1, at 41–45 (discussing market inefficiencies). Milton Friedman would subsequently argue that classical (nineteenth-century) liberalism "supported laissez faire at home as a means of reducing the role of the state in economic affairs ...; it supported free trade abroad as a means of linking the nations of the world together." Milton Friedman, Capitalism and Freedom 5 (1962).
10. Warren G. Harding, *The Return to Normalcy* (April 12, 1921); David M. Kennedy, Freedom From Fear 33 (1999) (Coolidge); Dumenil, supra note 6, at 35.
11. Statistical History, supra note 3 at 139 (Table: Gross National Product, Total and Per Capita, in Current and 1929 Prices); id. at 167 (Table: Percent Shares of Total Income); id. at 711 (Table: Summary of Federal Government Finances).
12. Christopher G. Tiedeman, The Unwritten Constitution of the United States 80 (1890).

13. Alexander Keyssar, The Right to Vote 128–129 (2000); Dumenil, supra note 6, at 53; Arthur S. Link and Richard L. McCormick, Progressivism 53–55 (1983).

14. *New Literacy Test Adopted by State*, New York Times, Aug. 9, 1923, at 30; William J. O'Shea, *Literacy Test of Voters is Pronounced a Success*, New York Times, Jan 4, 1925, at X12; *The Literacy Law*, New York Times, March 28, 1931, at 15.

15. Keyssar, supra note 13, at 226, 105–116; Austin, supra note 3, at 378–379 (Table: National Voter Turnout); Lin k and McCormick, supra note 13, at 53.

16. Walter Lippmann, The Phantom Public 30 (1925).

17. Block and Somers, supra note 1, at 35; Polanyi, supra note 1, at 234; see Friedrich A. Hayek, The Road to Serfdom 43 (1944) (discussing minimal government).

18. Bakan, supra note 2, at 112–113; Bowles and Gintis, supra note 1, at 3–7; Kuhner, supra note 1, at 24; Polanyi, supra note 1, at 3; Prindle, supra note 1, at x, 2; see Friedrich A. Hayek, The Constitution of Liberty 107–122 (2011 definitive ed.) (arguing that rationalistic social engineering undermines liberty).

19. The economist Joseph Schumpeter referred to this economic drive for innovation and profit as "creative destruction," partly because the new (such as a new product) often threatens the old (such as a less-desirable old product). Joseph A. Schumpeter, Capitalism, Socialism, and Democracy 82–83 (1942).

20. Fran Tonkiss, Contemporary Economic Sociology 60–61 (2006); Schumpeter, supra note 19, at 131–142 (aspects of democratic culture undermine capitalism); John Medearis, *Schumpeter, the New Deal, and Democracy*, 91 Am. Pol. Sci. Rev. 819, 820–826 (1997) (Schumpeter viewed democracy as transformative and as undermining capitalism).

21. Block and Somers, supra note 1, at 10–11, 24, 34–35. On professions and academic disciplines, see Andrew Abbott, The System of Professions (1988); Steve Fuller, Philosophy, Rhetoric, and the End of Knowledge 33 (1993); Magali Sarfatti Larson, The Rise of Professionalism: A Sociological Analysis (1977). On the economics discipline, specifically, see Galbraith, supra note 2, at 89–90; Krugman, supra note 1, at 115 (economists naturally tend to "free-market fundamentalism"); Rodrik, supra note 1, at 114–116, 121–122 (dividing economists into two groups); Richard A. Posner, *An Afterword*, 1 J. Legal Stud. 437, 437 (1972) (economics is an objective and scientific enterprise).

22. The historical connection between laissez-faire ideology and the disastrous events of the early-twentieth century is the subject of Polanyi's book, *The Great Transformation*. Polanyi, supra note 1; see Block and Somers,

supra note 1, at 11–15 (summarizing *The Great Transformation*); Barry
Eichengreen, Globalizing Capital 5–6, 191–192 (1996) (confirming and
extending Polanyi's argument).

23. Polanyi, supra note 1, at 25, 240. Polanyi referred to the connection
between laissez faire and social welfare as a "double movement." Polanyi,
supra note 1, at 79, 136, 223; Fred Block, *Introduction, in* Polanyi, supra
note 1, at xviii, xxv–xxix. On the tension between Progressivism and laissez faire, see Martin J. Sklar, The Corporate Reconstruction of American
Capitalism, 1890–1916 (1988); Charles W. McCurdy, *The "Liberty
of Contract" Regime in American Law, in* The State and Freedom of
Contract 161, 161–163 (Harry N. Scheiber ed., 1998).

24. Barbara W. Tuchman, The Proud Tower xiii (1966). On suddenness of
war, see Frieden, supra note 2, at 127–129; MacMillan, supra note 8,
at 633; Neiberg, supra note 8, at 1–9. On inequality, see Frieden, supra
note 2, at 25–27, 40, 109–111, 122; Piketty, supra note 1, at 26 (Figure:
The Capital/Income Ration in Europe, 1870–2010) (showing high capi-
tal/income ratio, and hence inequality, in Europe until World War I).

25. Statistical History, supra note 3 at 546–547 (Table: Exports of Selected
U.S. Merchandise); Micklethwait and Wooldridge, supra note 2, at 63;
Frieden, supra note 2, at 7–8. In the late-nineteenth century, many
American farmers were not prospering. They were instrumental in the
development of the Populist movement. Stephen M. Feldman, Free
Expression and Democracy in America: A History 187–190 (2008);
Michael Kazin, The Populist Persuasion 27–46 (1995).

26. Tuchman, supra note 24, at 356 (quoting John Atkinson Hobson, The
Social Problem 12 (1901)); Eichengreen, supra note 2, at 6; Frieden,
supra note 2, at 30.

27. Edward Hallett Carr, The Twenty Years' Crisis, 1919–1939, at 45–46
(1962); Eichengreen, supra note 2, at 6–7; Ray Ginger, Age of Excess
168, 181–188 (1975); Ira Katznelson, Desolation and Enlightenment 56
(2003); Polanyi, supra note 1, at 21–32, 231–244.

28. Frieden, supra note 2, at xvi, 128; Eichengreen, supra note 2, at 5–12;
Katznelson, supra note 27, at 56; MacMillan, supra note 8, at xxxii;
Polanyi, supra note 1, at 21–32, 231–244.

29. The Fourteen Points (Wilson's Address to Congress, Jan. 8, 1918),
reprinted in 2 Commager, supra note 7, at 137, 138; Carr, supra note 27,
at 50–57; Frieden, supra note 2, at 133–139; Polanyi, supra note 1, at
23–24. "Britain's return to gold in 1925 still stands as one of the most
transparently wrong decisions in the long and impressive history of economic error." Galbraith, supra note 2, at 231.

30. Eichengreen, supra note 2, at 3–4; Frieden, supra note 2, at 140–145,
160–167, 182; Katznelson, supra note 27, at 14. On Hoover and events

leading to his presidency and the Depression, see Maxwell Bloomfield, Peaceful Revolution 99 (2000); Kennedy, supra note 10, at 10–103.

31. Statistical History, supra note 3, at 91–93 (Tables: Hours and Earnings in Manufacturing, in Selected Nonmanufacturing Industries, and for 'Lower-Skilled' Labor); id. at 167 (Table: Percent Shares of Total Income); Eichengreen, supra note 2, at 12; Heilbroner and Milberg, supra note 2, at 102–104; Kennedy, supra note 10, at 35–38; Leuchtenburg, supra note 5, at 243–244; Donald R. McCoy, Coming of Age 172–175 (1973); Piketty, supra note 1, at 293; Polanyi, supra note 1, at 27.

32. Eichengreen, supra note 2, at xi; see id. at 4, 12–21, 258–259 (on gold standard).

33. Frieden, supra note 2, at 177, 179, 182; Heilbroner and Singer, supra note 2, at 282.

34. Heilbroner and Singer, supra note 2, at 281 (quoting Hoover).

35. Frieden, supra note 2, at 209; see id. at 184, 191–193, 209; Block and Somers, supra note 1, at 42; Carr, supra note 27, at 27 (many inter-war democracies "were the product of abstract theory, stuck no roots in the soil, and quickly shrivelled away"); Eichengreen, supra note 2, at 3–4; John Lewis Gaddis, The Cold War: A New History 92–93 (2005); Katznelson, supra note 27, at 14.

36. Walter J. Shepard, Democracy in Transition, 29 Am. Pol. Sci. Rev. 1, 6–7, 12–13, 19 (1935); Edward A. Purcell, Jr., The Crisis of Democratic Theory 119–127 (1973).

37. Charles E. Merriam, Political Power 4 (1934).

38. Bakan, supra note 2, at 87 (quoting Fortune). The General refused the proposal and went to the House Committee on Un-American Activities (HUAC). Id. at 85–94; Jules Archer, The Plot to Seize the White House (1973).

39. Purcell, supra note 36, at 120 (quoting Dewey); Martin H. Redish, The Logic of Persecution 71–72 (2005); Christina E. Wells, Fear and Loathing in Constitutional Decision-making, 2005 Wisconsin Law Review. 115, 121–122.

40. John E. Mulder, Democracy Must Introspect, 1 Bill Rts. Rev. 259, 260 (1941); Robert Brooks, Reflections on the "World Revolution" of 1940, 35 Am. Political Science Review. 1 (1941); Clarence Dykstra, The Quest for Responsibility, 33 Am. Political Science Review. 1 (1939).

41. William M. Wiecek, The Lost World of Classical Legal Thought 10 (1998); Leuchtenburg, supra note 5, at 271 (collapse of American insti-tutions).

42. Lizabeth Cohen, Making a New Deal 254–257, 362–366 (1990); Ira Katznelson, Fear Itself: The New Deal and the Origins of Our Time

6–9, 18–19 (2013); Franklin D. Roosevelt, *Commonwealth Club Speech* (Sept. 23, 1932), *reprinted in* III Great Issues in American History 335, 341–342 (Richard Hofstadter ed., 1982). Roosevelt was far more solicitous of African American interests than any previous president, yet he often sacrificed black interests and values so as to keep white Southerners aligned with the Democratic party. Katznelson, supra, at 20–25. Also, Roosevelt eventually broke with and became antagonistic toward big business. Feldman, supra note 25, at 318–319, 324.

43. Wilfred E. Binkley and Malcolm C. Moos, A Grammar of American Politics (1949); Cushman, supra note 56, at 6–7, 64–67; David B. Truman, The Governmental Process (1951); see Robert S. McElvaine, The Great Depression (1984) (development of acquisitive individualism).

44. Carr, supra note 27, at 43–48, 60, 62 (drawing this metaphor from Karl Mannheim); Gaddis, supra note 35, at 92–93; Heilbroner and Singer, supra note 2, at 297; Stiglitz, supra note 1, at 41; Deborah Boucoyannis, *The Equalizing Hand: Why Adam Smith Thought the Market Should Produce Wealth Without Steep Inequality*, 11 Perspectives on Politics 1051 (2013) (properly functioning market should not produce inequality).

45. David Harvey, A Brief History of Neoliberalism 10–11 (2005); *e.g.*, John Maynard Keynes, The General Theory of Employment, Interest, and Money (1936); see Frieden, supra note 2, at 153–154; Heilbroner and Singer, supra note 2, at 287–292; Daniel Stedman Jones, Masters of the Universe: Hayek, Friedman, and the Birth of Neoliberal Politics 24–26 (2012); Stiglitz, supra note 1, at 41–43. "The term 'embedded liberalism' [connotes] a commitment to free markets tempered by a broader commitment to social welfare and full employment." Eichengreen, supra note 22, at 4 n.1. Keynes admitted he changed his views on free trade during the interwar era. Rodrik, supra note 1, at 58.

46. William E. Leuchtenburg, Franklin D. Roosevelt and the New Deal 335 (1963); id. at 335–344; Bruce Ackerman, We the People: Foundations 116–119 (1991); Anthony J. Badger, The New Deal 61–65 (1989); Bakan, supra note 2, at 85–86; Carr, supra note 27, at 114–117; Kennedy, supra note 10, at 119–124, 285; Statistical History, supra note 3 at 139 (Table: Gross National Product, Total and Per Capita, in Current and 1929 Prices).

47. Bakan, supra note 2, at 187 (quoting Douglas); Eichengreen, supra note 2, at 4; Frieden, supra note 2, at 186; Polanyi, supra note 1, at 27.

48. Hayek, supra note 17, at 44, 133; Milton Friedman, *Neo-liberalism and Its Prospects*, 17 Farmand 89 (1951); see Greg Castillo, Cold War on the Home Front 122–123 (2010); Jones, supra note 45, at 3–8, 94–97. Hayek was an Austrian economist living and teaching in London in 1944.

49. 295 U.S. 330, 368, 374 (1935).

50. 298 U.S. 587, 609–611 (1936).
51. 81 Cong. Rec. 877 (1937); Howard Gillman, The Constitution Besieged: The Rise and Demise of *Lochner* Era Police Powers Jurisprudence 147–194 (1993); Jeff Shesol, Supreme Power: Franklin Roosevelt vs. the Supreme Court (2010).
52. 300 U.S. 379, 391–392, 398–400 (1937).
53. 301 U.S. 1, 33, 43–44, 46 (1937).
54. John Dewey, Freedom and Culture 176 (1939); John Dewey and James H. Tufts, Ethics (1932 ed.), *reprinted in* John Dewey, 7 The Later Works, 1925–1953, at 1, 359 (Jo Ann Boydston ed., 1985) (anticipating this argument).
55. Binkley and Moos, supra note 43, at 8–11; *e.g.*, V.O. Key, Jr., Politics, Parties, and Pressure Groups (1942); Truman, supra note 43; see Purcell, supra note 36, at 197–217.
56. Robert A. Dahl, Democracy and its Critics 172 (1989) [hereinafter Democracy]; Robert A. Dahl, A Preface to Democratic Theory 4, 143 (1956) [hereinafter Preface]; Dewey, supra note 54, at 162, 175.
57. David B. Truman, The Governmental Process 129, 138, 512–513 (2d ed. 1971). On the economic and middle-class foundations of the democratic culture, see id. at 520–523; Louis Hartz, The Liberal Tradition in America 50–64 (1955); V.O. Key, Jr., Politics, Parties, and Pressure Groups 54–57 (3d ed. 1953).
58. Daniel J. Boorstin, The Genius of American Politics 1, 162 (1953); Carr, supra note 27, at 27; Gaddis, supra note 35, at 102. For a more extensive discussion of the transition from republican to pluralist democracy, see Feldman, supra note 25, at 291–382.
59. Democracy, supra note 56, at 109, 170; see id. at 83, 106, 109–111, 130–131, 169–175; Preface, supra note 56, at 37–38, 50–51, 67–71; Thornhill v. Alabama, 310 U.S. 88, 96 (1940); Katznelson, supra note 27, at 107–176; Stephen Holmes, *The Secret History of Self-Interest*, *in* Beyond Self-Interest 267, 283–285 (Jane Mansbridge ed., 1990); Harry Kalven, Jr., *The New York Times Case*, 1964 Sup. Ct. Rev. 191, 208. Dahl also emphasized democratic culture. Democracy, supra note 56, at 172; Preface, supra note 56, at 4, 143.
60. Alexander Meiklejohn, Free Speech: And its Relation to Self-Government 18, 26 (1948).
61. G. Edward White, *The First Amendment Comes of Age: The Emergence of Free Speech In Twentiethcentury America*, 95 Michigan Law Review 299, 300–301 (1996).

62. Thornhill v. Alabama, 310 U.S. 88 (1940) (holding that labor picketing is protected free speech); Schneider v. State, 308 U.S. 147 (1939) (invalidating conviction for distributing handbills); Hague v. C.I.O., 307 U.S. 496 (1939) (upholding right of unions to organize in streets).
63. West Virginia State Board of Ed. v. Barnette, 319 U.S. 624, 642 (1943). The justices' elevation of free expression to lodestar status was one logical part of the Court's increased attention to the broader process of pluralist democracy. United States v. Carolene Products Company, 304 U.S. 144, 152–153 n.4 (1938); John H. Ely, Democracy and Distrust (1980).

CHAPTER 5

Pluralist Democracy Evolves: Free Expression, Judicial Conservatism, and the Cold War

Pluralist democracy evolved after emerging in the 1930s. As with republican democracy during the nineteenth and early-twentieth centuries, pluralist democracy retained its basic principles but changed in its details and applications. Two interrelated factors contributed significantly to this evolution: the Cold War and the consumer culture.[1] Putting this in more human terms, many Americans worried about the threat of Soviet communism, while many of those same Americans wanted, most of all, to enjoy the fruits of prosperity after the nation's victory in World War II.

During the post-World War II period, judicial interpretations of free speech—particularly, conservative interpretations—gradually shifted, partly because of the changes in pluralist democracy. Conservative interpretations of free speech are best understood within the broader context of postwar political developments. After World War II, two primary strands of American political conservatism emerged: traditionalism and libertarianism. Traditionalists reacted, in particular, against the pluralist democratic commitment to ethical relativism. While liberals increasingly celebrated the diverse values and interests roiling through a multicultural America, traditionalists emphasized moral clarity: a need to specify and cultivate the traditional values that had long undergirded the United States. Meanwhile, libertarians reacted against the expanding power of the national government. Thus, liberals might advocate to continue and strengthen New Deal (and subsequently, Great Society) social programs, but libertarians maintained that government power diminished individual liberty and dignity.

© The Author(s) 2017
S.M. Feldman, *The New Roberts Court, Donald Trump, and Our Failing Constitution*, DOI 10.1007/978-3-319-56451-7_5

And from the libertarian standpoint, individual liberty was the root source of American vitality, creativity, and power.[2] One important manifestation of libertarianism was neoliberalism which emphasized economic liberty and drew partly from classical liberal thinkers such as Adam Smith. As already mentioned, early neoliberal thought began to emerge even before World War II, and at that stage, it accepted government intervention in the market. But after the war, neoliberalism transformed, rapidly becoming more assertively libertarian and anti-government.[3]

Traditionalism (now, sometimes called social conservatism) and libertarianism united loosely in their opposition to liberalism and pluralist democracy. Nevertheless, traditionalism, with its emphasis on moral clarity, and libertarianism, with its emphasis on individual liberty, inevitably clashed in numerous situations. Quite simply, the promotion of specific moral values sometimes decreased the degree of individual freedom and vice versa. To be sure, some conservatives, including prominent neoconservatives, attempted to harmonize these conflicting goals for the sake of political advantage. Moreover, conflict between traditionalism and libertarianism is not logically necessary. Rather, conflict or harmony depends on the factual circumstances.[4]

THE EARLY-COLD WAR, FREE EXPRESSION, AND MORAL CLARITY

By the late 1930s, with pluralist democracy firmly entrenched, a broad-based coalition had emerged to support the protection of civil liberties. Many political conservatives reacted to the expanding power of the national government by aligning themselves with this coalition. If the government, now seemingly controlled by diverse political outsiders, was reaching into new realms, especially of economic activity, then conservatives recognized that the courts and civil liberties might usefully shield them from government control. In 1938, the president-elect of the American Bar Association reminded lawyers that civil liberties protect the "wealthy and privileged," while renowned corporate lawyer, Grenville Clark, encouraged "conservatives" to be "intelligent, enlightened guardians of ... civil rights." This conservative backing for civil liberties bolstered the transformation of free speech into a constitutional lodestar.[5]

But conservative support for civil liberties was brief. Pressure to suppress speech and writing increased during World War II and the Cold War, and led to the unraveling of the broad civil-liberties coalition.

During the 1940s and 1950s, conservatives frequently reasoned that government interests outweighed free-expression interests and thus justified suppression. For instance, in *Minersville School District v. Gobitis*, decided in 1940, with war looming, the Court upheld mandatory flag salutes. A Pennsylvania school board required teachers and students to salute the flag and recite the pledge of allegiance. When the Gobitis children, aged twelve and ten, refused to participate in the daily ceremony, they were expelled. The Gobitis family argued that the school board had violated the children's rights to free exercise of religion and free expression. The Court concluded, though, that a societal interest in unity and security outweighed both First-Amendment rights.[6]

The Court would soon overrule itself on the issue of mandatory flag salutes, emphasizing in *West Virginia State Board of Education v. Barnette* that free speech is a constitutional lodestar and that democracy cannot exist without it.[7] Yet, the onset of the Cold War immediately after World War II triggered strong impulses to suppress dissent. For many Americans, the conflict between the United States and the Soviet Union presented a moral choice between freedom and democracy, on the one side, and tyranny and communism, on the other. In a speech delivered on March 12, 1947, President Harry Truman announced that the United States would aid all democratic nations resisting communist takeovers. He justified this policy, which would be called the Truman Doctrine, in stark moral terms. "At the present moment in world history nearly every nation must choose between alternative ways of life. ... One way of life is based upon the will of the majority, and is distinguished by free institutions, representative government, free elections, guarantees of individual liberty, freedom of speech and religion, and freedom from political oppression. The second way of life is based upon the will of a minority forcibly imposed upon the majority. It relies upon terror and oppression, a controlled press and radio; fixed elections, and the suppression of personal freedoms."[8]

From this perspective, any dissent to American principles and policies amounted to an immoral betrayal of the nation's interests and the American way of life. By executive order, the President established a loyalty program for all federal employees. Under this program, "[m]embership in, affiliation with or sympathetic association with any foreign or domestic organization ... designated by the Attorney General as ... Communist, or subversive" constituted disloyalty that would disqualify the individual from federal employment.[9] Loyalty investigations were means for enforcing traditional American values, including certain less savory norms such as racism and anti-intellectualism. Loyalty review boards, for example, would ask: "Have you ever had Negroes in your homes?" Or they might ask: "Do you read Howard Fast? Tom Paine? Upton Sinclair?" One review board member explained: "Of course the fact that a person believes in racial equality doesn't *prove* that he's a communist, but it certainly makes you look twice, doesn't it?"[10]

Despite such executive actions, Red baiters, such as Republicans Joseph McCarthy and Richard Nixon, persistently attacked Truman and the Democrats as being too soft on communism. In 1947, a Republican-controlled Congress overrode Truman's veto and enacted the Taft-Hartley Act. Apart from its general anti-union purposes, Taft-Hartley required each union officer to sign an affidavit declaring that "he is not a member of the Communist Party or affiliated with such party." Refusal to sign would preclude a union from invoking NLRA protections and procedures.[11] In *American Communications Association v. Douds*, decided in 1950, the Supreme Court upheld this affidavit requirement in the face of a First-Amendment challenge. Chief Justice Frederick M. Vinson's majority opinion stressed the specific government interest (or legislative purpose) behind the statute. Congress had sought to protect the free flow of interstate commerce from what Communists "have done and are likely to do again," namely, call political strikes—labor strikes called to advance political rather than union-employee goals. Thus, Vinson reasoned, Congress had imposed the Taft-Hartley affidavit requirement to restrict harmful conduct and not to restrict unpopular expression. Even so, the Court acknowledged that the statutory restriction might interfere with the expression of ideas by Communists. Vinson therefore proceeded to balance the government interest against the infringement of First-Amendment freedoms. Concluding that the government interest predominated, the Court emphasized that Communists remained free to express their beliefs. The statute merely sought to discourage unions from having Communist officers because, once in such a position of power, they could then call a political strike—a dangerous possibility, particularly in a defense industry. The First Amendment, Vinson concluded, "does not require that [a Communist] be permitted to be the keeper of the arsenal."[12]

Conservative Republicans in Congress continued to push an anti-Communist agenda. On September 23, 1950, Congress enacted, again over Truman's veto, the McCarran Internal Security Act, which required all "Communist-action" and "Communist-front" organizations to register with the Attorney General, who then was required to publish the registrants. The Act further mandated that the Communist organizations divulge the names of their officers and the sources of their funds; Communist-action organizations also needed to identify their members.[13] Meanwhile, the House Committee on Un-American Activities (HUAC) investigated not only Hollywood insiders, most notoriously, but also doctors, lawyers, musicians, and others. Thousands of reputations and careers were destroyed. State legislatures, along with HUAC, investigated Communist influences in the public schools. Local school boards were apt to fire any teacher subject to an investigation, regardless of the result. States also imposed loyalty oaths to bar teachers who allegedly had Communist affiliations. In *Adler v. Board of Education of the City of New York*, decided in 1952, the Supreme Court upheld a New York law that compelled teachers to sign affidavits swearing they did not belong to subversive organizations. The Court reasoned that each individual had a right to free expression but not a right to be a public school teacher. The fear was that individuals with Communist affiliations were morally unfit to teach the young.[14] In the end, hundreds of school teachers as well as hundreds of college professors lost their jobs "because of their actual or suspected, past or present, membership in the Communist Party."[15]

Dennis v. United States might be the most renowned and significant Supreme Court anti-Communist decision of the post-World War II period. By a six-to-two vote, *Dennis* upheld the convictions of eleven leaders of the Communist Party of the United States (CPUSA) for advocating the violent overthrow of the government. Even though the prosecution had proven only that the defendants taught Marxist-Leninist doctrine, Chief Justice Vinson's plurality opinion reasoned that the advocated evil—the violent overthrow of the government—was so grave as to outweigh any First-Amendment free-expression concerns. The prosecution's success in *Dennis* then prompted the government to arrest and prosecute dozens of additional CPUSA members.[16]

Ironically, the nation, with the Court's approval, vigorously suppressed free expression during this Red Scare era for the overarching purpose of protecting the American way of life and traditional values. In *Adler*, the Court explicitly stated that it sought to protect "truth and free inquiry" in the public schools. To maintain such free inquiry, the government must "screen the officials, teachers, and employees as to their fitness to maintain the integrity of the schools." From this perspective, free inquiry depended on moral clarity. The morally unfit necessarily undermined free and open discussion and therefore had to be suppressed.[17]

The nation sought to proclaim its traditional values—those that distinguished the United States from the Soviet Union—in other overt ways. For instance, in 1954, Congress amended the law specifying the words of the Pledge of Allegiance to include the phrase, "under God."[18] The legislative history underscored the congressional purpose: "to distinguish the American system of government from communism and to underscore the commitment to inalienable, individual rights guaranteed by God."[19] In 1956, Congress officially declared "In God We Trust" to be the national motto.[20] For many Americans, religious values seemed central to democracy. In upholding the constitutionality of a released-time program—permitting students to be released early from public school for the purpose of receiving religious instruction—the Court stated: "We are a religious people whose institutions presuppose a Supreme Being. ... When the state encourages religious instruction or cooperates with religious authorities by adjusting the schedule of public events to sectarian needs, it follows the best of our traditions."[21] In his book, *Protestant-Catholic-Jew*, Will Herberg encapsulated the perception that traditional religious-cultural morality supplied "the crucial values" for "the American Way of Life." According to Herberg, Protestantism, Catholicism, and Judaism were together "the three 'religions of democracy.'"[22]

Even as the Supreme Court seemingly supported traditional values in the Cold War, some conservative constitutional theorists remained dissatisfied and pushed the Court to move rightward. Writing in 1957, Walter Berns, who had studied under political philosopher Leo Strauss, complained that "speech of almost any character, true or false, good or bad, enjoys a favored status before the Court," except in cases involving national security. The justices, continued Berns, were committed to the tenets of pluralist democracy, including ethical relativism, and thus acted as if "all judgments of better and worse are arbitrary." Berns condemned this judicial attempt to eschew value judgments vis-à-vis the content of expression. The "problem of free speech," he explained, was really "the problem of virtue." In resolving free-expression cases, the Court should attempt to "promote the virtue of citizens" and to pursue the common good. Hence, Berns recommended that the Court return to a doctrinal equivalent of the bad tendency test, which the Court had followed during the republican democratic era. The Court must distinguish between "good and evil," then must allow the government to cultivate citizens of "good character" while censoring the licentious. Otherwise, the United States would be unable to protect "against dangers to civility" and would no longer be a "decent society."[23]

Subsequently, in reaction to the 1960s counterculture and social unrest—including the anti-Vietnam War movement, the Black Power movement, the women's movement, and so on—conservative scholars increasingly followed a traditionalist path condemning relativism and advocating for moral clarity. Alexander Bickel worried that democracy and civil society could not survive without "a foundation of moral values." "A valueless politics and valueless institutions are shameful and shameless and, what is more, man's nature is such that he finds them, and life with and under them, insupportable."[24] Bickel's friend and Yale colleague, Robert Bork, emphasized the importance of such moral values to First-Amendment jurisprudence. He argued that the justices should follow an originalist approach to constitutional interpretation, thus sticking "close to the text and the history, and their fair implications." From Bork's perspective, the Court had unjustifiably expanded the First-Amendment protection of free expression. "There is no basis," Bork wrote, "for judicial intervention to protect ... scientific, literary or that variety of expression we call obscene or pornographic." Pornography, in particular, should be "seen as a problem of pollution of the moral and aesthetic atmosphere precisely analogous to smoke pollution."[25]

The Flip Side of the Cold War: Liberty and Equality in an Emerging Consumers' Democracy

During the early pluralist democratic era, the Cold War unquestionably generated suppression in the ostensible service of traditional American values, but the Cold War also had a flip side. Even as the nation tried to stamp out communism, America pushed to expand liberty in the realms of both political and economic rights.

Civil Rights and Democracy

America's long-running struggle against the Soviet Union forced the United States, for strategic reasons, to confront some of its own shortcomings. The ideal of pluralist democracy demanded that all citizens have an equal vote and an equal voice in democratic debates. But particularly in the South, governments systematically denied political rights to blacks. And this denial of political rights facilitated the enactment and enforcement of 'Jim Crow' laws, which imposed legal segregation in a host of public accommodations, ranging from buses to schools to parks to water fountains. In fact, throughout the New Deal and early-postwar years, the Democratic party often left loopholes in federal programs that, in effect, excluded black participation. These loopholes were the price to be paid to white southerners to retain their support for the Democrats.[26]

The Cold War, however, helped undermine Jim Crow in the South. In the struggle against the Soviets, the United States sought to win the allegiance of other nations, including emerging third-world nations, often populated by people of color. To appeal to these third-world nations, the United States claimed that American democracy stood for liberty and equality for all, regardless of race, color, creed, or gender. As the Soviets gleefully pointed out, though, such claims sounded woefully hollow when many African Americans continued to suffer under a type of apartheid. And federal officials were fully cognizant that the image of democracy presented to the world could be either a benefit or a detriment to the nation's Cold War interests. Thus, the federal government sought to improve the nation's image by burnishing the democratic glow, whether it was in relation to the mistreatment of blacks in the South or the impoverishment of a segment of the country (again, the South), another by-product of Jim Crow.[27] As early as 1947, President Truman's Committee on Civil Rights reported that racial segregation was no longer acceptable for reasons "of conscience, of self-interest, and of survival in a threatening world ... [o]r to put it another way, we have a moral reason, an economic reason, and an international reason" to attack segregation.[28] In the school segregation cases argued in the early 1950s, *Brown v. Board of Education* and its companion, *Bolling v. Sharpe*, the Justice Department filed an amicus curiae brief arguing that segregation was unconstitutional. Given that *Bolling* dealt with the segregated District of Columbia schools, the brief emphasized the treatment of people of color in Washington. "[F]oreign officials and visitors naturally judge this country and our people by their experiences and observations in the nation's capital; and the treatment of colored persons here is taken as the measure of our attitude toward minorities generally." Thus, the brief highlighted how racial segregation, including in the schools, contravened national interests: "[T]he existence of discrimination against minority groups in the United States has an adverse effect upon our relations with other countries. Racial discrimination furnishes grist for the Communist propaganda mills, and it raises doubts even among friendly nations as to the intensity of our devotion to the democratic faith."[29] When the Supreme Court followed the Justice Department's recommendation and held that school segregation violated the Constitution, Chief Justice Earl Warren's unanimous opinion emphasized that education was crucial for "good citizenship" in "our democratic society."[30] In fact, the national government immediately used the decision to its advantage in the Cold War. Within one hour after the Court announced *Brown*, "the Voice of America broadcast the news to Eastern Europe [emphasizing] that 'the issue was settled by law under democratic processes rather than by mob rule or dictatorial fiat.'"[31]

In short, the Cold War created an imperative for the United States to champion the principles of pluralist democracy. Likewise, to defeat the Soviets, the nation needed to temper any threat to American democracy—or at least to the appearance of democracy. Thus, non-violent civil rights protests were acceptable—because they underscored how America could change in accordance with the rule of law—but any protests that became too radical or disruptive were considered subversive of national interests. Violent protests suggested that the democratic process could not peacefully accommodate conflicting interests and values, while a judicial decision like *Brown* lent credibility to the nation's claim that the democratic rule of law was superior to communism. In fact, conservative opponents of civil rights were quick to denounce protestors as communists or communist sympathizers, especially if they even hinted at violence. "All the disgraceful episodes which have occurred in New York and other cities recently were certainly not directed by patriotic American Negro leaders," declared the magazine, *U.S. News and World Report*. "The time has come for the Government of the United States to do more to expose the infiltration in civic movements by the Communist Party and its agents, stooges, and allies inside this country."[32]

Regardless, after the Court decided *Brown*, the pro-democracy effects of the Cold War continued to snowball, as the nation moved toward the fulfillment of pluralist democratic principles. President Lyndon B. Johnson, a Southerner from Texas, proclaimed that "[i]t is wrongly—deadly wrong—to deny any of your fellow Americans the right to vote." In 1964, the Twenty-Fourth Amendment, proscribed poll taxes in federal elections, while the Voting Rights Act of 1965 (VRA) and parts of the Civil Rights Act of 1964 eradicated literacy, educational, and character tests that had been used to deny or discourage racial minorities from voting. The VRA, in particular, produced substantive change—not merely changes in the appearance or in the forms of democracy. For instance, the percentage of blacks registered to vote in Mississippi catapulted from 6.7 in 1964 to 66.5% in 1969.[33] The Court, too, continued to transform pluralist democracy by interpreting the Constitution to protect participation in the democratic process. In the 1960s, the Court decided many cases that explicitly protected the democratic process and made it more inclusive. *Gomillion v. Lightfoot*, decided in 1960, held that a state law transforming the city of Tuskegee, Alabama, "from a square to an uncouth twenty-eight-sided figure" violated the Fifteenth Amendment. The state statute, which removed "from the city all save four or five of its 400 Negro voters while not removing a single white voter or resident," amounted to unconstitutional gerrymandering that denied African Americans "the municipal franchise and consequent rights."[34] In *Baker v. Carr*, the Court overruled an earlier decision and held that an allegation of vote dilution arising from disproportional representation, whether in a state legislature or the House of Representatives, constituted a justiciable claim. *Baker* led to *Wesberry v. Sanders*, focusing on congressional districts, and *Reynolds v. Sims*, focusing on state legislative districts, which together established the doctrine of one person, one vote.[35]

Unsurprisingly, given how the self-governance rationale posits that free expression is a prerequisite for pluralist democracy, when the Court in the 1960s invigorated its protection of the democratic process, it also energized the First-Amendment guarantee of free speech. Many of the Court's most speech protective decisions came during that decade. Indeed, one could reasonably argue that the Court fulfilled the promise of free expression being a constitutional lodestar. Again and again, the justices in these cases emphasized the need for free and open discussions of political issues in a pluralist democratic regime. *New York Times v. Sullivan*, decided in 1964, asked whether the First Amendment protected the press from civil libel actions brought by government officials. The *Times* had published a full-page advertisement that solicited support for the civil rights movement while criticizing the Montgomery, Alabama, police commissioner. The advertisement, however, contained several minor factual errors. For instance, it stated that students in Montgomery, Alabama, had sung "'My Country,' Tis of Thee' on the State Capitol steps," but they had, in fact, sung the national anthem. The police commissioner successfully brought a civil action in the state courts for defamation. The Supreme Court had previously recognized defamation as constitutionally unprotected (or low-value) speech, yet this case resembled a criminal prosecution for seditious libel: The government, through the institution of the state courts, sought to punish the press for criticizing a public official, the police commissioner. Reversing the state court decision, a unanimous Court emphasized the self-governance rationale. "[W]e consider this case against the background of a profound national commitment to the principle that debate on public issues should be uninhibited, robust, and wide-open, and that it may well include vehement, caustic, and sometimes unpleasantly sharp attacks on government and public officials." After deeming government prosecution of seditious libel unconstitutional, the Court reasoned that if a state could not constitutionally punish criticisms of government policies and officials through a criminal prosecution, then it should not be able to impose punishment through a civil defamation action. Instead, a "public official" can recover "damages for a defamatory falsehood relating to his official conduct" only if "he proves that the statement was made with 'actual malice'—that is, with knowledge that it was false or with reckless disregard of whether it was false or not."[36]

Pickering v. Board of Education, decided in 1968, arose when a School Board dismissed a teacher for writing a letter to a newspaper. The letter criticized how the Board and the school superintendent had handled funding issues. The Court began by emphasizing that public school teachers cannot be forced, as a condition of employment, to relinquish their free-expression rights to comment on issues of public concern. While the state, as an employer, might have an interest in regulating for purposes of efficiency, the First Amendment protects an employee from being discharged for comments "on issues of public importance."[37] One year later, the Court decided *Tinker v. Des Moines Independent Community School District*, which also involved public schools, though in this case the schools had suspended students for wearing black armbands in protest against the Vietnam War. The Court categorized the armbands as "pure speech" rather than conduct and, therefore, as deserving of "comprehensive protection under the First Amendment." Like teachers, students do not lose their First-Amendment rights merely because they enter a school, the Court reasoned. Although students' presence in a school environment might require some diminishment of their rights, the Court articulated a highly speech-protective doctrine: Student expression is constitutionally protected unless it causes "material

and substantial interference with schoolwork or discipline." In concluding that the student speech in this case was constitutionally protected,
the Court underscored that public schools are training grounds where
students learn the skills prerequisite for participation in pluralist democracy—the skills needed to become citizens and leaders.[38] *Brandenburg
v. Ohio*, decided the same year as *Tinker*, directly confronted the issue
raised in the World War I Espionage Act cases: When, if ever, did the
Constitution protect expression encouraging unlawful conduct, particularly subversive advocacy criticizing the government? Compared
to the World War I decisions, which had upheld convictions of numerous defendants who had protested against the draft and the war, the
Court now dramatically enlarged free-expression guarantees. Under
the *Brandenburg* test, the First Amendment shields expression unless
the speaker specifically intends to incite imminent unlawful action, and
such unlawful action is likely to occur imminently.[39] In sum, in case after
case, from *Sullivan* to *Pickering* to *Tinker* to *Brandenburg*, the Court
expanded the First-Amendment protection of free expression—a judicial action induced partly by the Cold War imperative to uphold pluralist
democratic principles.

Capitalism and Democracy

The Cold War combined with other forces to contribute to the further
evolution of pluralist democracy in yet another manner. In particular, a maturing mass-consumer culture intertwined with the Cold War
to reshape the economic ground underlying the pluralist democratic
regime. In the 1920s, the development of mass-consumerism had helped
create a widely shared American culture revolving around the consumption of mass-produced items and the worship of mass-media celebri-
ties. This mass-consumer culture, in turn, helped fuse Americans into
a more encompassing and less exclusionary polity that would serve as a
springboard for pluralist democracy. But the development of the mass-
consumer culture did not end in the twenties. It continued in the 1930s
and, even more so, after World War II, as the nation emerged out of its
prolonged economic depression.[40]

Americans increasingly embraced mass-consumerism after the war.
Gross national product (GNP) nearly doubled from 1945 to 1955,
going to $397.5 billion. During those years, personal consump-
tion expenditures on manufactured products increased dramatically;

spending on the purchase of new and used cars alone jumped an incredible 44-fold. Significantly, the nation's prosperity empowered a growing percentage of Americans to enjoy these consumer goods; disparities of wealth diminished as the middle class grew.[41]

Changes in commercial advertising contributed to the further growth of the mass-consumer culture. The very nature of advertising transformed during the twentieth century. Early in the century, product advertisements provided potential consumers with information that would allow them to assess rationally the benefits of purchasing the respective products. During the 1920s, however, advertisers began to market images and lifestyles. Advertisements encouraged individuals to purchase particular products because the products symbolized certain attractive personality traits or ways of living. A particular automobile, for instance, might be marketed as conducive to a relaxed drive in the country on a Sunday afternoon.[42]

Of course, advertisers continued to experiment, to quest after evermore effective means for generating sales. Advertisements, for example, could generate previously unrecognized anxieties—oh no! my underarms look sweaty—which only a certain product could alleviate—thank goodness for my antiperspirant. After World War II, marketing analysts realized that they could increase sales by targeting distinct segments of the population with particularized advertisements and products—marketing one deodorant for males and another for females, one beer for the wealthy and another for the middle class. Such segmentation of the population for marketing purposes has, of course, become increasingly refined. An individual buying toothpaste today, for instance, must decide from a dizzying array of products. No longer must one choose between Crest and Colgate. Now one must puzzle over special whitening toothpaste, special tartar-removing toothpaste, special anti-cavity toothpaste, special mouthwash-striped toothpaste, special gum-disease toothpaste, and so on. Moreover, if a shopper checks the fine print on competing products, one frequently finds that the active ingredients are identical. What differentiates the hand lotion for normal skin from the lotions for dry skin, rough skin, and extra-dry skin? Nothing, at least oftentimes. The products are substance-wise the same. They merely target distinct segments of the market (or population).[43]

Meanwhile, changes in the mass media transformed advertising. In the early-twentieth century, advertisements were placed within the print media, primarily newspapers and magazines. The development of electronic mass media—radio in the 1920s, television in the 1950s, and the internet in the 1990s—opened additional pathways for reaching consumers. Given these new venues and the evident success of advertising as a means for increasing profits, the amount of money devoted to commercial advertising grew astronomically. In 1900, $542 million was spent on advertising; by 1929, the amount had jumped to $3426 million. After World War II, advertising volumes skyrocketed: In 1949, the amount had climbed over $5 billion, and by 1957, the amount was above $10 billion. The numbers continued their ascent: In 1990, amazingly, almost $130 billion was spent on advertising, a figure that nearly doubled by 2001.[44]

The expanding mass-consumer culture fused with American law and politics in multiple ways. Most important, pluralist democracy became, in effect, a consumers' democracy. From its outset, pluralist democracy had resonated with capitalist ideology because of the overlapping emphases on the individual pursuit of self-interest. But during the Cold-War period, the connection between democracy and capitalism grew stronger; politics grew increasingly like commercial consumption. Citizens followed their own values and interests, whether shopping for a product or a candidate. In the presidential campaigns of the 1950s, New York advertising agencies successfully marketed Dwight "Ike" Eisenhower. Then, when market analysts realized the effectiveness of aiming advertisements at targeted population segments, political analysts followed close behind. The John F. Kennedy campaign marketed to distinct segments of the political market in the 1960 election. Election campaigns became "indistinguishable in form (and often in content) from product marketing campaigns."[45]

Around this time, in the 1960s and 1970s, American jurisprudence saw the initial emergence of a law and economics movement. According to its early practitioners, such as Richard Posner, law and economics entailed "the application of scientific methods to the study of the legal system." Thus, law and economics is "an endeavor to make precise, objective, and systematic observations of how the legal system operates in fact and to discover and explain the recurrent patterns in the observations—the 'laws' of the system."[46] How could such scientific objectivity be possible? It rested on the ostensible predictability of each individual's behavior—behavior that was supposedly in accordance with certain assumptions. First, individuals act pursuant to "a stable set of preferences" and have access to all relevant information. Second, individuals rationally pursue self-interest, or in other words, they maximize their own utility. Third, the marketplace naturally coordinates the actions of buyers and sellers by shifting resources and prices.[47]

From the perspective of law and economics, the legal actor functions like homo economicus, the neoclassical economic self. Homo economicus was often criticized, however. Critics pointed out that when the economic self is neither making nor spending money, it appears to be empty and isolated. Community and tradition seem to be mere "revocable" affiliations. Although motivated by its preferences or interests, homo economicus cannot locate their ultimate source, other than itself. For many individuals, preferences appear to bubble up from within. Of course, the critics maintain that homo economicus takes its cues from the economic marketplace. Corporations saturate the broadcast and electronic media with advertisements that tell consumers what to drive, what to drink, what to wear, what to worry about, and so on. Other critics worry, though, that homo economicus is inevitable. They argue that, centuries ago, Enlightenment philosophers who separated the material from the spiritual, the mind from the body, inadvertently placed the western self on the road to homo economicus. In a disenchanted world of scientific objectivity, the economic self might be all that is possible.[48]

Despite the criticisms and regardless of whether it was inevitable, the conception of human nature embodied in homo economicus continued to grow in influence. At a cultural level, there were two crucial messages: first, the individual is a rational self-maximizer, and second, the consumer is sovereign. As a rational self-maximizer, the individual coldly calculates the most efficient means of satisfying its own interests. Meanwhile, consumer sovereignty means that the individual knows its own interests or preferences, or in other words, the individual knows what is best for itself. Therefore, the consumer knows what products to demand in the marketplace, and the marketplace (supposedly) satisfies. The individual chooses, and the world responds.[49]

The changing nature and role of corporations in American society strongly contributed to the growing connection between democracy and capitalism. During the first decades of the twentieth century, Americans often denounced corporations as "soulless leviathans" and corporate leaders as robber barons.[50] In 1933, Justice Louis Brandeis referred to large corporations as a "Frankenstein monster."[51] After World War II, though, the corporate public image improved: Corporations became increasingly associated with and even emblematic of American capitalism in its Cold

War battle against communism. And in the midst of the Cold War, the connection between corporate capitalism and the United States did not remain merely implicit; it was a weapon to be wielded openly against the Soviets. In 1959, Vice President Richard Nixon attended a trade show in Moscow. He boasted about the opulence of the American kitchen appliances on display, which the *New York Times* described as a "lavish testimonial to abundance."[52] Nixon did not hesitate to accentuate the differences between America and the Soviet Union. "The United States comes closest to the ideal of prosperity for all in a classless society," he proclaimed. The variety and availability of consumer goods in the United States symbolized "'our right to choose. We do not wish to have decisions made at the top by governmental officials,' whether about [our] 'kind of house' or [our] 'kind of ideas.'"[53] In a similar vein, in 1955, when Will Herberg celebrated the American Way of Life, he referred to more than democracy. He included the products and comforts that accompanied the American capitalist economy. The American Way of Life "synthesizes all that commends itself to the American as the right, the good, and the true in actual life," he wrote. "It embraces such seemingly incongruous elements as sanitary plumbing and freedom of opportunity, Coca-Cola and an intense faith in education—all felt as moral questions relating to the proper way of life."[54] In effect, American commercial products had become "icons of anticommunism."[55]

As the mass-consumer culture fused with pluralist democracy, corporations sought to exercise greater control over democracy and government. Starting in the 1960s and 1970s, the number of organized interest groups lobbying in Washington, D.C., began to increase rapidly. While 5843 national non-profit associations existed in 1959, that number had nearly tripled to 14,726 by 1980, and it had jumped to 22,289 by 1990. To be sure, these proliferating interest groups represented a wide variety of viewpoints and concerns, including professional associations like the American Medical Association, religious organizations like the Christian Coalition, and anti-abortion and pro-choice advocates like the National Right to Life Organization and the National Abortion and Reproductive Rights Action League. Yet, by far, the largest number of associations fell into the "trade, business, and commercial" category. Basically, corporations became more resolute at using their bureaucratic organizations and accumulated wealth to intervene in the pluralist democratic marketplace. Over the last 5 years of the 1970s, for instance, the number of corporate political action committees zoomed from 300 to 1200. Even more extreme, from the early 1970s to the early 1980s, the number of corporations with registered lobbyists in Washington expanded nearly 15-fold.[56]

During this era, in 1971, corporate attorney and future Supreme Court Justice Lewis Powell wrote an influential memorandum to his friend and neighbor, an official for the U.S. Chamber of Commerce, an organization dedicated to promoting and protecting business interests. Maintaining that the free enterprise system was under attack from the American left, Powell proposed a detailed program of response. For instance, he advocated for the creation of conservative think tanks that would help counter liberalism on college campuses. He also argued that business should use the corporate-owned media to shape public opinion. In doing so, corporate spokespersons should emphasize that any threat to business was a threat to "individual freedom." Corporate America, Powell was suggesting, should expressly equate the interests of business with the liberty interests of individual Americans. What was bad for business was bad for America. Finally, he insisted that business must begin to assert political power more directly, whether through lobbying or other means. Business, he wrote, must learn "that political power is necessary; that such power must be assiduously [sic] cultivated; and that when necessary, it must be used aggressively and with determination."[57]

Businesses answered Powell's call to action with enhanced and aggressive politicizing. Membership in the Chamber of Commerce more than quadrupled over the next decade. In 1972, Chief Executive Officers (CEOs) of some of America's largest corporations formed the Business Roundtable, committed to expanding corporate political power. Significantly, as part of this effort, corporations explicitly advocated that their expenditures fell within the compass of First-Amendment protections. During the seventies, Mobil Oil paid to publish in the *New York Times* numerous essays, which effectively appeared as op-eds, arguing that corporate speech was integral to American liberty and democracy. Such corporate advocacy proved incredibly successful. In the 1960s and early 1970s, corporations were forced to confront issues related to public health, consumer safety, and labor—the types of issues pressed by consumer advocate Ralph Nader. By the late 1970s and early 1980s, corporations had transformed public debate to focus on the costs of the so-called big government and the benefits of the marketplace. And not incidentally, Powell was sitting on the Supreme Court less than 6 months after he had written his memorandum.[58]

Despite these corporate advances, the Cold War inherently constrained the extension of capitalism and corporate power. Specifically, the Cold War tempered laissez-faire dreams on both the international and domestic fronts. On the international front, the United States after World War II did not immediately attempt to reinstate the laissez-faire ideal of a wide-open and unregulated international marketplace. First, political geography imposed boundaries on corporate reach. Corporations seek new consumers, regardless of nationality or ethnicity, because new consumers produce additional profits. But even as corporations went multinational, they could not go global. With few exceptions, corporations could not open markets behind the "Iron Curtain." Second, the Bretton Woods monetary system, negotiated toward the end of the war, was designed to nurture an international capitalist market among the non-Iron Curtain countries, but with limits protecting against the types of economic crises and disasters witnessed during the early-twentieth century. Bretton Woods created the International Monetary Fund (IMF) and the World Bank (the International Bank for Reconstruction and Development). The IMF would monitor and manage exchange rates and currencies with an eye to avoiding crises. The World Bank would provide funds to underdeveloped and war-ravaged nations. To be sure, Bretton Woods contained elements that resonated with the interwar international market and gold standard. The 44 member nations agreed to peg their currencies to the United States dollar, and the United States agreed to ground the dollar on its gold reserves. Yet, Keynes, who helped create the system, said that it was "the exact opposite of the gold standard."[59] Overall, the postwar system was designed to avoid economic crises by maintaining stable currencies and coordinating government actions with marketplace operations.[60]

The American and western European leaders had learned from history: International economic prosperity should not be left to the whims of an invisible hand. The Soviets were the utopians: They insisted that history must fit Marxist theory and that a proletarian paradise could be achieved. The democratic-capitalists of the West had become pragmatists: They now sought practical solutions for economic and government problems while eschewing utopian verities, whether laissez faire or otherwise. Thus, as soon as the Bretton Woods system appeared inadequate for rebuilding the war-shattered western European economies, the United States announced the Marshall Plan—named for Secretary of State George Marshall—which funneled 12–13 billion dollars in grants to western European nations. Although aspects of the Marshall Plan might, in the short run, contravene the concept of a laissez-faire international marketplace, Marshall and President Truman emphasized its practical economic benefits.[61]

On the domestic front, no matter how strongly corporate capitalists quested after additional wealth, they could not aggressively attack the government or undermine democratic culture—so long as American democracy was locked in battle with Soviet communism. For better or worse, corporate capitalists were, in effect, teammates with the government in the fight against communism. If widespread middle-class economic attitudes generated the cultural willingness to negotiate and compromise politically, to engage in the pluralist democratic process— as numerous political theorists maintained—then the economic middle class had to be preserved. Corporate greed could not squeeze the middle class too excessively, at least not yet. And, in fact, Nixon was not alone in proclaiming that capitalism and mass consumption demonstrably created "a classless society [which countered] Soviet charges that capitalism created extremes of wealth and poverty." This assertion, that capitalism engendered widespread economic equality, which in turn promoted democratic equality, was a staple of American Cold War propaganda. The documentary film, *Despotism*, produced by Encyclopaedia Britannica, emphasized the inverse: If wealth became too concentrated in an upper class, if the divisions between the haves and have-nots became too distinct, "then despotism threatened."[62]

To be sure, neoliberals, often called libertarians during the 1950s, became more strident defenders of the economic marketplace during this post-World War II era. In the context of the Cold War, their conservative defense of the market took on "apocalyptic" proportions. Even so, because neoliberals viewed themselves as "foot-soldiers in the fight against communism," they still needed to restrain their questioning of democratic government.[63] After all, the government was leading the fight against the communists. Whenever the United States government successfully persuaded a third-world nation to align against the Soviet Union, American corporations stood to profit as their markets expanded. In fact, many conservatives were moved to support government-funded research. More specifically, government support for particular industries and research related to national defense seemed not only justified but also urgently needed, whether it involved the development of a hydrogen (fusion) bomb or the exploration of outer space. As Margaret Pugh

O'Mara points out, "Cold War geopolitics prompted new political attention to science," and transformed scientists into "elites." Massive sums of money flowed to research universities, such as Stanford, MIT, and Harvard, creating affluent "cities of knowledge."[64]

The evolution of pluralist democracy into a consumers' democracy profoundly influenced the Supreme Court justices, especially in free-expression cases. In 1942, soon after pluralist democracy had supplanted republican democracy, the Supreme Court held that the First Amendment did not protect commercial expression. The regulation of commercial advertising, at the time, seemed no different from other permissible government regulations of the economic marketplace.[65] But during the Cold War, as the mass-consumer culture became increasingly entangled with democratic processes, the Court modified its treatment of commercial expression. *Bigelow v. Virginia*, decided in 1975, arose when a newspaper editor ran an advertisement for the Women's Pavilion, which provided abortion services in another state. The state of Virginia convicted the editor for violating a statute that proscribed any "advertisement" that would "encourage or prompt the procuring of abortion." Justice Harry Blackmun wrote an opinion for a seven-justice majority, which included now-Justice Powell, holding the conviction unconstitutional. He began by acknowledging the Court's prior recognition of several low-value "categories of speech—such as fighting words, or obscenity, or libel, or incitement—[which] have been held unprotected." Nonetheless, Blackmun insisted that "commercial advertising enjoys a degree of First Amendment protection." Advertising was no longer "unprotected per se," though the Court allowed that it could "be subject to reasonable regulation." Then, by applying a balancing test, weighing the government interest in regulation against the First-Amendment interest in free expression, the Court held this particular statutory proscription unconstitutional.[66]

One year later, in *Virginia State Board of Pharmacy v. Virginia Citizens Consumer Council*, the Court held unconstitutional a state law that prohibited licensed pharmacists from advertising prescription drug prices. The majority opinion, which Powell again joined, reasoned that democracy entails the allocation of resources in society, but that most resource-allocation decisions are made through the economic marketplace. "So long as we preserve a predominantly free enterprise economy, the allocation of our resources in large measure will be made through numerous private economic decisions." The economic marketplace, from this perspective, had become a situs of democracy. The private sphere was engulfing the public sphere. Alluding to the self-governance rationale, the Court reasoned that commercial speech or advertising was now essential to democracy, for "the proper allocation of resources in a free enterprise system." Spending money had become a form of politics—of political expression. "Advertising, however tasteless and excessive it sometimes may seem, is ... dissemination of information as to who is producing and selling what product, for what reason, and at what price." Given this viewpoint, consumer sovereignty, liberty, had to be protected. The government (and the Court) should "assume ... that people will perceive their own best interests if only they are well enough informed." Government restrictions on advertising are "highly paternalistic" intrusions into the marketplace—and, consequently, democracy. The Court even suggested that the American citizen looked like homo economicus: "As to the particular consumer's interest in the free flow of commercial information, that interest may be as keen, if not keener by far, than his interest in the day's most urgent political debate." As an economic self, the American was more motivated to learn about the prices and ostensible qualities of shampoo brands than about the policy positions of senate candidates.[67]

The Court continued to resolve commercial-expression issues pursuant to a balancing test, with the definitive statement of this approach coming in *Central Hudson Gas and Electric Corporation v. Public Service Commission of New York*, decided in 1980. This time, Powell wrote the majority opinion invalidating a state ban on promotional advertising by utility companies. Powell articulated, albeit awkwardly, a four-part balancing test to determine the constitutionality of commercial speech regulations. "For commercial speech to come within [the protection of the First Amendment], it at least must concern lawful activity and not be misleading. Next, we ask whether the asserted governmental interest is substantial. If both inquiries yield positive answers, we must determine whether the regulation directly advances the governmental interest asserted, and whether it is not more extensive than is necessary to serve that interest." Despite the clumsiness of Powell's four-part test, the Court would continue to invoke it in numerous subsequent cases. Significantly, then, the reasoning in Powell's *Central Hudson* opinion echoed his 1971 memorandum and clarified the Court's growing affinity for homo economicus. Quoting from *Virginia State Board*, Powell reiterated the principle of consumer sovereignty: The economic self knows its own interests and generally should not be restricted by the government. He equated the interests of individual Americans with the interests of business: "Commercial expression not only serves the economic interest of the [business] speaker, but also assists consumers and furthers the societal interest in the fullest possible dissemination of information." Finally, he asserted the importance of the private sphere vis-à-vis the public sphere. "[M]any, if not most, products," he noted, "may be tied to public concerns with the environment, energy, economic policy, or individual health and safety."[68]

The commercial speech cases had obvious potential ramifications for campaign finance issues. If the economic marketplace had become a situs of democracy, and spending money had become a form of political expression, then governmental restrictions on campaign finance spending might also contravene the First Amendment. This issue surfaced the same year the Court decided *Virginia State Board*. In the seminal *Buckley v. Valeo*, the Court upheld a statutory restriction on campaign contributions to candidates but invalidated a restriction on campaign expenditures, whether made by candidates, individuals, or groups (including political action committees). A contribution is money given directly to a candidate (and therefore within the candidate's control), while an expenditure is money spent on a campaign but never within a candidate's immediate control. With Powell joining a per curiam majority opinion, the Court stressed the political importance of spending money in our consumers' democracy. "A restriction on the amount of money a person or group can spend on political communication during a campaign necessarily reduces the quantity of expression by restricting the number of issues discussed, the depth of their exploration, and the size of the audience reached." Money had now become speech "because virtually every means of communicating ideas in today's mass society requires the expenditure of money." The Court nonetheless upheld the limits on campaign contributions largely because money given directly to a candidate created at least the appearance of corruption, if not constituting actual corruption. When it came to campaign expenditures, however, the Court reasoned that the danger of corruption or the appearance of corruption was greatly diminished. Thus, emphasizing the confrontational political battles characteristic of pluralist democracy (rather than the supposedly virtuous civil exchanges that might generate the republican democratic common good), the Court evoked the self-governance rationale and concluded that limits on expenditures were unconstitutional.

> [T]he concept that government may restrict the speech of some elements of our society in order to enhance the relative voice of others is wholly foreign to the First Amendment, which was designed "to secure 'the widest possible dissemination of information from diverse and antagonistic sources,'" and "to assure unfettered interchange of ideas for the bringing about of political and social changes desired by the people."[69]

The *Buckley* Court did not explicitly discuss restrictions on *corporate* campaign expenditures, but the justices addressed that issue 2 years later in *First National Bank of Boston v. Bellotti*. With a majority opinion written by Powell, the Court invalidated a state law that prohibited business corporations from spending money to influence voters in referendum elections. Once again, Powell's reasoning echoed his 1971 memorandum. He equated corporate interests with individual interests, and then explicitly extended First-Amendment protections to corporations. Powell explained that the source, corporate or otherwise, of speech was irrelevant, while the nature of the speech was crucial. Building on this premise, Powell could invoke the self-governance rationale to support corporate speech. "[T]here is practically universal agreement that a major purpose of [the First] Amendment was to protect the free discussion of governmental affairs," Powell began. "If the speakers here were not corporations, no one would suggest that the State could silence their proposed speech. It is the type of speech indispensable to decision making in a democracy, and this is no less true because the speech comes from a corporation rather than an individual. The inherent worth of the speech in terms of its capacity for informing the public does not depend upon the identity of its source, whether corporation, association, union, or individual." By focusing on the self-governance rationale, the conservative justices underscored the importance of free speech. And by protecting free speech, the justices simultaneously enhanced the protection of liberty vis-à-vis economic wealth.[70]

In sum, the development of the consumers' democracy changed how the justices, particularly the conservative ones, viewed free expression.[71] Free expression no longer was merely a civil liberty to be asserted by minorities and dissidents. Because of the fusion of democracy and the mass-consumer culture, the expenditure of wealth had become integral to politics. Spending money had become a form of political expression. Thus, the conservative justices sought to energize the protection of liberty, as manifested in free speech. In short, libertarian conservatism had come to the Court, albeit from an unexpected direction. Conservative constitutional scholars and Supreme Court justices had begun to follow the traditionalist path, with its focus on moral clarity, largely for the same reason that other conservatives had done so. They rebelled against the ethical relativism of pluralist democracy and its manifestation in multiculturalism. In general, libertarianism had also gained a foothold in American conservatism in reaction against an aspect of pluralist democracy: namely, its expansion of national government power. To be sure, conservative constitutional scholars eventually followed this libertarian path to argue against exercises of congressional power. And the conservative justices would begin in the 1990s to implement this libertarian approach in congressional power and Tenth Amendment cases.[72] Yet, in free-speech cases, conservative justices had already moved in the libertarian direction: The Court decided *Bigelow* and *Virginia State Board of Pharmacy* in the mid-1970s. And in those commercial speech cases, the conservative justices did not react against pluralist democracy. Instead, they acted in accord with pluralist democracy—as transformed into a consumers' democracy—relying on the self-governance rationale, characteristic of the pluralist democratic era. In the context of the consumers' democracy, in other words, the conservative justices seized upon the libertarian emphasis on individual liberty, particularly vis-à-vis the economic marketplace.[73]

NOTES

1. Helpful sources on the Cold War cited in this chapter include: H.W. Brands, The Devil We Knew: Americans and the Cold War (1993); Greg Castillo, Cold War on the Home Front (2010); Richard B. Day, Cold War Capitalism: The View From Moscow, 1945–1975 (1995); Mary L. Dudziak, Cold War Civil Rights (2000); John Lewis Gaddis, The Cold War: A New History (2005); Melvyn P. Leffler, A Preponderance of Power (1992); Richard Saull, The Cold War and After (2007); Martin Walker, The Cold War: A History (1993).

2. George H. Nash, The Conservative Intellectual Movement in America Since 1945, at 1–83 (2008 ed.); Peter Berkowitz, Constitutional

Conservatism 9 (2013). On traditionalism, see Russell Kirk, The Conservative Mind: From Burke to Santayana (1953); Nash, supra, at 104–115. On libertarianism, see Nash, supra, at 1–49; Peter Berkowitz, *Introduction, in* Varieties of Conservatism in America xvii–xviii (2004).

3. Daniel Stedman Jones, Masters of the Universe: Hayek, Friedman, and the Birth of Neoliberal Politics 6–11, 101–102 (2012); *e.g.*, Friedrich A. Hayek, The Road to Serfdom 17 (1994 ed., 1st ed. 1944).

4. Berkowitz, supra note 2, at 9; Stephen M. Feldman, Neoconservative Politics and the Supreme Court: Law, Power, and Democracy 3–4, 52–54 (2013); Murray Friedman, The Neoconservative Revolution 183 (2005); Irving Kristol, Neoconservatism: The Autobiography of an Idea (1995); Nash, supra note 2, at 197–198, 235–243; George H. Nash, *The Uneasy Future of American Conservatism, in* The Future of Conservatism 1–19 (Charles W. Dunn ed., 2007).

5. Richard W. Steele, Free Speech in the Good War 11 (1999) (quoting Frank Hogan); Grenville Clark, *Conservatism and Civil Liberty*, 24 A.B.A. J. 640, 640–644 (1938) (address to Nassau County Bar Association, June 11, 1938); Ken I. Kersch, Constructing Civil Liberties 112–117 (2004).

6. 310 U.S. 586, 593–596 (1940), *overruled*, West Virginia State Board of Ed. v. Barnette, 319 U.S. 624 (1943); Stephen M. Feldman, Free Expression and Democracy in America: A History 430–431 (2008).

7. 319 U.S. 624, 640–642 (1943).

8. The Truman Doctrine (March 12, 1947), *reprinted in* 2 Documents of American History 525, 527 (Henry Steele Commager ed., 3d ed. 1947) [hereinafter Commager]; Gaddis, supra note 1, at 7–8, 98–102.

9. Truman Loyalty Order (March 21, 1947), *reprinted in* 2 Commager, supra note 8, at 529, 532. Commager dates Truman's executive order on March 22, but the government archives date it on March 21. http://www.archives.gov/federal-register/executive-orders/1947.html.

10. Robert Goldstein, Political Repression in Modern America 303–304 (2001) (emphasis in original); Geoffrey R. Stone, Perilous Times 345–346 (2004).

11. Taft-Hartley Act (June 23, 1947), *reprinted in* 2 Commager, supra note 8, at 537, 539–540; Goldstein, supra note 10, at 290–291; Geoffrey R. Stone, *Free Speech in the Age of Mccarthy: A Cautionary Tale*, 93 Cal. L. Rev, 1387, 1388–1396 (2005).

12. 339 U.S. 382, 396, 402–403, 412 (1950). For a discussion of whether Communists truly threatened to weaken the nation's defenses by calling political strikes, see Martin H. Redish, The Logic of Persecution 29–31 (2005); Ellen Schrecker, Many Are the Crimes 183–190 (1998). The

scholarly consensus is that political strikes did occur, but they were far less common and serious than the government claimed.

13. Internal Security Act (Sept. 23, 1950), 64 Stat. 987; Goldstein, supra note 10, at 322–323.
14. 342 U.S. 485 (1952); James T. Patterson, Restless Giant 185 (2005) (university professors).
15. Stone, supra note 10, at 422.
16. *Dennis*, 341 U.S. 494, 508–511 (1951). The defendants were also convicted for conspiring to organize the CPUSA. Id. at 495–497. On subsequent prosecutions, see Goldstein, supra note 10, at 332–333; Patterson, supra note 14, at 193; Freda Kirchwey, *The Shape of Things*, The Nation, Jan. 31, 1953, at 89.
17. 342 U.S. at 490, 493.
18. Pub. L. No. 396, 68 Stat. 249 (1954).
19. Vincent Blasi and Seana V. Shiffrin, *The Story of West Virginia State Board of Education v. Barnette: The Pledge of Allegiance and the Freedom of Thought, in* Constitutional Law Stories 433, 471 (Michael C. Dorf ed., 2004) (citing legislative history).
20. Anson Phelps Stokes and Leo Pfeffer, Church and State in the United States 570–571 (1964); Thomas C. Berg, *Anti-Catholicism and Modern Church-State Relations*, 33 Loyola U. Chi. L. J. 121, 148–149 (2001).
21. Zorach v. Clauson, 343 U.S. 306, 313–314 (1952).
22. Will Herberg, Protestant-Catholic-Jew 88, 166 (1955).
23. Walter Berns, Freedom, Virtue, and the First Amendment 26, 47, 70, 72, 126, 225, 242, 250–251, 255–256 (1957); Leo Strauss, Natural Right and History (1953).
24. Alexander M. Bickel, The Morality of Consent 23–24 (1975).
25. Robert H. Bork, *Neutral Principles and Some First Amendment Problems*, 47 Ind. L. J. i. 1, 8, 20, 29 (1971); Robert H. Bork, *The Impossibility of Finding Welfare Rights in the Constitution*, 1979 Wash. U.L.Q. 695; Steven M. Teles, *Transformative Bureaucracy: Reagan's Lawyers and the Dynamics of Political Investment*, 23 Studies in American Political Development 61, 76 (2009).
26. Michael K. Brown, et al., Whitewashing Race 193–194 (2003); Ira Katznelson, When Affirmative Action was White (2005).
27. Dudziak, supra note 1, at 11–13, 79; Gaddis, supra note 1, at 123; Walker, supra note 1, at 162; Derrick A. Bell, *Brown v. Board of Education and the Interest-Convergence Dilemma*, 93 Harvard Law Review. 518, 523–525 (1980); Michael J. Klarman, *Brown, Racial Change, and the Civil Rights Movement*, 80 Va. L. Rev. 7, 26–29 (1994).

28. To Secure These Rights: The Report of President Harry S. Truman's Committee on Civil Rights 158 (1947; 2004 reprint); id. at 158–167 (elaborating reasons for change). Many white southerners initially resisted social change even though they would ultimately benefit economically from desegregation. Gavin Wright, Sharing the Prize: The Economics of the Civil Rights Revolution in the American South 1–31, 259–260 (2013); Klarman, supra note 27, at 37–51 (explaining how economic pressures were brought to bear in the South).

29. Dudziak, supra note 1, at 99–100 (quoting amicus brief); *Brown*, 347 U.S. 483 (1954); *Bolling*, 347 U.S. 497 (1954).

30. 347 U.S. at 493.

31. Dudziak, supra note 27, at 107; Stephen M. Feldman, *Do the Right Thing: Understanding the Interest-Convergence Thesis*, 106 Nw. U. L. Rev. Colloquy 248 (2012) (elaborating interest convergence as historical thesis).

32. Brands, supra note 1, at 110 (quoting *U.S. News and World Report*, May 4, 1964); id. at 108–115; Derrick Bell, Race, Racism, and American Law 280–285 (2d ed. 1980); Dudziak, supra note 1, at 11–17, 249–251; Charles R. Lawrence, *If He Hollers Let Him Go: Regulating Racist Speech on Campus*, 1990 Duke L.J. 431.

33. Alexander Keyssar, The Right to Vote 263 (2000) (quoting Johnson from 1965); Manning Marable, The Great Wells of Democracy 71 (2002); U.S. Const. amend. XXIV; Voting Rights Act of 1965, 79 Stat. 437; Civil Rights Act of 1964, 78 Stat. 241.

34. 364 U.S. 339, 340–341, 347 (1960).

35. 369 U.S. 186 (1962), *overruling* Colegrove v. Green, 328 U.S. 549 (1946); *Reynolds*, 377 U.S. 533 (1964); *Wesberry*, 376 U.S. 1 (1964).

36. 376 U.S. 254, 258–259, 270, 279–280 (1964).

37. 391 U.S. 563, 574 (1968).

38. 393 U.S. 503, 505–506, 511–512 (1969).

39. 395 U.S. 444, 447 (1969).

40. Stewart Ewen, Captains of Consciousness 23–50 (1976); Feldman, supra note 6, at 298–303, 322–333.

41. Lizabeth Cohen, A Consumers' Republic 113 (2003); Gary Cross, An All-Consuming Century (2000); Walker, supra note 1, at 162; Ronald K.L. Collins and David M. Skover, *Commerce and Communication*, 71 Tex. L. Rev. 697 (1993); The Statistical History of the United States from Colonial Times to the Present 139 (1965) (Table: Gross National Product) [hereinafter Statistical History]; id. at 178 (Table: Personal Consumption Expenditures).

42. Lynn Dumenil, The Modern Temper 89 (1995); Ewen, supra note 40, at 25, 35–36; Collins and Skover, supra note 41, at 700–702.

43. Cohen, supra note 41, at 336–338; Dumenil, supra note 42, at 90; Ewen, supra note 40, at 35; Collins and Skover, supra note 41, at 703. Empirical support for this paragraph can be found at Walmart.

44. Cross, supra note 41, at 34, 77, 100; Paul Starr, The Creation of the Media 327–384 (2004) (radio and television); Statistical History, supra note 41, at 526 (Table: Volume of Advertising); U.S. Census Bureau, Statistical Abstract of the United States: 2002 (122d ed.) 772 (Table No. 1253: Advertising—Estimated Expenditures by Medium) [hereinafter Abstract].

45. Collins and Skover, supra note 41, at 724–725; Cohen, supra note 41, at 9, 113–342.

46. Richard A. Posner, An Afterword, 1 J. Legal Stud. 437, 437 (1972); Richard Posner, Economic Analysis of Law (1973); Ronald H. Coase, The Problem of Social Cost, 3 J. L. & Econ. 1 (1960).

47. Gary S. Becker, The Economic Approach to Human Behavior 5, 14 (1976); Robin Paul Malloy, Law and Economics: A Comparative Approach to Theory and Practice 32–33, 54 (1990); Richard Posner, Economic Analysis of Law 3–4 (7th ed. 2007). Different economists characterize the assumptions in slightly different ways. See Malloy, supra, at 32–33, 54; A. Mitchell Polinsky, An Introduction to Law and Economics 10 (1983).

48. Charles Taylor, Sources of the Self 508 (1989); Robert Bellah et al., Habits of the Heart 6, 75, 154 (1985); Philip Cushman, Constructing the Self, Constructing America 78–79, 210–211 (1995); Peter Gay, 2 The Enlightenment: An Interpretation 567 (1969); Max Horkheimer and Theodor W. Adorno, Dialectic of Enlightenment (John Cumming trans., 1972); Ira Katznelson, Desolation and Enlightenment 36–39 (2003); Max Weber, From Max Weber: Essays in Sociology 139 (H. H. Gerth and C. Wright Mills trans., 1946) (emphasizing disenchantment). "The neoclassical economists' Homo Economicus has several characteristics, the most important of which are (1) maximizing (optimizing) behavior; (2) the cognitive ability to exercise rational choice; and (3) individualistic behavior and independent tastes and preferences." Chris Doucouliagos, A Note on the Evolution of Homo Economicus, 28 Economic Journal. Issues, No.3 (1994); see Christine Jolls et al., A Behavioral Approach to Law and Economics, 50 Stanford Technology Law Review. 1471 (1998); Tanina Rostain, Educating Homo Economicus: Cautionary Notes on the New Behavioral Law and Economics Movement, 34 Law & Society Review. 973 (2000).

49. John Kenneth Galbraith, The Essential Galbraith 31 (2001); Polinsky, supra note 47, at 10; Abba P. Lerner, The Economics and Politics of Consumer Sovereignty, 62 American Economic Review. 258 (1972).

50. Joel Bakan, The Corporation 16–17 (2004); Robert L. Kerr, The Corporate Free-Speech Movement 19–21 (2008); Kevin Phillips, Wealth and Democracy 39 (2002).

51. Liggett v. Lee, 288 U.S. 517, 566–567 (1933) (Brandeis, J., dissenting in part).

52. Patterson, supra note 14, at 317 (quoting *Times*); Kerr, supra note 50, at 31–32; Castillo, supra note 1, at vii-xi; Dudziak, supra note 1, at 243; Thomas J. Sugrue, Sweet Land of Liberty 117 (2008); Sheldon S. Wolin, Democracy Incorporated 26 (2008); Sheldon S. Wolin, Politics and Vision 552 (Expanded ed. 2004) [hereinafter Vision].

53. Cohen, supra note 41, at 126 (quoting Nixon).

54. Herberg, supra note 22, at 88–89, 91; Vision, supra note 52, at xvi–xvii, 552–553.

55. Castillo, supra note 1, at xiii.

56. Abstract, supra note 44, at 776 (Table No. 1261: National Nonprofit Associations, compiled from *Encyclopedia of Associations*); Gene M. Grossman and Elhanan Helpman, Special Interest Politics 2–3 (2001); Jacob S. Hacker and Paul Pierson, Winner-Take-All Politics 118–119 (2010); Kerr, supra note 50, at 7–8; 33–34; Mark P. Petracca, *The Rediscovery of Interest Group Politics, in* The Politics of Interests: Interest Groups Transformed 11–14 (1992).

57. Lewis Powell, *Confidential Memo: Attack of American Free Enterprise System*, Aug. 23, 1971. The memo was addressed to "Mr. Eugene B. Sydnor, Jr., Chairman, Education Committee, U.S. Chamber of Commerce."

58. Cohen, supra note 41, at 354–387; Chris Hedges, Death of the Liberal Class 176–177 (2010); Jones, supra note 3, at 43–44; Kerr, supra note 50, at 48–53, 67–68; Patterson, supra note 14, at 713, 725.

59. M.J. Stephey, *Bretton Woods System*, Time (Oct. 21, 2008) (quoting Keynes); Jeffry A. Frieden, Global Capitalism 475 (2006); Saull, supra note 1, at 62–63; Wyatt Wells, American Capitalism, 1945–2000, at 13–14 (2003); Benjamin J. Cohen, *Bretton Woods System, in* Routledge 1 Encyclopedia of International Political Economy 95, 95–97 (R.J. Barry Jones ed., 2001). Winston Churchill introduced the term, Iron Curtain, in 1946. Gaddis, supra note 1, at 95.

60. Gaddis, supra note 1, at 93; Dani Rodrik, The Globalization Paradox xvi–xvii, 69–76 (2011).

61. Gaddis, supra note 1, at 30–32, 116–117; Leffler, supra note 1, at 157–164; Saull, supra note 1, at 64–68; Wells, supra note 59, at 23–24.

62. Cohen, supra note 41, at 125–126; David B. Truman, The Governmental Process 520–523 (2d ed. 1971); Louis Hartz, The Liberal Tradition

in America 50–64 (1955); V.O. Key, Jr., Politics, Parties, and Pressure Groups 54–57 (3d ed. 1953).

63. Jones, supra note 3, at 120, 141; Nash, supra note 2, at 32–37, 46–49; see Milton Friedman, Capitalism and Freedom (1962).

64. Margaret Pugh O'Mara, Cites of Knowledge 2, 5 (2005); id. at 1–9; Gérard Duménil and Dominique Lévy, Capital Resurgent 1 (2004); Gaddis, supra note 1, at 35–36, 61–63; Jones, supra note 3, at 281–282; Joseph D. Phillips, *Economic Effects of the Cold War, in* Corporations and the Cold War 173, 186–188 (David Horowitz ed., 1969).

65. Valentine v. Chrestensen, 316 U.S. 52, 54–55 (1942); see Wickard v. Filburn, 317 U.S. 111 (1942) (upholding regulation of the economic marketplace, specifically in this case, production quotas).

66. 421 U.S. 809, 812–813, 819–821, 826 (1975).

67. 425 U.S. 748, 763, 765, 770 (1976); see id. at 787 (Rehnquist, J., dissenting) (complaining that advertising about shampoos should not be deemed as important as political discussion).

68. 447 U.S. 557, 561–562 & n.5, 566 (1980); see Lorillard Tobacco Co. v. Reilly, 533 U.S. 525 (2001) (applying *Central Hudson* test); 44 Liquormart, Inc. v. Rhode Island, 517 U.S. 484 (1996) (same).

69. 424 U.S. 1, 19, 26, 46–49 (1976); see id. at 143 (summarizing holding). In *Buckley*, the justices, for the first time, used the phrase, "money is speech." Stewart used the phrase during oral argument, and White used it in his opinion. Id. at 262–263 (White J., concurring in part, dissenting in part); Gordon Silverstein, Law's Allure 167–168 (2009).

70. 435 U.S. 765, 776–777, 778–786 (1978).

71. Rehnquist was one conservative justice who did not go down this path. Id. at 781 (Rehnquist, J., dissenting); *Bellotti*, 435 U.S. 765, 822 (1978) (Rehnquist, J., dissenting) (arguing that corporate campaign finance restrictions are constitutional).

72. City of Boerne v. Flores, 521 U.S. 527 (1997) (focusing on Fourteenth Amendment, section five); United States v. Lopez, 514 U.S. 549 (1995) (focusing on Commerce Clause); New York v. United States, 505 U.S. 144 (1992) (focusing on Tenth Amendment); Richard A. Epstein, *The Proper Scope of the Commerce Power*, 73 Va. L. Rev. 1387 (1987).

73. Virginia State Bd. of Pharmacy v. Virginia Citizens Consumer Council, 425 U.S. 748 (1976); Bigelow v. Virginia, 421 U.S. 809 (1975).

CHAPTER 6

Democracy, Inc., and the End of the Cold War

By the end of the Cold War—and the end arrived gradually, from 1989 to 1992—conservative constitutional scholars had long been in the traditionalist camp, condemning relativism and advocating for moral clarity.[1] But partly because of a change in Court personnel—particularly the replacement of the liberal Thurgood Marshall with the conservative Clarence Thomas—this focus on moral clarity became a hallmark in the early 1990s of not only conservative scholarship but also conservative Supreme Court decision making. Among scholars, Bork still led the way. He condemned the Court's free-speech jurisprudence for protecting mere "self-expression, personal autonomy, or individual gratification." In *Cohen v. California*, for example, the defendant had worn into a courthouse a jacket inscribed with the message, "Fuck the Draft." Bork condemned the Court's reversal of the defendant's conviction for disturbing the peace. The majority opinion had "asked 'How is one to distinguish this from any other offensive word?' and answered that no distinction could be made since 'one man's vulgarity is another's lyric.'" Bork did not similarly stumble over this distinction. To him, 'Fuck the Draft' was vulgar—nothing lyrical about it. Governmental and non-governmental institutions must be allowed and encouraged to promote the appropriate values. "[I]n a republican form of government where the people rule," Bork wrote, "it is crucial that the character of the citizenry not be debased."[2]

The conservative justices heeded this clarion call by promoting moral clarity in numerous contexts. For example, in an Establishment

© The Author(s) 2017   159
S.M. Feldman, *The New Roberts Court, Donald Trump, and
Our Failing Constitution*, DOI 10.1007/978-3-319-56451-7_6

Clause case, the Court upheld a school voucher program that allowed parents to use public money to pay for religious-school education.[3] Some important moral clarity cases encompassed both free expression and religion. In the typical case, a private (non-government) actor sought to express religious views or values on government-owned property. The Court consistently analyzed such religious-expression cases pursuant to public forum doctrine. Under the Court's free-expression jurisprudence, government-owned property can be divided into three categories: public forums, non-public forums, and designated public forums. A public forum is government property, particularly the streets and parks, that has traditionally—from time immemorial—been held open for public speaking. On such property, the government cannot impose a content-based restriction on expression unless it can satisfy the strict scrutiny test, showing that the restriction is necessary or narrowly tailored to achieve a compelling government interest. All other government-owned property is non-public forum. On such property, the government can impose any reasonable restrictions on expression. If, however, the government has specially designated the property for public speaking, then the property is transformed into a designated or limited public forum, and the speech-protective public forum rules control.[4]

Applying this public forum doctrine in the religious-expression cases, the Court concluded that the government must allow Christian organizations to spread their messages on public (school) properties. In *Rosenberger v. Rectors and Visitors of the University of Virginia*, decided in 1995, the five conservative justices—William Rehnquist, Scalia, Thomas, Sandra Day O'Connor, and Kennedy—held that the First Amendment required the University of Virginia to fund a student newspaper, *Wide Awake*, dedicated to evangelical proselytizing. *Wide Awake* explicitly challenged "Christians to live, in word and deed, according to the faith they proclaim and to encourage students to consider what a personal relationship with Jesus Christ means." The *Rosenberger* Court reasoned that the University's funding program for student organizations created a limited public forum and that denial of funding to *Wide Awake* constituted unconstitutional viewpoint discrimination.[5] The justices reached a similar result in a grade school setting. In *Good News Club v. Milford Central School*, decided in 2001, the five conservative justices, joined by Stephen Breyer, held that a public school violated free expression by denying access to "a private Christian organization for children ages six to twelve" that sought to hold club meetings on school property. Writing for the majority, Thomas chastised the lower court for its ostensible hostility toward Christianity; prior cases already had established the constitutional protection of Christian education and proselytizing on public property, including schools, and the *Good News Club* case was indistinguishable.[6]

To be clear, in these cases, the conservative justices did not appear to be motivated by an unshakable desire to protect free expression in all contexts—because free expression should be treated as a constitutional lodestar—but rather by a desire to bolster moral clarity through the promotion of traditional religious (Christian) values. In other cases where the protection of free speech might undermine the promotion of moral clarity, the justices have sacrificed free speech. For instance, a 2007 decision, *Morse v. Frederick*, rejected a student's First-Amendment claim and deferred to the school principal's decision to suspend the student for displaying a banner, "BONG HiTS 4 JESUS."[7] A 2009 decision, *Pleasant Grove City v. Summum*, appeared to present a religious-expression issue subject to a public forum analysis. Pleasant Grove displayed in its city park several privately donated monuments, including one showing the Ten Commandments, contributed years earlier by the Fraternal Order of Eagles. Summum, a minority religious group, offered to donate a monument showing its Seven Aphorisms (also called the Seven Principles of Creation). The city refused to accept the monument. Was this case like *Rosenberger* and *Good News Club* and, therefore, governed by the public forum doctrine? The Supreme Court held otherwise. "[T]he display of a permanent monument in a public park is not a form of expression to which forum analysis applies," Alito reasoned for the majority. "Instead, the placement of a permanent monument in a public park is best viewed as a form of government speech and is therefore not subject to scrutiny under the Free Speech Clause." As Alito explained the government-speech doctrine: "The Free Speech Clause restricts government regulation of private speech; it does not regulate government speech." Comparing *Summum* with *Rosenberger* and *Good News Club*, the justices, it would seem, will allow (or require) the government to adopt and display traditional (Christian) values and symbols while refusing to adopt and display other values and symbols.[8]

THE RISE OF DEMOCRACY, INC.:
AN ATTACK ON GOVERNMENT

The end of the Cold War ushered in a significant change in American society that, in turn, would influence the Supreme Court so strongly as to outweigh the conservative justices' commitment to moral clarity. The American celebration of the nation's victory in the Cold War obscured potential untoward ramifications of that success. Just as the Cold War had helped shape the evolution of pluralist democracy from the 1940s to 1990, the end of the Cold War would shape its further evolution. As already discussed, the Cold War had constrained corporate capitalism on both the international and domestic fronts. For instance, the political geography of the Cold War had limited the international scope of corporate markets. Quite simply, McDonald's could not open a franchise in Prague or Moscow in 1975. Perhaps more important, the Cold War struggle against communism had limited the degree to which corporations could attack the process and culture of democratic government. If the alternative to pluralist democracy was totalitarian communism, then American critics of democracy needed to curb their denunciations.[9] With the end of the Cold War, these constraints on corporate capitalism evaporated.[10]

To be sure, at the level of theory, neoliberal libertarianism had evolved during the years of the Cold War by gradually shedding its earlier acceptance of government interventions in the economic marketplace. Neoliberals became market fundamentalists, insisting that the unregulated market could best resolve all social and economic problems. Any type of government planning or regulation smacked of hubris.[11] Hayek had led the way in this attack on government. "Human reason can neither predict nor deliberately shape its own future," he wrote in 1960. "Progress by its very nature cannot be planned."[12] The real world was too complex for government to predict and control through rational planning, neoliberals asserted. The invisible hand and the market were far more efficient in accounting for human desires and actions. "[The invisible hand] is a highly sophisticated and subtle insight," explained Milton Friedman in 1976. "The market, with each individual going his own way, with no central authority setting social priorities, avoiding duplication, and coordinating activities, looks like chaos to the naked eye. Yet through [Adam] Smith's eyes we see that it is a finely ordered and delicately tuned system, one which arises out of man's actions, yet is not deliberately created by man. It is a system which enables the dispersed knowledge and skill of millions of people to be coordinated for a common purpose." By this time, then, Friedman was unequivocally preaching laissez faire. Neoliberals completely rejected Keynesian economics, the New Deal, and social welfare legislation. The unregulated market, they asserted, maximized individual liberty and human dignity.[13]

A growing American conservative movement absorbed these views in the 1970s and 1980s. Significantly, the neoliberal message had been simplified to a great degree, and thus had become more politically pointed and useful. The early neoliberals had sought to mediate between laissez faire and New Deal liberalism—an intermediate position difficult to stake out and to communicate. Yet, shortly after World War II, Hayek explicitly recommended that neoliberals needed to articulate a "Utopian" program to influence public opinion and inspire enthusiasm. As it turned out, Hayek was right on this account: A straightforward laissez-faire utopianism was far easier to explain and sell. Not only was it clearer, but it also resonated closely with traditional American individualism as well as other forms of libertarianism.[14]

This more aggressive neoliberal libertarian thinking gained political traction in the late 1970s and 1980s. Perhaps, most important, the post-World War II Bretton Woods system had collapsed. Consistent with Keynesian economics, Bretton Woods had blended the capitalist marketplace with democratic welfare government. Overall, this system had produced long-running and widespread (though not universal) prosperity, especially for the United States. But in the 1970s, both high inflation and high unemployment hit the United States and other western industrialized nations. Suddenly, Keynesian policies seemed unable to deal with this so-called stagflation. These economic problems provided political ammunition for advocates of neoliberal libertarianism. Adding to this political shift in America, the wealthy or upper class became dissatisfied with their share of the economic pie. For nearly three decades after World War II, the top 1% of income earners accrued approximately 8% of the national income on an annual basis. When the American economy was booming, the wealthy appeared to find this income distribution acceptable. But when stagflation hit, the upper class became dissatisfied with its share of income and wealth. Many wealthy Americans consequently threw their political weight behind the neoliberal views being expressed by Ronald Reagan when he ran for president in 1980.[15]

Once elected, Reagan nominated law and economics practitioners Richard Posner and Frank Easterbrook to the federal bench. They both still sit on the Seventh Circuit Court of Appeals. More important,

Reagan in the United States, and Margaret Thatcher in Britain, began to introduce neoliberal elements into their economic policies. For instance, the Reagan administration started deregulation, relaxing anti-trust policies that then facilitated corporate mergers, such as between oil giants Gulf, Texaco, and Chevron. Reagan's anti-union stances, as evidenced by his pro-employer appointments to the National Labor Relations Board, enhanced corporate strength in the marketplace. Meanwhile, Reagan cut the top marginal tax rate from 70 to 28% while claiming that supply-side or "trickle-down" economics would generate more revenue for the government and greater prosperity for rich and poor alike. Yet, the Reagan tax cuts, when combined with those of his successor, President George H.W. Bush, more than quadrupled the national debt over a 12-year period while contributing to growing income and wealth disparities.[16]

When the Cold War ended, the political constraints came off neoliberal libertarianism. Corporate capitalist power was unleashed. An increasing number of corporations went multinational, with many flocking into former Iron-Curtain countries. For example, "Daewoo spent $1.5 billion to build two Polish auto plants; Sony set up state-of-the-art factories to make consumer electronics in Hungary; Goodyear took over a Polish tiremaker; Volkswagen bought up the Czech Republic's respected Skoda automaker."[17] From the end of the Cold War to 2002, the number of multinational corporations jumped from approximately 37,000 to 63,000. These multinationals reached ever deeper into new markets. McDonald's, in effect, became "McWorld," opening in Prague, Moscow, East Berlin, and dozens of other cities formerly behind the Iron Curtain.[18] Multinationals aggressively sought to reach as many consumers as possible, wherever they lived. From the corporate standpoint, all potential consumers had preferences that could be exploited, and if those preferences did not fit the products, then advertising could reshape the preferences. "A consumer is a consumer is a consumer." Corporate business and investment began to flow around the globe as if national borders no longer existed.[19]

How diverse and far-reaching is a multinational corporation? Unilever provides one example. Unilever began as a producer of margarine in 1914, but was producing more than 1600 brands by the end of the twentieth century. After a corporate restructuring, which entailed selling some of its brands, Unilever still produces Lipton (teas), Hellmann's (mayonnaise), Knorr (foods), Vaseline (petroleum jelly), Dove (soaps), Bertolli (oils), Slim Fast (diet foods), Ben & Jerry's (ice cream), Breyers (ice cream), and many other brands. Their products are used in most households in the United States, the United Kingdom, Canada, Indonesia, and Vietnam. As of 2001, 27% of their quarter-million employees were in Europe, 8% in North America, 18% in Africa and the Middle East, 32% in Asia and the Pacific, and 14% in Latin America. Meanwhile, McDonald's was serving 3 million burgers per day in at least 100 nations by the mid-1990s. Mattel, at that point, made "the quintessentially American Barbie Doll" into a global affair by drawing materials from and manufacturing parts in an international array of countries, including the United States, Taiwan, Japan, China, Indonesia, Malaysia, and Hong Kong.[20] By the year 2000, more than half of the world's largest economies, based on gross domestic product, were corporations, rather than nations. By 2002, approximately 50 multinational corporations were wealthier than between 120 and 130 nations. Multinational corporations could rightly be called the "new Leviathans," as they challenged the power and wealth of nation-states.[21]

Besides the end of the Cold War, multiple causes contributed to globalization and the spread of multinational corporations. Deregulation, reduced taxes, government perks, and technological changes all played roles. For instance, and most obviously, communication technologies based on the internet facilitated the development of international businesses and international financial markets. Likewise, innovations in transportation, leading to less expensive and more rapid shipping of products, also contributed to globalization. Advanced communication and transportation technologies, together with freely circulable capital, allow corporations to manufacture products wherever labor costs are low and environmental restrictions are lax and then to sell the products where incomes are high. And the corporations can still locate their offices where taxes are minimal, the views are enticing, the culture is exciting, or anywhere else. Indeed, because of the combined corporate capabilities to shift capital and to ship products rapidly around the world, corporations can pressure nations to minimize labor demands, lower taxes, and diminish environmental regulations. Ultimately, though, the overriding cause of globalization was the pursuit of profit: Multinational corporations sought to maximize profits regardless of where they could be accrued.[22]

To be clear, the quest for maximum profits requires corporations to minimize costs, and the corporate minimization of costs requires shifting costs to others, whenever possible. In other words, the corporate profit motive practically mandates the externalization of costs or harms, such as pollution. The fact that others, outside the corporation, must pay the costs or suffer the harms cannot deter the corporation in search of maximum profits. In effect, a corporation wants to create selective market failures that accrue to its benefit; for instance, a corporation that prevents competitors from entering a market can realize higher profits. In a perfect market, a corporation would bear its own costs and reap its own profits. But market failures allow a corporation to change its costs into externalities, shifting them onto others, while still retaining its profits. To be certain, some corporate officers are pleasant moral people who would not purposely harm their friends and neighbors. But place them in their official corporate positions, and the corporate veil becomes a veil of ignorance. They seemingly forget morality and social relationships. As Sidney Shapiro and Joseph Tomain put it: In the economic marketplace, the "tendency to cheat is perfectly economically rational."[23]

In the United States, in particular, multinational corporations dominate the mass-consumer culture as never before. In the twenty-first century, individuals rarely buy their mass-produced items at independent Mom-and-Pop stores. Instead, people shop at Target, a Walmart Supercenter, or online at Amazon.com. The American economy has thoroughly transformed into a *corporate* capitalist system. Previously, corporations in the United States had followed Lewis Powell's memorandum by increasing their determination to influence public opinion and interest-group machinations. With the end of the Cold War, the increased wealth and power of large and multinational corporations was also brought to bear. The result? The democratic system became corporate-dominated. Our consumers' (pluralist) democracy transformed into Democracy, Inc.[24] Not only has democratic politics become more capitalistic or market oriented, but also corporate capitalism has become more politically potent. With ever-increasing proficiency, corporations manipulate elections and government for their own advantage—benefiting the respective corporations as well as corporate business in toto. Citizens still vote, but corporate muscle manages elections and shapes government policy (in the gaps between election seasons).[25] Corporate and government power coexist incestuously, with officials going back and forth between corporate and government positions. Government agencies often suffer from "regulatory capture": The officials appointed to monitor an industry either worked previously in that same industry or are otherwise strongly sympathetic to its needs. For example, when the time comes for an appointment to the Federal Reserve, which regulates banking, bank lobbyists will push for a candidate who believes banks do not need government monitoring because the market is self-regulating. Given these types of arrangements, the system readily self-propagates: Corporate wealth skews electoral outcomes and government policies, while government officials and policies further contribute to wealth inequality, in general, and corporate power, more specifically.[26]

At the end of the Cold War, the neoconservative Francis Fukuyama had metaphorically called the collapse of the Soviet Union the "end of history."[27] American democracy and capitalism had been locked in ideological struggle with Soviet communism. The United States had won the battle. Democratic government and free market economics had no more serious competitors. At that point in time, most observers assumed that "capitalism and democracy would evolve along compatible lines and mutually reinforce each other."[28] After all, during the Cold-War era of consumers' democracy, capitalism and pluralist democracy had appeared to coexist harmoniously, even buttressing each other. But the emergence of Democracy, Inc., called into question this assumption of an ongoing consonant relationship. Maybe, American democracy and capitalism had not *together* won the Cold-War battle over Soviet communism. Instead, neoliberal libertarianism—laissez-faire capitalism on steroids—had conquered all. It was as if the Cold War had been a scab covering a deep cut between the logics of capitalism, on the one hand, and democratic government, on the other. The end of the Cold War had scraped off the scab, and suddenly, the tensions between capitalism and democracy were bleeding all over the floor.[29]

To be sure, at the global level, the end of the Cold War engendered transitions to democracy in numerous nations formerly behind the Iron Curtain. Hungary, Poland, the Czech Republic, East Germany, as well as former geographical regions of the Soviet Union, such as Russia, Lithuania, and Estonia, were among the host of burgeoning democracies. At least initially, then, winning the Cold War yielded a democracy dividend. Yet, also on a global basis, an outburst of laissez-faire ideology accompanied the Cold-War end and the related rise of Democracy, Inc. The free market was endowed with a "divine status." The United States and Britain pressured the rest of the world, especially Europe and Japan, to follow neoliberal libertarian principles for a global economy. The so-called "Washington Consensus" —emphasizing "tax reform, trade liberalization, privatization, deregulation, and strong property rights"—took hold of international markets.[30] Ironically, the IMF and World Bank, originally formed to implement the Bretton Woods Keynesian-inspired policies, now switched to neoliberal approaches. New institutions and policies, including the World Trade Organization (WTO), the European Union (EU), and the North American Free Trade Agreement (NAFTA), were formed to implement free-market principles and further promote global capitalism. Business and financial interests from the wealthiest nations dominated these international institutions, which predictably emphasized maximizing profits.[31]

Thus, the former communist nations were taught a lesson in market fundamentalism, with the teachers being the United States, Britain, the IMF, and other neoliberal institutions. From the neoliberal standpoint, history, culture, and social structures should not affect capitalist marketplace transactions. If a laissez-faire market can be introduced, it should produce economic efficiency. The former communist nations lacked the traditional institutions of democratic-capitalism, including banks, structured employer–employee relations, and the rule of law in contractual agreements. But from the neoliberal standpoint, these inadequacies were minor annoyances rather than serious obstacles. Let the market operate, keep the government out of the way, and all should be well. Except, in reality, many of these nations did not respond well to this "shock therapy" approach to laissez-faire capitalism.[32] For instance, during the 1990s, many people in the nations of the former Soviet Union were plunged into privation; "the proportion of the population in poverty went from 2 percent to over 50 percent." The sudden fortunes of a handful of new millionaires did not ameliorate the sufferings of so many people. In the year 2000, "real income per person in the former Soviet Union was barely half what it had been a decade earlier."[33] Russia was hit particularly hard. Income inequality skyrocketed, and the middle class was decimated. For the poor, this transition led to a diminished quality of life and, in fact, lower life expectancies. Significantly, economic inequality and its consequences undermined the development of democracy. People who had eagerly repudiated totalitarianism now looked nostalgically to the Soviet past. Desperate individuals will take desperate measures. In many of the former Soviet nations, and especially in Russia, many people consequently turned to former Communist party leaders. Elements of authoritarian government resurfaced. Today, in Russia, ruled by former KGB officer, Vladimir Putin, "elections are not fair, courts are not independent, and political opposition is not tolerated."[34]

Meanwhile, in the United States, the rise of Democracy, Inc., and the concomitant flourishing of laissez faire produced aggressive attacks on democratic government. From the perspective of neoliberal libertarianism, government determinations of means and goals are irrational and inefficient.[35] According to pluralist democratic theory, public (government) goals are determined through the negotiations and compromises of a wide-open process in which all individuals and groups are able to contribute their values and interests. Neoliberals questioned this government process on multiple grounds, but primarily by comparing it to economic transactions in the marketplace. For instance, public choice theorists applied economic analysis to public decision making and concluded that majority voting, as in democracy, is frequently an irrational means for making group decisions. Unlike an unregulated economic marketplace, democracy cannot maximize the satisfaction of individual interests, at least under certain conditions. Consequently, public choice theorists maintained that when the government legislates—for example, by imposing economic regulations—the legislative decisions do not rest on a rational calculation of costs and benefits. Rather, they arise from interest group machinations unrelated to individual preferences and social utility.[36]

Public choice theory illustrates how neoliberal libertarianism pushed beyond nineteenth-century laissez faire. Laissez faire ideology celebrated the free market; government regulations were criticized because they interfered with the marketplace. Neoliberal libertarianism goes further by directly attacking, by demonizing, democratic government. Milton Friedman and other neoliberals insisted that the economic marketplace is a wondrous device because of the invisible hand. According to Friedman, the market operates so that "the voluntary actions of millions of individuals can be coordinated through a price mechanism without central direction." Each individual's interests and knowledge lead him or her to pursue desired goals and, simultaneously, lead society as a whole to pursue appropriate goals. But the government, Friedman argued, operates like a backward reflection of the marketplace. There is an "invisible hand in politics [that] is as potent a force for harm as the invisible hand in economics is for good." Government actors might very well have the best of intentions, yet they cannot help but pursue harmful goals. "In politics, men who intend only to promote the public interest, as they conceive it, are 'led by an invisible hand to promote an end which was no part of' their intention. They become the front-men for special interests they would never knowingly serve." Private interests necessarily manipulate political processes in ways that cannot arise in market transactions.[37]

Moreover, even if private interests did not manipulate the government, democratic processes are inherently inefficient, according to neoliberals. If pluralist democracy were to stumble onto an appropriate public goal, such a goal nonetheless would still be tentative because of the constant and ongoing political battles inherent to a pluralist society. Next week, the government might settle on a different tentative goal. And if not next week, then next month, or next year. Partly for this reason, the choice of means for achieving a government-designated goal becomes problematic. Suppose the government is able to determine a cost-efficient means for achieving its democratically established goal. By the time the government institutionalizes the means, the pluralist democratic process might have established a different goal. The government is trapped in a kaleidoscopic hall of mirrors, where means and ends are constantly shifting and unstable. Is this any way to run a business? No, of course not. Unlike government, business corporations need not equivocate about goals. They all pursue a single overarching goal: profit. Consequently, corporations can focus on constructing the most efficient means for achieving their profit goals. Rationality unequivocally becomes economic efficiency. Thus, while corporations have the virile confidence of heroic certainty, government appears timid and wasteful.[38]

In short, in Democracy, Inc., neoliberal libertarians denigrate government, in general, and public (or group) decision making pursuant to democratic processes, more specifically. From the neoliberal perspective, the private sphere should subsume the public sphere. Friedman suggested as much when he argued that politics and economics were not "separate and largely unconnected." Political freedom, he insisted, cannot exist unless individuals enjoy complete economic freedom, which could exist only with an unregulated marketplace. Economics is primary, while politics is secondary and derivative. As Friedman put it, "economic freedom is an end in itself, [but] economic freedom is also an indispensable means toward the achievement of political freedom." In a free society, according to Friedman, economic power provides "a check to political power."[39] The key to political freedom, consequently, is a laissez-faire marketplace. The best society is one that leaves the maximum degree of decision making to the market and the minimum to politics and government. From the neoliberal standpoint, with its celebration of the market, the public realm is degraded and dangerous. Arthur Brooks, president of the American Enterprise Institute, declared: "The best government philosophy is one that starts every day with the question, 'What can we do today to get out of Americans' way?'"[40] Consequently, neoliberal libertarians advocate for the privatization or outsourcing of numerous government functions and institutions, such as schools, prisons, and policing. In theory, privately owned and run schools, private prisons, and so on, will naturally operate for the good of society because they will function in accordance with economic principles. While government-run institutions are wasteful and corrupt, according to neoliberals, privatized institutions will allocate resources efficiently because they operate in accord with market incentives, primarily profit and loss.[41]

If doubt still existed about whether the dominant conception of the American self equated with homo economicus, that doubt had dissipated by the beginning of the twenty-first century. The self not only focuses on its own personal satisfaction, but now satisfaction largely depends on the consumption of products or the turning of profits. As a rational self-maximizer, homo economicus thrives in the proper environment, a responsive and unregulated marketplace, where it can profit or consume. Homo economicus is especially comfortable visiting the shopping mall and buying online at Amazon.com and other virtual department stores. One click of the computer mouse brings the instant gratification of a purchase. Reason is crucial to homo economicus, but it is an instrumental reason. Goals are based on the self's preferences— the individual's self-interest. The consumer is sovereign. The economic self rationally assesses the various means of attaining its pre-determined goal and chooses the most efficient—the means that achieves the greatest benefit at the lowest cost. Of course, based on such assessments, homo economicus might shift goals. Perhaps, the individual's first goal cannot be attained efficiently with the current allocation of resources. At that point, the rational self-maximizer would evaluate the possibility of attaining an alternative goal. Rationality might therefore have implications for setting one's goals, but it does not directly affect one's preferences (or interests).[42]

During its slightly more than 200 years of existence, the American self has shriveled to an alarming extent. In the twenty-first century, homo economicus is but a remnant of the framers' citizen-self. The framers' Janus-faced self had been a complex subject who sought to use virtue and reason to control passion and interest—sometimes unsuccessfully so. It enjoyed commercial transactions in the private sphere, but it also found fulfillment and liberty in the public sphere. Under pluralist democracy, the citizen-self lost its concern for virtuous deliberation in pursuit of the common good, but it remained a citizen. It still sought to be involved in the public sphere. Nowadays, the economic self cares about government in only two instances. First, the self will seek to remove any governmental obstacles, such as environmental regulations, which threaten to reduce profits. Second, when possible, homo economicus will attempt to manipulate government to create laws or policies that will increase its rents (or profits), even if doing so harms others. Compared to the framers' citizen-self, homo economicus is diminished and simple, a scientifically predictable self who follows interests without compunction. For homo economicus, the private sphere does not merely predominate over the public sphere. The private subsumes the public.[43]

While democracy- and government-bashing are are part-and-parcel of neoliberal libertarianism, corporations (and the super-rich) do not merely denounce democratic government in Democracy, Inc.[44] They use a multi-layered systematic strategy to manipulate government and to thwart government efforts to regulate business. First, if Congress (or a state legislature) begins debating an economic regulatory bill, corporate lobbyists will seek to prevent its enactment. Second, if Congress nonetheless passes the regulatory legislation, then corporate lobbyists will attempt to block congressional funding for its implementation. Third, if Congress perseveres and supplies funding, then the lobbyists will work to insure the appointment of sympathetic regulators and, at the agency level, the making of favorable administrative rules (or no rules at all). Fourth, if an agency still manages to adopt restrictive rules implementing the regulatory law, then the corporations will challenge in court the validity of the congressional action and the agency rules. To be clear, corporate businesses do not view their multi-layered opposition to government as contravening a public interest or good. To the contrary, from an economic standpoint, they view such anti-government actions as legitimate means to promote the public interest.[45]

Furthermore, corporations not only seek to thwart government regulations of business, but also attempt to manipulate government to pass pro-business legislation. Both types of corporate control over government are illustrated in the actions of the American Legislative Exchange Council (ALEC). ALEC identifies itself as a non-profit that "works to advance limited government, free markets, and federalism at the state level through a nonpartisan public–private partnership of America's state legislators, members of the private sector and the general public." Its membership consists of nearly 2000 state legislators, almost all of whom are Republicans, as well as corporations and corporate officers. The organization tracks proposed state legislation and flags bills that it deems anti-business. Once such a bill is flagged, then ALEC advises legislative members from the respective state of the drawbacks to the proposed legislation. While such organizational actions are significant, ALEC is more renowned (or notorious) for its drafting of model legislation which lawmakers seek to enact at the state level. Most of ALEC's funding comes from corporations, including Pfizer, Bank of America, Best Buy, Walmart, AT&T, Verizon, and so on. Corporate members can effectively veto any proposed model legislation.[46]

In other words, through ALEC, corporations exercise close control over state legislators and state legislative processes. A prototypical example involves ExxonMobil, one of the corporate leaders in hydraulic fracturing, better known as fracking. ExxonMobil sponsored ALEC model legislation that supposedly would force corporations to disclose information about chemicals used in fracking fluids. The legislation was "promoted as a victory for consumers' right to know about potential drinking water contaminants," but in reality, it contained loopholes allowing corporations to withhold information about important chemicals or fluids, those "deemed trade secrets." State lawmakers thus advocated for the model legislation as a consumer-protection bill, while not revealing that ExxonMobil helped mold it to be pro-business. ALEC, however, was not being duplicitous when it declared in a member-only newsletter that membership was "a good investment." In a normal year, the newsletter explained, ALEC lawmakers introduce "more than 1,000 bills based on [its] model legislation" and successfully enact "about 17 percent of them." The newsletter emphasized: "Nowhere else can you get a return that high." ALEC's operations, one might fairly conclude, are the quintessence of Democracy, Inc. [47]

THE EARLY ROBERTS COURT IN DEMOCRACY, INC

If a legislature enacts a regulatory statute and corporate challengers then lose in the lower courts—that is, the courts uphold the legislation and agency rules—then the corporations can petition for certiorari to the United States Supreme Court. Fortunately for corporations, the early Roberts Court ranked as the most pro-business Supreme Court since World War II. Of course, some conservatives insisted that the early Roberts Court—including the late Antonin Scalia—was not conservative enough, that it was not truly pro-business, but empirical studies persuasively show otherwise. In fact, five of the justices ranked among the top ten justices most favorable to business from the 1946 through the 2011 terms. Remarkably, Alito and Roberts stood first and second on the list (Powell, incidentally, ranked number eight, one spot in front of Scalia).[48] Moreover, in free expression cases in particular, the conservative justices supported the First-Amendment claims of conservative speakers far more strongly than those of liberal speakers. Liberal justices also showed an in-group bias toward liberal speakers, but it was not as strong as that of the conservative justices.[49] And as one might expect, the conservative justices shaped the Court's docket in accord with their political concerns. A study focusing on the period from May 19, 2009 to August 15, 2012 concluded that the U.S. Chamber of Commerce, representing business, filed more amicus briefs supporting petitions for certiorari (cert.-stage amicus briefs) than any other organization. Unsurprisingly, the Chamber had the second highest success rate. Compared with a similar study conducted 5 years earlier—partially during the Rehnquist Court years—the new study underscored that the top 16 filers of cert.-stage amicus briefs are now "more conservative, anti-regulatory, and pro-business" than the previous top 16, which already were strongly pro-business. The findings also showed that these briefs influence the justices' decisions when shaping the Court's docket. A pro-business Court responds positively to pro-business petitioners.[50]

The early Roberts Court, it seems, perfectly fit its times. The conservative justices, in particular, fully accepted and bolstered Democracy, Inc. They decided cases and wrote opinions that guarded the economic marketplace, promoted business (especially corporate business), and protected homo economicus. Occasionally, in those cases, the Court explicitly invoked economic principles or assumptions. More often, the Court relied on traditional legal reasoning to reach decisions that nonetheless supported and harmonized with Democracy, Inc. Of course, some cases did both, relying on economic principles and assumptions as well as traditional legal reasoning. And while this book focuses on constitutional jurisprudence, with particular attention to free expression, the early Roberts Court also decided numerous significant non-constitutional cases supporting Democracy, Inc. While those non-constitutional cases did not, by definition, turn on express constitutional issues, they nonetheless involved the democratic-capitalist system because they accepted and bolstered Democracy, Inc.

The conservative justices' excessive support for corporate businesses had serious consequences even when the cases did not involve millions of dollars. The case of *Ledbetter v. Goodyear Tire & Rubber Co.* puts a human face on such consequences.[51] Lilly Ledbetter worked at a Goodyear Tire and Rubber Company plant in Alabama for nearly two decades, starting in 1979. For years, Ledbetter's supervisor ranked her performance generally below that of her male colleagues for purposes of merit-pay increases. Consequently, Ledbetter, an area manager, received relatively small annual raises. In early 1998, another employee left an anonymous note in Ledbetter's mailbox. The note revealed that Goodyear paid Ledbetter significantly less than it paid men who held the same job. With this information in hand, Ledbetter filed a charge for sex discrimination with the Equal Employment Opportunity Commission (EEOC). Later that year, in November 1998, Ledbetter retired, and soon filed a lawsuit in federal district (or trial) court under Title VII of the Civil Rights Act of 1964. After a trial, the jury found that Goodyear had discriminated against Ledbetter. In fact, Goodyear paid Ledbetter $3727 per month, while paying male area managers between $4286 and $5236 per month.[52] The district court awarded Ledbetter $360,000 in damages.

Goodyear appealed to the Supreme Court. In a five-to-four decision, with a majority opinion by Alito, the conservative bloc ruled in favor of the corporation and against Ledbetter. The Court concluded that Ledbetter's claim was time barred under Title VII.[53] Alito reasoned that an employee must file a discrimination charge with the EEOC no later than 180 days after the alleged discriminatory action. Once the employee files with the EEOC, she can recover for discriminatory acts that occurred during the prior 180 days but cannot recover for any previous discrimination. In Ledbetter's case, she would have literally needed to sue before she knew about the discrimination, even though Goodyear purposefully kept its pay scales confidential. As Justice Ruth Bader Ginsburg explained in her dissent, Goodyear's furtiveness was typical; employers often try to hide comparative pay information from their employees.[54] Because of the Roberts Court's decision, Goodyear did not have to pay a penny of compensation to Ledbetter despite unlawfully discriminating against her for years.[55]

Statutory and Other Non-constitutional Cases

Some early Roberts Court pro-business cases arose in areas, such as intellectual property, which involved overt governmental regulations of the marketplace.[56] In such cases, the Court was most likely to invoke economic principles and assumptions. In *Mayo Collaborative Services v. Prometheus Laboratories, Inc.*, decided in 2012, the Court dwelled on how patents affect the financial incentives for those questing after innovations. The Court even quoted Richard Posner and his occasional co-author, William Landes, regarding the potential for patent law to generate efforts at rent-seeking.[57] But many key cases arose in legal realms, both constitutional and non-constitutional, which did not focus on overt marketplace restrictions. Non-constitutional cases often revolved around the judicial process and access to the courts. In a 2008 decision, *Exxon Shipping Co. v. Baker*, the issue was whether a punitive damage award against a corporation was excessive under federal (maritime) common law. The Court suggested that punitive damages should reflect an "optimal level of penalty and deterrence." Thus, the Court treated the corporate-defendant and other potential future defendants as rational maximizers who would behave in accordance with proper economic incentives. "[A] penalty should be reasonably predictable in its severity," the Court explained, "so that [a potential defendant] can look ahead with some ability to know what the stakes are in choosing one course of action or another." Based on this emphasis on marketplace rationality and predictability, the Court held that punitive damages in maritime cases should be limited by a "punitive-to-compensatory ratio of 1:1."[58]

Multiple Roberts Court decisions limited the capacity of individuals to sue corporate businesses in the first place (so the question of punitive or any other type of damages does not even arise). The *Ledbetter* case, decided in 2007, is but one example.[59] In a subsequent employment discrimination case, *Wal-Mart Stores, Inc. v. Dukes*, the Court interpreted the Federal Rules of Civil Procedure (FRCP) to protect the corporation. Women employees brought a class action under Title VII alleging that Walmart, the nation's largest private employer, had sexually discriminated in pay and promotions. Federal Rule 23(a)(2) requires the party seeking class certification to demonstrate that "there are questions of law or fact common to the class." The Court refused to certify the class because the employees supposedly had failed to satisfy this commonality requirement. As interpreted by the Court, Rule 23 now requires "significant proof" that the "common contention [is] of such a nature that ... determination of its truth or falsity will resolve an issue that is central to the validity of each one of the claims in one stroke." Basically, the Court increased the burden of proof for class certification and, in so doing, protected Walmart (and other corporations, in the future) from costly litigation—regardless of wrongdoing.[60]

Indeed, the early Court's conservative bloc—Roberts, Alito, Scalia, Thomas, and Kennedy—often found the denial of class certification to be a congenial means for protecting corporations from unexpected expenses. After the *Wal-Mart Stores* decision, the Court followed a similar line of reasoning in *Comcast Corp. v. Behrend*. Subscribers of cable television services brought a class action alleging a violation of antitrust laws. The subscribers sought to have their class certified under Rule 23(b)(3), which requires that "the questions of law or fact common to class members predominate over any questions affecting only individual members." Again applying Rule 23 rigorously, the Court concluded that the subscribers' model of damages would not adequately measure losses across the entire class.[61]

In yet another case, decided less than 2 months before *Wal-Mart Stores*, the conservative bloc denied class certification, though based on its interpretation of the Federal Arbitration Act (FAA) rather than the FRCP. In *AT&T Mobility LLC v. Concepcion*, customers brought a class action against a cellular telephone service provider alleging false advertising and fraud. This time, the Court relied on a standard customer–contract provision that required arbitration of each unresolved dispute but precluded arbitration on a class-wide basis. The lower court found this contractual provision unconscionable pursuant to state law, but the Court held that the FAA preempted the state unconscionability doctrine.[62] The Court followed *AT&T Mobility* in *American Express Co. v. Italian Colors Restaurant*, holding that the FAA required the enforcement of a contractual waiver of class arbitration, even though the costs of individual lawsuits would exceed the potential recoveries.[63] Because of these decisions, large corporations "can impose no-class-action-arbitration clauses on people with little or no bargaining position—through adhesion contracts involving securities accounts, credit cards, mobile phones, car rentals, and many other social amenities and necessities." In practice, then, corporations will be insulated from lawsuits because individuals frequently will forego seeking any remedy for even clear violations of law.[64] These cases, while numerous, do not exhaust the many imaginative ways the early Roberts Court protected large corporate businesses from government regulation in the form of lawsuits.[65] In two more recent five-to-four decisions, for example, the Court's conservative bloc interpreted Title VII to make proof of discrimination more difficult for plaintiff-employees.[66] To be sure, corporations did not win every Supreme Court case,[67] but the Court clearly endorsed Democracy, Inc. Consistent with that position, the Court generally assumed that economic selves know and do what is best for themselves. If an individual signs an adhesion contract with an arbitration clause, then the individual must have wanted to do so. Consumer sovereignty suggests nothing else.

Free-Expression and Other Constitutional Cases

The extent to which the conservative justices accepted and bolstered Democracy, Inc., was nowhere clearer than in free-expression cases involving campaign finance. In cases after *Buckley* (1976) and *Bellotti* (1978), the Court had waffled over how much the government could regulate corporate political expression.[68] The entrenchment of Democracy, Inc., and the establishment of the early Roberts Court ended this uncertainty.[69] In 2010, in the monumental five-to-four decision, *Citizens United v. Federal Election Commission*, the conservative bloc of justices invalidated provisions of the Bipartisan Campaign Reform Act of 2002 (BCRA) that imposed limits on corporate (and union) spending for political campaign advertisements. Justice Kennedy's majority opinion, joined by Roberts, Scalia, Thomas, and Alito, began by articulating two First-Amendment premises. First, Kennedy reiterated the maxim, initially stated in *Buckley*, that spending on political campaigns constitutes speech. Second, Kennedy emphasized that, as stated in *Bellotti*, free-speech protections extend to corporations. With those premises in hand, the Court moved to the crux of its reasoning, that the self-governance rationale mandates free expression to be a constitutional lodestar. "Speech is an essential mechanism of democracy," Kennedy wrote. "The right of citizens to inquire, to hear, to speak, and to use information to reach consensus is a precondition to enlightened self-government and a necessary means to protect it." From the Court's perspective, then, corporate expenditures on political campaigns go the core of the First Amendment. Restrictions on such political speech and writing destroy "liberty" and are necessarily unconstitutional, unless the government can satisfy strict scrutiny by showing that the regulation is necessary (or narrowly tailored) to achieve a compelling purpose.[70]

Whether the government could satisfy strict scrutiny appeared to be, at least partly, an empirical question. Was the campaign finance regulation necessary or narrowly tailored to achieve the compelling purpose of avoiding corruption or the appearance of corruption in the democratic process? Indeed, Justice John Paul Stevens's *Citizens United* dissent stressed that Congress had relied on "evidence of corruption" when enacting the BCRA campaign finance restrictions.[71] Moreover, extensive social science research shows that excessive spending, whether corporate or otherwise, can in fact corrupt or distort democracy in two ways. First, it can skew electoral outcomes. Because running for office requires massive funding, personal wealth and friendship (or association) with wealthy contributors can determine who can even be a candidate. More broadly, social and cognitive psychology research demonstrates that wealth can be used to fund campaign strategies that purposefully manipulate the electorate and "induce sub-optimal vote decisions."[72] In a 2008 book-length empirical study of the connections between wealth and democracy, Larry Bartels concluded that if fundraising had been equal over the previous 50 years, then the number of Republican presidential victories would have been cut in half (Bartels, incidentally, revealed that the last time he voted in a presidential election, he voted for Ronald Reagan).[73] Second, wealth can influence the behavior of government officials after their elections. As one might expect, large campaign contributors implicitly buy privileged access to government officials and processes. For instance, contributors receive special consideration from legislative committee members who have benefitted from the contributors' largess. Empirical evidence also demonstrates a predictable corollary to this enhanced influence: Government officials are especially unresponsive to the interests of low-income citizens.[74]

Nonetheless, the Court's application of strict scrutiny is only *partly* an empirical question; it is also partly a normative question. For instance, in a campaign finance case, the definition of corruption is crucial to the Court's determination of whether the government has identified a compelling purpose. And in perhaps the most significant aspect of the Court's reasoning, *Citizens United* severely narrowed the concept of corruption. Indeed, the majority used such a cramped notion of corruption that the empirical evidence (of corruption) was rendered irrelevant.

From Kennedy's perspective, only a direct contribution to a candidate or officeholder can constitute corruption or its appearance. An independent expenditure, even on behalf of a specific candidate or officeholder, cannot do so. Thus, apparently, the government cannot ever justify its regulation of expenditures, whether by corporations or others. Anything short of a bribe or the appearance of a bribe is permissible. Ultimately, then, the *Citizens United* majority concluded that the government interest in avoiding corruption or its appearance was insufficient to satisfy strict scrutiny. The BCRA restrictions on expenditures were unconstitutional.[75]

Conservatives often assert that originalism is the best (or only) method of legitimate constitutional interpretation. Originalism supposedly requires the justices to uphold either the original public meaning of the Constitution or the framers' intentions.[76] On the early Roberts Court, Scalia and Thomas were avowed originalists, but the other conservative justices also invoked originalist arguments and joined originalist opinions.[77] Unsurprisingly, then, the *Citizens United* majority supported its holding with originalist flourishes, even though the Court did not rely heavily on originalist arguments. Kennedy characterized the statutory restriction on corporate campaign expenditures as "censorship … vast in its reach." "By suppressing the speech of manifold corporations," he explained, "the Government prevents their voices and viewpoints from reaching the public and advising voters on which persons or entities are hostile to their interests." But the framers, Kennedy reasoned, would have found such censorship or suppression impermissible, as he supposedly demonstrated with a quotation from Madison's *Federalist, Number 10*: "Factions will necessarily form in our Republic, but the remedy of 'destroying the liberty' of some factions is 'worse than the disease.' Factions should be checked by permitting them all to speak, and by entrusting the people to judge what is true and what is false." Kennedy concluded that "[t]here is simply no support for the view that the First Amendment, as originally understood, would permit the suppression of political speech by media corporations. … the most important means of mass communication in modern times."[78]

In a telling statement, Kennedy reasoned that "[t]he Government has 'muffle[d] the voices that best represent the most significant segments of the *economy*.'" Speech, it seems, no longer emanates from the people, from citizens, but from "segments of the economy."[79] From this standpoint, the private economic sphere has subsumed the public sphere.

The market governs the state. Numerous commentators have described this phenomenon by explaining, albeit imprecisely, that our democracy is now based on "one dollar, one vote," rather than "one person, one vote."[80] *Citizens United* amounted to a judicial proclamation that corporations and other wealthy entities and individuals can spend unlimited sums in their efforts to control elections and government policies. The D.C. Circuit Court of Appeals recognized as much in *SpeechNow. org v. Federal Election Commission*, decided barely 2 months after the Supreme Court handed down *Citizens United*. The D.C. Circuit invalidated limits on contributions to political action committees that would subsequently use the funds for campaign expenditures (which would never come within the direct control of an individual candidate). In conjunction with *Citizens United*, this decision opened the door to the creation of the so-called Super PACs, wielding enormous sums of money. Thus, in the democratic sphere, wealth and corporate power are unfettered. According to the conservative Supreme Court justices, the liberty embodied in the First-Amendment protection of free speech demands as much. Unsurprisingly, after *Citizens United* and *SpeechNow.org*, the flow of funds into the 2010 and 2012 political campaigns increased dramatically from previous election cycles. For the 2012 elections, $7 billion were spent.[81] Regardless, subsequent cases showed that the conservative justices were steeled to stand strong for Democracy, Inc. The Court not only reaffirmed the *Citizens United* holding but also extended it. It is as if Democracy, Inc. , has become official judicial and government dogma.

In one case, *Arizona Free Enterprise Club's Freedom Club PAC v. Bennett*, the state of Arizona created a legislative "matching funds scheme" for campaign financing. Under this scheme, a candidate for state office who accepted public financing would receive additional funds if a privately financed opponent spent more than the publicly financed candidate's initial allocation. Publicly and privately financed candidates would be able to spend roughly the same amounts on their respective campaigns. In a five-to-four decision, the conservative majority held this campaign finance scheme unconstitutional. The Court, once again, emphasized the self-governance rationale, and then reasoned that the flexible public financing system imposed a "penalty" by diminishing the privately financed candidate's expression. In dissent, Justice Elena Kagan suggested that the majority's reasoning was exactly backwards: The public financing, she explained, "subsidizes and so produces *more* political speech." But the conservative majority was adamant: Any regulation of campaign financing constituted an unconstitutional burden on free speech. "[E]ven if the matching funds provision did result in more speech by publicly financed candidates and more speech in general, it would do so at the expense of impermissibly burdening (and thus reducing) the speech of privately financed candidates and independent expenditure groups."[82]

In a second case, *American Tradition Partnership, Inc. v. Bullock*, a Montana statute provided that a "corporation may not make ... an expenditure in connection with a candidate or a political committee that supports or opposes a candidate or a political party." The Montana Supreme Court upheld this statute in the face of a First-Amendment challenge based on *Citizens United*. The Montana Court reasoned that the specific history in the state—of corporate corruption of democracy—supported the state's claim that the regulation was narrowly tailored to achieve a compelling purpose. In yet another five-to-four decision, the conservative justices on the United States Supreme Court disagreed. In a per curiam opinion reversing the Montana Court, the justices reasoned that "[t]here can be no serious doubt" that *Citizens United* controlled and precluded the state from even attempting to demonstrate that its factual situation was unique.[83]

And in the most recent campaign finance case, *McCutcheon v. Federal Election Commission*, the Court invalidated federal statutory limits on the aggregate contributions of campaign donors. *Buckley* had upheld both base and aggregate limits on contributions. A base limit restricts the amount a donor can give directly to a single candidate or committee, while an aggregate limit restricts the total amount a donor can give to all candidates and committees. In *McCutcheon*, Roberts's plurality opinion emphasized the narrow definition of corruption articulated in *Citizens United*. "The hallmark of corruption is the financial quid pro quo: dollars for political favors." Therefore, government restrictions on contributions must be "closely drawn" or "narrowly tailored" to prevent "'quid pro quo' corruption or its appearance." In concluding that aggregate limits on contributions were not closely enough tied to corruption, as narrowly defined, Roberts stated that contributing large sums of money to political campaigns amounts to "'robustly exercis[ing]' [one's] First Amendment rights." This view suggests that the more money an individual spends, the more vigorous is his or her exercise of free expression. Of course, this viewpoint makes perfect sense if one conceptualizes the citizen as homo economicus: The economic self acts, politically or otherwise, by spending (or making) money. *McCutcheon*, it should be noted, left intact the base contribution limits, which were not in issue, though Roberts characterized them as a "prophylactic measure." One might reasonably wonder, in the context of Democracy, Inc., whether the conservative justices will long abide a mere prophylactic that limits spending on political campaigns. In fact, Justice Thomas has already declared that he views all campaign finance restrictions, including the base limits on contributions, as unconstitutional.[84]

With the conservative Gorsuch having replaced Scalia, the conservative bloc appears intact. The change in personnel is unlikely to change the bloc's outlook—more on this later, though. The early Roberts Court's constitutional decisions suggest that the new Court will find any regulation of the economic self—any restriction on economic liberty, on the spending or accumulation of wealth—to be constitutionally suspect. In such cases, the justices are likely to rely on the First-Amendment Free-Speech Clause, as they did in the campaign finance decisions, but they might invoke other constitutional provisions as well. The conservative justices' interpretation of the Commerce Clause in *National Federation of Independent Business v. Sebelius*, the *Affordable Care Act Case*, illustrates. In Roberts's opinion, he stressed a distinction between activity and inactivity: Congress, he said, can regulate activity pursuant to its commerce power but cannot regulate inactivity. The individual mandate provision in the Patient Protection and Affordable Care Act requires most Americans to maintain "minimum essential" health insurance coverage. Any individual who does not comply with the mandate, and is not otherwise exempt, must pay a penalty to the government. According to Roberts, the constitutional problem with the individual mandate is that it "does not regulate existing commercial activity." Instead, it "compels individuals to *become* active in commerce by purchasing a product [namely, health insurance]." The other conservative justices (the joint dissenters) completely agreed with Roberts on this point, even though they did not join his opinion.[85]

The conservative bloc, in effect, protected the economic self and consumer sovereignty. Most often, individuals who choose not to buy health insurance are, in Roberts's words, "healthy ... young adults who are less likely to need significant health care and have other priorities for spending their money." These healthy young adults, like any good economic selves, know what is best for themselves. Roberts admitted that, at some point, "[e]veryone will likely participate in the markets for food, clothing, transportation, shelter, or energy." But, he insisted, Congress is not, therefore, authorized "to direct [the people] to purchase particular products in those or other markets today." Why not? Because the individual consumer—homo economicus—must remain at liberty to choose what and when to buy. As Roberts said, individuals choose to "do things," or not to do them, "for reasons of their own." If the individual chooses to remain inactive, to not buy health insurance, then the government should not be allowed to interfere in the marketplace by forcing the individual to purchase insurance.[86]

During the Rehnquist Court years, the conservative justices sought to protect traditional moral values while also protecting economic liberty. The early Roberts Court conservatives maintained the judicial support of moral values. For instance, in *Town of Greece v. Galloway*, a 2014 five-to-four decision, the conservative bloc upheld the opening of town board meetings with overtly sectarian Christian prayers. The Court found that such prayers did not violate the First-Amendment Establishment Clause because they were integral to American traditions, even though this particular town did not begin the practice until 1999.[87] Significantly, however, along with such moral clarity decisions, the Roberts Court conservatives intensified the constitutional shielding of economic liberty. And in cases where the bolstering of traditional moral values clashes with the protection of economic liberty, the early Roberts Court appeared to favor the latter. Two cases, in particular, involved businesses that used arguably immoral expressive activities to garner economic profits. Both cases held that the First Amendment protected the expression. Thus, the Court allowed the immoral but profitable activities to continue. In *United States v. Stevens*, a federal statute prohibited animal crush videos by criminalizing "the commercial creation, sale, or possession of certain depictions of animal cruelty." The Court held the statute to be substantially overbroad on its face and therefore unconstitutional under the First Amendment. The crush videos, the Court reasoned, did not fit into a previously recognized low-value (or unprotected) category of free speech. Moreover, the government could not justify the creation of a new low-value category.[88] In *Brown v. Entertainment Merchants Association*, a state law prohibited "the sale or rental of 'violent video games' to minors." Video games, the Court began, are a form of expression generally within the compass of the First Amendment. Then, as in *Stevens*, the Court reasoned that this expression neither fell into a low-value category of unprotected speech nor otherwise could be justifiably restricted.[89] To be sure, the Court did not emphasize in either *Stevens* or *Brown* that the expressive activities were commercial and profitable, but at the same time, the Court unquestionably understood that both cases involved economic activities.[90]

Of course, from a statistical standpoint, *Stevens* and *Brown* represent too small of a sample size to draw any definite conclusion about the Roberts Court's relative weighing of moral clarity versus economic liberty. Such cases, where the conservatives' two primary concerns conflict, arise infrequently. Indeed, the Court might be just as likely to decide cases where the concerns for moral clarity and economic liberty coincide. In the recent five-to-four decision, *Burwell v. Hobby Lobby Stores, Inc.*, the conservative bloc of justices was able to protect both corporate wealth and traditional religious values. The Court decided this case pursuant to a statute, the Religious Freedom Restoration Act (RFRA), rather than under the Free Exercise Clause. Regulations under the Affordable Care Act required corporations to provide health insurance coverage to employees for various types of contraceptives. In *Hobby Lobby*, closely held and for-profit corporations argued that complicity in supplying certain types of contraceptives—which the corporations claimed were actually abortifacients—violated their rights to religious freedom as protected under RFRA. The government replied, in part, that corporations do not exercise religion and therefore do not have rights under RFRA. The Court disagreed and held in favor of the corporations. Alito wrote for the majority: "Protecting the free-exercise rights of corporations like Hobby Lobby," controlled by conservative Christians, "protects the religious liberty of the humans who own and control those companies." In dissent, Justice Ginsburg castigated the majority's "expansive notion of corporate personhood."[91]

Ultimately, the Roberts Court's stretching of the First Amendment to protect economic liberty might be boundless, as demonstrated in the purported free-speech case, *Sorrell v. IMS Health Inc*, decided in 2011. When pharmacies process prescriptions, they routinely record information such as the prescribing doctor, the patient, the dosage, and so forth. Data mining businesses, such as IMS Health Inc., buy this information, analyze it, and sell or lease their reports to pharmaceutical manufacturers. When armed with this information, pharmaceutical salespersons are able to market their drugs more effectively to doctors. Vermont enacted a law to prevent pharmacies from selling this information. The legislature had two primary purposes: first, to protect the privacy of patients and doctors, and second, to improve public health by, for example, encouraging doctors to prescribe drugs in their patients' best interests rather than because of effective pharmaceutical marketing. Stephen Breyer's dissent, joined by Ruth Bader Ginsburg and Elena Kagan, characterized the statute as a police power regulation of the economic marketplace that did not trigger free-speech concerns. The Court disagreed, reasoning that the statute raised an unusual commercial speech issue. Commercial speech cases typically involve advertising, and as the Court admitted, the statute in *Sorrell* did not restrict advertising per se. Yet, the Court reasoned that the First Amendment not only applied but also required "heightened judicial scrutiny." The Court then invalidated the statute pursuant to this standard, more rigorous than the *Central Hudson* four-part balancing test ordinarily applied in commercial speech cases.[92] In *Sorrell*, then, the Roberts Court went even farther down the neoliberal libertarian road by extending the First Amendment to protect economic activities only tenuously connected to expression.[93]

NOTES

1. John Lewis Gaddis, The Cold War: A New History 237–257 (2005) (discussing end of Cold War); James T. Patterson, Restless Giant 194–195 (2005) (same).
2. Robert H. Bork, Slouching Towards Gomorrah 99, 141 (1996); Robert H. Bork, *Adversary Jurisprudence*, New Criterion, May 2002, at 4; *Cohen*, 403 U.S. 15 (1971).
3. Zelman v. Simmons-Harris, 536 U.S. 639 (2002).
4. Perry Education Assn. v. Perry Local Educators' Assn., 460 U.S. 37, 45 (1983).
5. 515 U.S. 819, 826, 829–831 (1995); id. at 874 (Souter, J., dissenting).
6. 533 U.S. 98, 103, 108–112 (2001).
7. 551 U.S. 393 (2007); Holder v. Humanitarian Law Project, 130 S. Ct. 2705 (2010) (upholding punishment of speech that might provide material support to foreign terrorist organizations, even without proof of likely harm); Beard v. Banks, 548 U.S. 521 (2006) (severely limiting prisoner access to written materials and photographs); Erwin Chemerinsky, *Not a Free Speech Court*, 53 Arizona Law Review 723, 724 (2011) (overall, the Roberts Court has a "dismal record" in free-speech cases); David Kairys, *The Contradictory Messages of Rehnquist-Roberts Era Speech Law: Liberty and Justice for Some*, 2013 U. Illinois Law Review 195 (Rehnquist and Roberts Courts' inconsistencies in free-expression cases).

8. 555 U.S. 460, 464, 467 (2009). "If petitioners [the city] were engaging in their own expressive conduct, then the Free Speech Clause has no application." Id. at 467. The conservative commitment to moral clarity, especially as embodied in traditional religious values, was again demonstrated in *Christian Legal Society v. Martinez*, 130 S.Ct. 2971 (2010). The CLS chapter at the University of California, Hastings College of the Law, argued that the school's "all comers" policy, prohibiting student funded organizations from discriminating against gays and lesbians (and others), violated the First Amendment. Id. at 2979–2981. Kennedy and the four liberal justices formed a majority upholding the policy. Alito wrote a dissent, joined by the three other conservatives, that repeatedly emphasized the importance of protecting CLS, a religious organization dedicated to encouraging a Christian outlook and moral clarity. According to Alito, the only way to explain the school's policy and the Court's decision was that the school and the Court reacted against the Christian identity of the student organization and the content of its message. Id. at 3008–3009 (Alito, J., dissenting). Citing *Rosenberger* and *Good News Club*, Alito stressed that a public forum analysis should have proscribed government (school) suppression of religious viewpoints. Id. at 3009 (Alito, J., dissenting). Whereas, from a conservative standpoint, the government should support efforts by religious organizations to promote morality, the school's policy and the Court's decision would necessarily lead to the "marginalization" of religion. Id. at 3019 (Alito, J., dissenting).

9. Helpful sources on the relationship between democracy and capitalism cited in this chapter include: Fred Block and Margaret R. Somers, The Power of Market Fundamentalism (2014); Timothy K. Kuhner, Capitalism v. Democracy (2014); Thomas Piketty, Capital in the Twenty-first Century (Arthur Goldhammer trans., 2014); Dani Rodrik, The Globalization Paradox (2011); Sidney A. Shapiro and Joseph P. Tomain, Achieving Democracy (2014); Joseph E. Stiglitz, The Price of Inequality (2013 ed.).

10. Sources in this chapter discussing economic developments, including globalization, include: Joel Bakan, The Corporation (2004); Jeffry A. Frieden, Global Capitalism (2006); Robert Heilbroner and Aaron Singer, The Economic Transformation of America (1999); John Micklethwait and Adrian Wooldridge, The Company: A Short History of a Revolutionary Idea (2003); Kenichi Ohmae, The End of the Nation State (1995); Joseph E. Stiglitz, Globalization and Its Discontents (2002); Wyatt Wells, American Capitalism, 1945–2000 (2003); Alfred D. Chandler and Bruce Mazlish, *Introduction, in* Leviathans 1 (Alfred D. Chandler and Bruce Mazlish eds., 2005); Brian Roach, *A Primer on Multinational*

Corporations, in Leviathans 19 (Alfred D. Chandler and Bruce Mazlish eds., 2005).

11. Daniel Stedman Jones, Masters of the Universe: Hayek, Friedman, and the Birth of Neoliberal Politics 109 (2012); Block and Somers, supra note 9, at 3.

12. Friedrich A. Hayek, The Constitution of Liberty 94–95 (2011 definitive ed.).

13. Milton Friedman, *Adam Smith's Relevance for 1976*, Selected Papers No. 50, at 1, 15–16; Jones, supra note 11, at 8, 118; David Harvey, A Brief History of Neoliberalism 5 (2005). Hayek emphasized the superiority of the empirical practices and institutions of the economic marketplace over rationalist attempts at social improvement. Hayek, supra note 12, at 118–125.

14. Friedrich A. Hayek, *The Intellectuals and Socialism*, 16 The University of Chicago Law Review 417, 432–433 (1949); Block and Somers, supra note 9, at 99–100; Jones, supra note 11, at 9, 86–87; see John Dewey, Individualism: Old and New (1930); Robert Nozick, Anarchy, State, and Utopia (1974) (philosophical defense of libertarianism).

15. Harvey, supra note 35, at 15; Frieden, supra note 10, at 359–363; Robert B. Horwitz, America's Right: Anti-Establishment Conservatism from Goldwater to the Tea Party 16 (2013); Rodrik, supra note 9, at xvii; Facundo Alvaredo et al., *The Top 1 Percent in International and Historical Perspective*, 27 Journal of Economic Perspectives 3, 4 (Table: Top 1 Percent Income Shared in the United States); Benjamin J. Cohen, *Bretton Woods System, in* Routledge 1 Encyclopedia of International Political Economy 100–101 (R.J. Barry Jones ed., 2001); Chad Stone et al., *A Guide to Statistics on Historical Trends in Income Inequality*, Center on Budget and Policy Priorities 7 (December 5, 2013) (Fig. 1: Income Gains Widely Shared in Early Postwar Decades—But Not Since Then); see Paul Craig Roberts, *The Breakdown of the Keynesian Model, reprinted in* Supply-Side Economics: A Critical Appraisal 1 (Richard H. Fink ed., 1982) (criticizing Keynesian approach).

16. Stiglitz, supra note 9, at 8–9, 89, 277; Frieden, supra note 10, at 378; Jones, supra note 11, at 19, 263–269; Wells, supra note 10, at 129–135; George Gilder, *The Supply-Side, in* Supply-Side Economics: A Critical Appraisal 14 (Richard H. Fink ed., 1982). Income distribution started to change dramatically in America in the 1980s. Piketty, supra note 9, at 24 (Figure: Income Inequality in the United States, 1910–2010).

17. Frieden, supra note 10, at 378, 430–432; Jones, supra note 11, at 332; Wells, supra note 10, at 179.

18. Benjamin R. Barber, Jihad vs. McWorld (2001 ed.); Micklethwait and Woolridge, supra note 10, at 173–174; Kevin Phillips, Wealth and

Democracy 147–156 (2002); Chandler and Mazlish, supra note 10, at 2; Roach, supra note 10, at 24–25.

19. Barber, supra note 18, at 23; Ohmae, supra note 10, at 2–5, 7.

20. Frieden, supra note 10, at 417; Roach, supra note 10, at 21–22; Micklethwait and Woolridge, supra note 10, at 175. Unilever's website lists many brands: http://www.unileverusa.com/brands-in-action/view-brands.aspx. Unilever did not originate as a United States firm. Heilbroner and Singer, supra note 10, at 343.

21. Chandler and Mazlish, supra note 10, at 1, 12; Roach, supra note 10, at 25–26.

22. Bakan, supra note 10, at 22–25; Frieden, supra note 10, at 395–396; Ohmae, supra note 10, at 2–5; Stiglitz, supra note 9, at 74–76; Roach, supra note 10, at 30, 35–36.

23. Shapiro and Tomain, supra note 9, at 61; Bakan, supra note 10, at 34, 60–61, 72–73; Stiglitz, supra note 9, at 41–45. I am obviously twisting Rawls's philosophical notion of a veil of ignorance. John Rawls, A Theory of Justice (1971).

24. David S. Allen, Democracy, Inc. (2005); Sheldon S. Wolin, Democracy Incorporated (2008); Barber, supra note 18, at 23–154; Phillips, supra note 18, at 229–232, 284–286

25. Jacob S. Hacker and Paul Pierson, Winner-Take-All Politics 118–119 (2010); Dara Strolovitch, Affirmative Advocacy 209–210 (2007) (statistics showing corporations and businesses dominate lobbying); Wolin, supra note 24, at 149.

26. Stiglitz, supra note 9, at 59–60; Wolin, supra note 24, at 63, 135–136. When an official is sympathetic to the industry, it is sometimes called "cognitive capture." Stiglitz, supra note 9, at 59. Thomas Piketty's graphing of American income inequality shows a sharp increase starting in the early 1990s, at the end of the Cold War. Piketty, supra note 9, at 24 (Figure: Income Inequality in the United States, 1910–2010).

27. Francis Fukuyama, *The End of History?*, 16 The National Interest 3–18 (Summer 1989).

28. Sheldon S. Wolin, Politics and Vision 596 (Expanded ed. 2004) [hereinafter Vision].

29. Francis Fukuyama, *The Future of History: Can Liberal Democracy Survive the Decline of the Middle Class?*, 91 Foreign Affairs 53 (2012); Fran Tonkiss, Contemporary Economic Sociology 60–61 (2006); Vision, supra note 28, at 597. As Foa and Mounk note, the luster of democracy began to dull once it became the "only game in town." Roberto Stefan Foa and Yascha Mounk, *The Danger of Deconsolidation: The Democratic Disconnect*, 27 Journal of Democracy 5, 15–16 (2016).

30. Jones, supra note 11, at 338; Gaddis, supra note 1, at 258–260; Harvey, supra note 35, at 93; Stiglitz, supra note 10, at 53–88; Martin Walker, The Cold War: A History 310–314 (1993).
31. Jones, supra note 11, at 8; Stiglitz, supra note 10, at 10–20.
32. Stiglitz, supra note 10, at 138–141; Frieden, supra note 10, at 430–431, 438–439; Jones, supra note 11, at 332–333.
33. Frieden, supra note 10, at 438–439.
34. Kathy Lally and Will Englund, *Russia, Once Almost a Democracy*, The Washington Post (Aug. 18, 2011); Andrew Jack, Inside Putin's Russia (2004); Anna Politkovskaya, Putin's Russia: Life in a Failing Democracy (2007); Mikhail Shishkin, *Poets and Czars, From Pushkin to Putin: The Sad Tale of Democracy in Russia*, The New Republic (July 1, 2013); Frieden, supra note 10, at 431, 439; Harvey, supra note 35, at 154–56; Stiglitz, supra note 10, at 133–34, 151–53.
35. Jones, supra note 11, at 109–110; e.g., Milton Friedman, *Adam Smith's Relevance for 1976*, Selected Papers No. 50, at 11.
36. Daniel A. Farber and Philip P. Frickey, Law and Public Choice 1–11, 38–62 (1991); Jones, supra note 11, at 126–132; e.g., William H. Riker, Liberalism Against Populism 1 (1982) (arguing social choice theory calls democracy into question); Frank Easterbrook, *Statutes' Domains*, 50 The University of Chicago Law Review 533 (1983) (arguing courts should not presume that legislative decisions are rational); George Stigler, *The Theory of Economic Regulation*, 2 Bell J. Economics 3 (1971) (discussing regulatory capture); see Mark Kelman, *On Democracy-Bashing: A Skeptical Look at the Theoretical and 'Empirical' Practice of the Public Choice Movement*, 74 Virginia Law Review 199 (1988) (criticizing public choice).
37. Friedman, supra note 35, at 15, 18.
38. Barber, supra note 18, at 7; J. Mark Ramseyer, *Public Choice, in* Law and Economics 101 (Eric A. Posner ed., 2000).
39. Milton Friedman, Capitalism and Freedom 7–8, 15 (1962).
40. Arthur Brooks, *Why the Stimulus Failed*, National Review (Sept. 25, 2012); James M. Buchanan and Gordon Tullock, The Calculus of Consent: Logical Foundations of Constitutional Democracy (1962); Friedman, supra note 39, at 24; Jones, supra note 11, at 270.
41. Randy Barnett, The Structure of Liberty 179–180, 261 (1998) (supporting the privatization of prisons and law enforcement); Privatization and Economic Performance (Matthew Bishop et al. eds. 1994); Bakan, supra note 10, at 113–138; Jones, supra note 11, at 332; Kimberly N. Brown, *"We the People," Constitutional Accountability, and Outsourcing Government*, 88 Ind. L.J. 1347, 1348 (2013) (examples of privatization creating problems).

42. Gary S. Becker, The Economic Approach to Human Behavior 5 (1976); Jeffrie Murphy and Jules Coleman, The Philosophy of Law 212–218 (on efficiency); Philip Cushman, Constructing the Self, Constructing America 68–69, 82 (1995); John Kenneth Galbraith, The Essential Galbraith 31 (2001); A. Mitchell Polinsky, An Introduction to Law and Economics 10 (1983) (individual preferences are stable, unaffected by external influences); Chris Doucouliagos, *A Note on the Evolution of Homo Economicus*, 28 J. Econ. Issues, No. 3 (1994); Abba P. Lerner, *The Economics and Politics of Consumer Sovereignty*, 62 Am. Econ. Rev. 258 (1972); Richard A. Posner, *Values and Consequences: An Introduction to Economic Analysis of Law, in* Chicago Lectures in Law and Economics 189, 191–192 (Eric Posner ed., 2000).

43. Farber and Frickey, supra note 36, at 15 n.10, 34 (rent-seeking); Albert O. Hirschman, The Passions and the Interests 49–55 (1997 ed.) (predictability and economic interest); Charles Taylor, Sources of the Self 322, 508 (1989); Richard Posner, *An Economic Approach to Legal Procedure and Judicial Administration*, 2 J. Legal Studies 399 (1973).

44. Theda Skocpol and Alexander Hertel-Frenandez, *The Koch Network and Republican Party Extremism*, 14 Perspectives on Politics 681 (2016) (emphasizing the influence of the Koch brothers on Republican politics).

45. Bakan, supra note 10, at 97–107; Gary Rivlin, *Wall Street Fires Back*, The Nation (May 20, 2013), at 11. For examples of statutes that conservatives fought in this manner, see Dodd-Frank Wall Street Reform And Consumer Protection Act, Public Law 111–203, 124 Stat. 1376 (July 21, 2010); Patient Protection and Affordable Care Act, Public Law 111–148, 124 Stat. 119 (March 23, 2010).

46. ALEC: American Legislative Exchange Council http://www.alec.org/. Additional Information on ALEC is drawn from the following sources: The Center for Media and Democracy, *ALEC Exposed*; Mike McIntire, *Conservative Nonprofit Acts as a Stealth Business Lobbyist*, New York Times (April 21, 2012); John Nichols, *ALEC Exposed*, The Nation (July 12, 2011).

47. McIntire, supra note 46.

48. Lee Epstein et al., *How Business Fares in the Supreme Court*, 97 Minn. L. Rev. 1431, 1449–1451, 1472–1473 (2013); J. Mitchell Pickerill, *Is the Roberts Court Business Friendly? Is the Pope Catholic?, in* Business and the Roberts Court 35 (Jonathan H. Adler ed., 2016) (empirical study showing concluding that Roberts Court is business friendly though it continues a trend starting years ago with Nixon's appointees); Corey Ciocchetti, *The Constitution, the Roberts Court, and Business*, 4 William & Mary Business Law Review 385 (2013). For claims that the Roberts Court is not conservative enough, see Ramesh Ponnuru, *Supreme Court*

Isn't Pro-Business, But Should Be, Bloomberg (July 5, 2011); Jonathan Adler, *Business, the Environment, and the Roberts Court: A Preliminary Assessment*, 49 Santa Clara Law Review 943 (2009); Eric Posner, *Is the Supreme Court Biased in Favor of Business?*, Slate (March 17, 2008). But according to Mark Tushnet, the "Roberts Court's overall balance sheet in business cases fits the 'pro-business' view of the Court reasonably well." Mark Tushnet, In the Balance: Law and Politics on the Roberts Court 213 (2013); id. at 187–214 (discussing evidence).

49. Lee Epstein et al., *Do Justices Defend the Speech They Hate? In-Group Bias, Opportunism, and the First Amendment* (APSA 2013 Annual Meeting Paper).

50. Adam D. Chandler, *Cert.-stage Amicus "All Stars": Where Are They Now?*, Scotusblog (April 4, 2013); Adam D. Chandler, *Cert.-stage Amicus Briefs: Who Files Them and To What Effect?*, Scotusblog (Sept. 27, 2007) (earlier study).

51. Facts about this case are drawn from the following: the Supreme Court decision, 550 U.S. 618 (2007); the Circuit Court decision, 421 F.3d 1169 (11th Cir. 2005); Ann Friedman, *TAP Talks With Lilly Ledbetter*, The American Prospect (April 23, 2008).

52. 550 U.S. at 643 (Ginsburg, J., dissenting).

53. Id. at 623–632.

54. Id. at 545, 650 (Ginsburg, J., dissenting).

55. In this instance, Congress effectively overturned the Court's decision by enacting the *Lilly Ledbetter Fair Pay Act of 2009*, Public Law No. 111–112, 123 Stat. 5 (2009), which changed the statute of limitations for discrimination claims.

56. Even before Roberts became chief justice, the Court conceived of individuals as economic selves in antitrust cases (another area involving overt marketplace regulations). See Albert A. Foer, *The Third Leg of the Antitrust Stool: What the Business Schools Have To Offer To Antitrust*, 47 New York Law School Law Review 21, 30 (2003) (discussing *Matsushita v. Zenith*, 475 U.S. 574 (1986)). Posner himself had advocated that "predatory pricing complaints should be killed off whenever possible at the summary judgment stage of an antitrust case" because an economic self would not rationally engage in such practices. Foer, supra, at 30. In other words, from this perspective, courts should presume that a business-defendant would not have implemented a pricing scheme for predatory purposes because a rational self-maximizer would be unlikely to do so. In fact, the Court has so closely followed Posner in this area that he has declared a "unilateral victory." Id. at 31 (citing Richard A. Posner, Antitrust Law IX (2d ed. 2001)).

57. 132 S. Ct. 1289, 1301–1302 (2012) (citing William Landes and Richard Posner, The Economic Structure of Intellectual Property Law 305–306 (2003)). In *Association for Molecular Pathology v. Myriad Genetics, Inc.*, 133 S. Ct. 2107 (2013), another patent case, the Court again considered incentives to innovate. Breyer, influenced by law and economics, sometimes follows an economic perspective and cites Posner. E.g., Leegin Creative Leather Products, Inc. v. PSKS, Inc., 551 U.S. 877, 909–911 (2007) (Breyer, J., dissenting) (antitrust case); see Golan v. Holder, 132 S. Ct. 873, 900 (2012) (Breyer, J., dissenting) (copyright case); Stephen Breyer, *The Uneasy Case for Copyright: A Study of Copyright in Books, Photocopies, and Computer Programs*, 84 Harvard Law Review 281 (1970); Posner, supra note 42, at 191 (describing Breyer as alumnus of the law and economics movement).

58. 554 U.S. 471, 500, 502, 514 (2008). One should not assume that when the Court relies on economic principles or assumptions, it necessarily applies those principles and assumptions correctly. Joni Hersch and W. Kip Viscusi, *Punitive Damages by Numbers: Exxon Shipping Co. v. Baker*, 18 Supreme Court Economic Review 259 (2010).

59. 550 U.S. 618 (2007). Posner has long advocated for interpreting rules of judicial administration to maximize efficiency. Richard Posner, *An Economic Approach to Legal Procedure and Judicial Administration*, 2 The Journal of Legal Studies 399 (1973).

60. 131 S. Ct. 2541, 2548, 2551, 2553, 2556–2557 (2011); Arthur R. Miller, *Simplified Pleading, Meaningful Days in Court, and Trials on the Merits: Reflections on the Deformation of Federal Procedure*, 88 New York University Law Review 286, 318–320 (2013).

61. 133 S. Ct. at 1426, 1432–1435 (2013).

62. 131 S. Ct. 1740, 1744–1753 (2011).

63. 133 S. Ct. 2304 (2013). For additional cases upholding contractual provisions requiring arbitration, see *Marmet Health Care Center, Inc. v. Brown*, 132 S. Ct. 1201 (2012), and *Compucredit Corp. v. Greenwood*, 132 S. Ct. 665 (2012). See Miller, supra note 60, at 326–327 (discussing these cases).

64. Miller, supra note 60, at 322–325.

65. *Kiobel v. Royal Dutch Petroleum Co.*, 133 S. Ct. 1659 (2013), limited human rights suits against corporations despite complicity in human rights violations abroad. *Rapanos v. United States*, 547 U.S. 715 (2006), limited the reach of the Clean Water Act. In *Pliva, Inc. v. Mensing*, the Court held that federal drug regulations preempted state tort-law claims against generic drug manufacturers. 131 S. Ct. 2567 (2011). The Court followed *Pliva* in *Mutual Pharmaceutical Co., Inc. v. Bartlett*, again

holding that federal law preempted a state law claim against a generic drug manufacturer. 133 S.Ct. 2466 (2013).

66. *Vance v. Ball State University* limited who qualifies as a supervisor under Title VII. When an employee claims that a co-worker discriminated (in this case, the claim was for racial harassment), the plaintiff's burden of proof is higher if the co-worker was not a supervisor. 133 S. Ct. 2434 (2013). *University of Texas Southwestern Medical Center v. Nassar* imposes a more rigorous burden of proof on a plaintiff-employee who alleges under Title VII that an employer retaliated because the employee had previously complained of discrimination. Under the new standard, the plaintiff must prove that retaliation was the determinative factor rather than one of several motivating factors leading to the employer's action. 133 S. Ct. 2517 (2013).

67. Wyeth v. Levine, 555 U.S. 555 (2009) (upholding state law judgment against drug manufacturer arising from amputation of patient's arm).

68. Austin v. Michigan Chamber of Commerce, 494 U.S. 652 (1990) (upholding restriction on corporate political spending); FEC v. Massachusetts Citizens for Life, 479 U.S. 238 (1986) (invalidating restriction on non-profit corporations); FEC v. National Right to Work Committee, 459 U.S. 197 (1982) (upholding restriction on non-profit corporations); see McConnell v. FEC, 540 U.S. 93 (2003) (reaffirming *Buckley* and upholding main sections of Bipartisan Campaign Reform Act of 2002).

69. Given Rehnquist's stance on commercial speech—he preferred to defer to legislative decisions, Virginia State Board of Pharmacy v. Virginia Citizens Consumer Council, Inc., 425 U.S. 748, 781 (1976) (Rehnquist, J., dissenting)—he unsurprisingly also often sided with the liberal justices in campaign finance cases. E.g., Nixon v. Shrink Missouri Government PAC, 528 U.S. 377 (2000); Austin v. Michigan Chamber of Commerce, 494 U.S. 652 (1990). O'Connor also voted to uphold some campaign finance restrictions. McConnell v. FEC, 540 U.S. 93 (2003); Nixon v. Shrink Missouri Government PAC, 528 U.S. 377 (2000). Thus, when Roberts and Alito replaced Rehnquist and O'Connor, respectively, the conservative bloc of justices was ready to act in accord with Democracy, Inc.

70. 558 U.S. 310, 336–342, 354 (2010); Pub. L. No. 107–155, 116 Stat. 81. In several cases preceding *Citizens United*, the Roberts Court invalidated campaign finance restrictions. Davis v. FEC, 554 U.S. 724 (2008) (invalidating federal provisions allowing certain candidates to have increased contribution and expenditure limits based on spending of opponents); FEC v. Wisconsin Right To Life, Inc., 551 U.S. 449 (2007) (limiting restrictions on expenditures by corporations and unions); Randall v. Sorrell, 548 U.S. 230 (2006) (invalidating state limits on contributions).

71. 558 U.S. at 452 (Stevens, J., concurring in part and dissenting in part).
72. Molly J. Walker Wilson, *Behavioral Decision Theory and Implications for the Supreme Court's Campaign Finance Jurisprudence*, 31 Cardozo L. Rev. 679, 684 (2010); Stiglitz, supra note 9, at 184; Larry M. Bartels et al., *Inequality and American Governance, in* Inequality and American Democracy 88, 113–117 (Lawrence R. Jacobs and Theda Skocpol eds., 2005).
73. Larry M. Bartels, Unequal Democracy 125 (2008) [hereinafter Unequal]; id. at ix–x (voting for Reagan); Molly J. Walker Wilson, *Too Much of a Good Thing: Campaign Speech After Citizens United*, 31 Cardozo Law Review 2365, 2374–2377 (2010). The empirical evidence does not show, however, that the better financed candidate always wins. Bradley A. Smith, Unfree Speech: The Folly of Campaign Finance Reform 48–51 (2001); Jamin B. Raskin, *The Campaign-Finance Crucible: Is Laissez Fair?*, 101 Michigan Law Review 1532, 1535 (2003).
74. Bartels, supra note 72, at 116–117; Unequal, supra note 73, at 2–3, 285–286; Martin Gilens, Affluence and Influence (2012); Martin Gilens and Benjamin I. Page, *Testing Theories of American Politics: Elites, Interest Groups, and Average Citizens*, 12 Perspectives on Politics 564 (2014).
75. 558 U.S. at 348–362; Samuel Issacharoff, *On Political Corruption*, 124 Harvard Law Review 118, 118–121 (2010); Michael S. Kang, *The End of Campaign Finance Law*, 98 Virginia Law Review 1, 25–26 (2012); Wilson, supra note 72, at 740–745.
76. Randy E. Barnett, *An Originalism for Nonoriginalists*, 45 Loyola Law Review 611 (1999); John O. McGinnis and Michael B. Rappaport, *Original Interpretive Principles as the Core of Originalism*, 24 Constitutional Commentary 371 (2007).
77. District of Columbia v. Heller, 554 U.S. 570, 576–626 (2008).
78. 558 U.S. at 353–355; Tushnet, supra note 48, at 279–280.
79. 558 U.S. at 354 (quoting McConnell v. FEC, 540 U.S. 93, 257–258 (2003) (Scalia, J., concurring in part, concurring in judgment in part, dissenting in part)) (emphasis added). For a similar example, see *Davis v. FEC*, where Alito suggested that the strength of a candidate depends on wealth, the wealth of contributors, or celebrity. 554 U.S. 724, 742 (2008).
80. Stiglitz, supra note 9, at xlix–l, 149; Kuhner, supra note 9, at 26; Shapiro and Tomain, supra note 9, at xii.
81. 599 F.3d 686 (D.C. Cir. 2010); Marcia Coyle, The Roberts Court 275 (2013); Kuhner, supra note 9, at 1–4; Kang, supra note 75, at 5–6; see McCutcheon v. FEC, 134 S.Ct. 1434, 1457 (2014) (amount spent).
82. 131 S. Ct. 2806, 2813, 2816–2818, 2821 (2011); id. at 2833 (Kagan, J., dissenting) (emphasis in original).
83. 132 S. Ct. 2490, 2491 (2012); id. at 2491–92 (Breyer, J., dissenting) (discussing Western Tradition Partnership v. Attorney General, 363 Mont. 220 (2011)).

84. 134 S.Ct. 1434, 1441, 1449, 1457–1458 (2014); id. at 1462–1463 (Thomas, J., concurring in the judgment); *Buckley*, 424 U.S. 1, 26, 38 (1976).
85. 132 S. Ct. 2566, 2587 (2012); id. at 2644, 2648–2649 (joint dissent); Patient Protection and Affordable Care Act of 2010, 124 Stat. 119; 26 U.S.C. §5000A.
86. 132 S. Ct. at 2589–91. Roberts and the four liberals nonetheless upheld the individual mandate pursuant to Congress's taxing power. Id. at 2599–2600.
87. 134 S.Ct. 1811 (2014).
88. 130 S. Ct. 1577, 1582, 1584–1592 (2010).
89. 131 S. Ct. 2729, 2732–2733 (2011). After discussing low-value categories, id. at 2734–2738, the Court reasoned that the state could not justify the restriction under the strict scrutiny test. Id. at 2738–2741.
90. *Stevens*, 130 S. Ct. at 1585, 1592; *Brown*, 131 S. Ct. at 2732, 2735. Of note, in both *Stevens* and *Brown*, the conservative bloc divided. Even *Snyder v. Phelps*, 131 S. Ct. 1207 (2011), which held that the First Amendment shields church members from tort liability for speech of public concern, can be interpreted as protecting homo economicus. Conservatives generally view tort claims as threats to business. See, e.g., Exxon Shipping Co. v. Baker, 554 U.S. 471 (2008) (limiting punitive damages). Thus, although *Phelps* did not specifically involve a tort claim against a *business*, the justices' general hostility to tort claims might have influenced them. One could argue similarly about *Agency for International Development v. Alliance for Open Society International, Inc.* 133 S. Ct. 2321 (2013). A federal statute provided funding to non-governmental organizations to fight HIV/AIDS worldwide. The statute required organizations, however, to agree that they opposed prostitution. Thus, the case can be construed as pitting moral clarity (opposing prostitution) against marketplace restrictions (attaching conditions to funding). Again, the Court held that the restrictions violated the First Amendment.
91. 134 S. Ct. 2751 (2014); Religious Freedom Restoration Act of 1993 (RFRA), 107 Stat. 1488.
92. 131 S. Ct. 2653, 2659–2663, 2667–2668 (2011); id. at 2673 (Breyer, J., dissenting).
93. Interestingly, when the government is an employer, the Roberts Court protects the economic marketplace and the sanctity of contract by allowing the government-employer to restrict the speech of its employees. Borough of Duryea v. Guarnieri, 131 S. Ct. 2488 (2011) (limiting government employee's First-Amendment right to petition the government); Garcetti v. Ceballos, 547 U.S. 410 (2006) (limiting free-speech rights of government employees by distinguishing between speech as a citizen and speech as an employee).

PART III

The Early and New Roberts Courts

Constitution Betrayed: The Endangerment of the American Democratic-Capitalist System

In numerous constitutional and non-constitutional cases, the early Roberts Court conservatives fully accepted and bolstered Democracy, Inc.[1] Their expansive constitutional protection of homo economicus, economic liberty, and the marketplace harmonized with neoliberal libertarianism and its underlying laissez-faire ideology. In *Citizens United* and other cases, the conservative justices interpreted the Constitution so that the private sphere subsumed the public. Rational self-maximization, apropos in the private sphere, became the governing rule of conduct in the public sphere, as Milton Friedman and other neoliberals have advocated. Homo economicus replaced the framers' complex citizen-self.[2] Moreover, the conservative justices maintained that originalist methodology—focusing on the original public meaning or the framers' intentions—supported at least some of their decisions, including *Citizens United*.

Renowned libertarian legal scholars such as Randy Barnett and Richard Epstein bolstered the Court's constitutional approach. Epstein, for instance, exhaustively defended "the original classical liberal constitutional order," as he put it. Following a "guarded originalist view," Epstein argued that "classical liberal theory" animated the framers in their drafting of the Constitution. That is, according to Epstein, the framers committed normatively to "the twin pillars of private property and limited government." When Epstein said 'limited government,' though, he meant minimal government because government, to him, is no more than "a necessary evil." Epstein maintained that

© The Author(s) 2017
S.M. Feldman, *The New Roberts Court, Donald Trump, and Our Failing Constitution*, DOI 10.1007/978-3-319-56451-7_7

the "Constitution embraces a theory of laissez-faire," under which the government can perform functions such as enforcing peace and defending against foreign enemies, but little else. The government, Epstein insisted, cannot implement any programs that would entail "income redistribution." From his perspective, the predominant purpose of the constitutional system is to protect "competitive markets" and the rights of individuals "to enter and exit" those markets. Economic competition is the "highest good" and "unregulated market forces" produce a "desirable social equilibrium."[3]

With the conservative Neil Gorsuch having replaced the late Justice Scalia, the new Roberts Court is unlikely to change direction in any substantial way. In fact, Gorsuch views Scalia as the model justice.[4] Nevertheless, this chapter and the next explain how the early Roberts Court's neoliberal libertarian interpretation of the Constitution is problematic on multiple counts. In fact, with the Court's support, our American constitutional democracy is now weaker than at any point since the mid-1930s.[5] In this crisis, will the new Roberts Court abet in the potential demise of our democratic-capitalist system? This chapter critiques the early Roberts Court's interpretation of the Constitution from three perspectives: the framing and originalism, social and political theory, and the practical effects of laissez faire in history. And as will be discussed in the next chapter, this three-pronged critique can serve as a roadmap for the new Court to repudiate Democracy, Inc., and to reinvigorate our constitutional system.

THE FRAMING AND ORIGINALISM

Originalism cannot justify a neoliberal libertarian interpretation of the Constitution, despite the claims of the conservative justices and scholars such as Epstein.[6] The framers sought balance between the public and private spheres—a balance inconsistent with the neoliberal emphasis on the private sphere. True, the framers gave great importance to the private sphere and property rights. They believed that individuals, in the private sphere, would and should act as self-interested commercial and economic strivers. Moreover, the framers realized that many individuals would try to pursue their own passions and interests not only in the private realm but also in the public sphere. This realization had arisen from the hard experiences of the 1780s, during which the framers witnessed the formation of factions that then seized government power in various states. From the framers' perspective, the state constitutions, following the Revolution's civic republican ideology, had been built on utopian illusions about the average citizen's degree of virtue. Such utopianism had allowed corruption to permeate state governments and to threaten national survival. The framers rejected such utopianism for a pragmatic realism. Not all citizens would virtuously pursue the common good. Many would seek to manipulate government power for their own private advantage.

The framers nonetheless did not surrender to a cynicism that would have denied the possibility of government in accord with republican principles. They did not believe that government should be based on the individual pursuit of self-interest. Instead, they insisted that the public sphere must be distinguished from the private sphere. They maintained that virtue and reason should and could overcome passion and interest in public affairs. Government should and could be conducted in accord with the civic republican principles of virtue and the common good. The foundation for the framers' political-economic vision was the American citizen-self—complex in its motivations. Passion and interest must be acknowledged—that was part-and-parcel of the framers' realistic conception of human nature. Yet, the framers also believed that enough Americans were imbued with sufficient civic virtue to sustain republican democratic government. And even when reason and virtue could not defeat passion and interest, the framers structured the Constitution to channel self-interest toward pursuit of the common good. The crux of the framers' constitutional system was the balance between the public and private spheres. The constitutional structures would promote the virtuous pursuit of the common good in the public sphere while simultaneously protecting individual rights and liberties in the private sphere.

When the Roberts Court conservatives invoke the framers, the justices often misconstrue the framers' words and intentions, largely because they filter those words and intentions through the prism of neoliberal libertarianism. For example, recall that in *Citizens United* the Court reasoned that the framers would have found the disputed campaign finance restrictions to be constitutionally impermissible suppression. Kennedy's majority opinion drew support by quoting in part from Madison's *Federalist, Number 10*. "Factions will necessarily form in our Republic, but the remedy of 'destroying the liberty' of some factions is 'worse than the disease.' Factions should be checked by permitting them all to speak, and by entrusting the people to judge what is true and what is false." The Court correctly reasoned that, according to Madison, liberty frequently causes factionalism but nonetheless should not be limited. After that point, however, the Court veered askew. It suggested Madison believed that factions should be given free rein and that the people can then discern the truth. This interpretation of Madison was deeply flawed. Most important, Madison sought to control the effects of factionalism in multiple ways (or at multiple levels). True, at one level, Madison argued that, by allowing faction to fight faction, the one might offset the other. But before reaching that level, Madison expressed the hope that the constitutional system would promote the election of a virtuous elite as governmental officials. Madison did not believe in "entrusting the people to judge what is true and what is false," as the Court put it. To the contrary, Madison believed that too many of the people followed their passions and interests while ignoring reason and virtue. The main thrust of *Federalist, Number 10*, was that, despite this propensity of the people, the nation should not succumb to passions, interests, and factional rule. Instead, Madison firmly believed that, in the public sphere, reason and virtue should control passion and interest. Passion and interest might have free rein in the private sphere—but not in the public sphere. Yet, the *Citizens United* Court could not recognize this possibility: that the public should predominate over the private. The Court's diminished concept of the self obscured (or even precluded) such recognition. An economic self that relentlessly pursues its own self-interest can know nothing of public-sphere virtue and reason. Thus, in the name of preserving liberty, the Court gave free rein to economic interests not only in the private sphere but also in the public sphere. Homo economicus rules. Spending on politics is no different from other spending in the marketplace. One spends or does not spend because of rational self-maximization. When the Court declared that "[t]he First Amendment confirms the freedom to think for ourselves," the justices seemed to protect consumer sovereignty as much as free speech. Ultimately, homo economicus can spend as much money on politics as it desires. Any government restriction amounts to a constitutionally suspect constraint on the economic self's liberty.[7]

Moreover, as conceived by the early Roberts Court conservatives, the economic self is a shape shifter. Yes, it can be an individual, but it also can be a profit-driven corporation.[8] And while the framers conceptualized separate public and private spheres, they never imagined a private sphere dominated by the billionaires and profit-crazed corporate behemoths that characterize Democracy, Inc. Founding-era corporations, few in number, were specially chartered to perform functions for the common good, such as building and operating a bridge. Otherwise, a legislative grant of a corporate charter—for example, for a purely profit-seeking enterprise—would be constitutionally suspect as advancing partial or private interests and hence contrary to republican democratic principles. During the early years of nationhood, corporations resonated more with mercantilism than with capitalism. Corporations operated to support government goals and functions rather than merely maximizing profits in a competitive free market.

Indeed, more generally, some of the framers had, at most, a partial vision of a competitive free-market. At that time, Americans largely understood the economic market as a quasi-mercantilist system, with the constrained conception of corporations being merely one part of that system. The state and the economy closely intertwined as they worked together for common purposes. Courts and legislatures still conceived of property and contract rights in premodern terms, at least in part, not as components of a modern capitalist free market. The legal institutionalization of slave labor underscored the premodern, pre-capitalist, status of the market. Moreover, neither in 1789 nor in 1791, when the Bill of Rights was ratified, would any American even have imagined that free speech or a free press directly protected a capitalist marketplace or economic liberty. Certainly, some Americans believed the press could serve as a watchdog for government corruption, and therefore might indirectly protect property rights. Yet, such oversight of republican government was a far cry from the neoliberal libertarian ideology endorsed by the Roberts Court. And for more than a century after the adoption of the First Amendment, courts would continue to conceptualize free expression in narrow republican democratic terms. The government could punish any speech or writing that might contravene the common good or undermine civic virtue.

In short, the Roberts Court conservatives betrayed constitutional principles when they treated economic interests, especially corporate interests, as sacrosanct rights. The framers not only aimed for a pragmatic balance, but also believed the government ultimately must have the power to control the private sphere, not vice versa—particularly when private interests threatened the common good, including the crucial public–private balance. Possibly, then, the conservative justices in *Citizens United* and *McCutcheon* did not rely heavily on originalist arguments for this very reason: The historical evidence suggests that the *Citizens United* and *McCutcheon* decisions contravene the framers' intentions and the original public meaning of the Constitution, including the First Amendment. The liberal dissenters in those cases, in fact, atypically invoked originalist sources more extensively than did the conservative majorities.[9] Disregarding the dissenters, the conservative justices allowed the framers' hopes for government in accord with reason and virtue— for government power in balance with individual rights to property and wealth—to be crushed under the weight of hundreds of millions of dollars.

If the Court's protection of Democracy, Inc., and glorification of a laissez-faire private sphere merely contravened the framers' intentions and the original public meaning, then the justices might, perhaps, have been able to justify their neoliberal libertarian interpretation of the Constitution by some other mode of constitutional reasoning— if the conservative justices, including the avowed originalists Scalia and Thomas, had been willing to repudiate originalism. But even apart from originalist sources, the neoliberal libertarian approach seems problematic. Both theory and history suggest it is wrongheaded—that the Court is going in a risky direction.

SOCIAL AND POLITICAL THEORY

For several decades now, a diverse collection of political philosophers and social theorists have warned that either excessive mixing of the public and private realms or undue weakening of one realm at the expense of the other seriously endangers the entire societal system, both the public and private. These theorists range from the seminal neoconservative social theorist, Daniel Bell, to the renowned liberal political philosopher, Jürgen Habermas, and would include Hannah Arendt, Benjamin Barber, and Michael Walzer.[10] A common theme running among these diverse scholars is that the economic and political spheres need to remain relatively separate. The logic, structure, and culture of each sphere are distinct. We need to be wary not only of government unduly controlling the economy—as with a centralized or planned economy—but also of economic institutions, particularly corporations, unduly controlling the government. In the words of Walzer, "What democracy requires is that property should have no political currency, that it shouldn't convert into anything like sovereignty, authoritative command, sustained control over men and women."[11] When economic concepts and reasoning are allowed to invade or colonize the political realm, these theorists all argue that democracy is threatened.

Writing in the late 1970s, when corporations were beginning to assert themselves in the democratic arena, Bell cautioned against the dangers of mixing money and politics in a democratic-capitalist system. Bell divided society into three realms: the techno-economic (or social), the cultural, and the political. The three realms, he suggested, will contribute to a stable society if they either remain separate or operate in ways that reinforce each other. Early in the development of capitalism, a culture of hard work, self-discipline, and self-denial—characterized by Max Weber as the Protestant ethic—bolstered the capitalist economy by encouraging individuals to devote themselves to employment in bureaucratically organized workplaces. By the second half of the twentieth century, however, the three realms overlapped and intersected in ways that were not mutually reinforcing; rather, they contradicted each other, causing societal instability. For instance, the capitalist economy required an ethos of "work, delayed gratification, career orientation, [and] devotion to the enterprise," but the modernist culture imbued individuals with a hedonistic desire for self-gratification. More to the point of this book, tensions between the economic and political realms would also prove problematic, according to Bell. The operative principle of the capitalist economy was efficiency, maximizing one's benefits while minimizing costs, while the operative principle of the pluralist democratic polity was equality, requiring that all individuals be "able to participate fully" as citizens. If the two realms had remained distinct, each could successfully fulfill its respective principle. But the two realms were bleeding into each other, Bell argued, producing discordance. Capitalism, aiming for efficiency, relied on hierarchically structured bureaucratic organizations that collided with the political desire for participatory equality. Meanwhile, citizens pressed political demands that confounded equality and efficiency, thus generating group conflict and societal instability. And to be clear, Bell perceived these dangers in the 1970s, in the midst of our consumers' democracy. The emergence of Democracy, Inc., only exacerbates the threat.[12]

The crucial point, whether one reads the neocon Bell or the liberal Habermas, is that much is at stake, far more than who wins the next election or what rate should be set for taxing corporations. The distinct economic and democratic realms, their respective logics and cultures, should not be allowed to intertwine excessively. As Habermas would put it, our democratic system is suffering from a "legitimation crisis." The democratic lawmaking process can retain its legitimacy only if citizens believe participatory equality structures the process. If strategic manipulations characteristic of the economic marketplace distort the democratic process, then legitimacy fades like an old black-and-white photograph. Viewers might be able to discern the general shapes of what remains, but the images are clouded and indistinct. Unsurprisingly, then, Democracy, Inc.—the extension of the corporate-dominated economic marketplace into the political realm of pluralist democracy—threatens the ongoing legitimacy and functionality of American democracy.[13]

Starting with the inveterate idea of American exceptionalism, the meaning of exceptionalism has varied over time, as different theorists have discerned it in different aspects of the American experience. In the colonial era, the Puritans of Massachusetts believed that America could be God's "City upon a Hill." Subsequently, early-nineteenth century Americans viewed the nation as exceptional because it could last longer than prior republics, which had succumbed to the seemingly natural rise and fall of civilizations. Indeed, at least until the Civil War, many Americans believed that the nation could escape the ravages of historical time. In the mid-twentieth century, liberal political theorists saw American exceptionalism in the nation's lack of a feudal past. In the late-twentieth century, neoconservatives viewed American exceptionalism as rooted in the nation's principled commitment to democracy and individual rights, thus justifying the American exercise of power in other countries.[14]

But today, if the concept of American exceptionalism retains any coherence, it lies in the historical persistence of our democratic culture. Both the republican and pluralist democratic regimes were built on the foundation of a democratic culture, which itself rested on the public perception of a rough material equality—or, at least, the lack of gross inequality, as found traditionally in European societies with entrenched aristocracies. Under republican democracy, the material equality engendered by widespread land ownership contributed to a sense that citizens were political equals with a shared commitment to the common good. Under pluralist democracy, widely shared middle-class attitudes generated a willingness to negotiate and compromise politically. Because America lacked an aristocratic class, citizens believed they were political equals; they all might, at different times, be democratic winners and losers, despite sharp disagreements over various policies. As Francis Fukuyama puts it, a "robust" democracy requires a "healthy middle-class."[15] In fact, the significance of a persistent democratic culture grounded on perceptions of a rough material equality—running from republican democracy through the consumers' democracy—is evident in prior iterations of American exceptionalism, such as the mid-twenti-eth century emphasis on the lack of a feudal past. Long ago, Alexis de Tocqueville emphasized material equality as the unique key to under-standing America.

> Amongst the novel objects that attracted my attention during my stay in the United States, nothing struck me more forcibly than the general equal-ity of conditions. I readily discovered the prodigious influence which this primary fact exercises on the whole course of society, by giving a certain direction to public opinion, and a certain tenor to the laws; by imparting new maxims to the governing powers, and peculiar habits to the governed. I speedily perceived that the influence of this fact extends far beyond the political character and the laws of the country, and that it has no less empire over civil society than over the Government; it creates opinions, engenders sentiments, suggests the ordinary practices of life, and modi-fies whatever it does not produce. The more I advanced in the study of American society, the more I perceived that the equality of conditions is the fundamental fact from which all others seem to be derived, and the central point at which all my observations constantly terminated.[16]

Most important, then, Democracy, Inc., undermines the stability of our democratic culture. Democracy, Inc., enfeebles belief in even the rough-est material equality because income and wealth are concentrated in an incredibly small sliver of the population. From 1974 to 2007, the share of national income going to the top-earning 0.1% of American families more than quadrupled (with adjustments for inflation) and continued to remain disproportionately high in subsequent years. From 2009 to 2012, 95% of income gains went to the top 1%. We went from being a nation in which most of its "income gains accrue to the bottom 90 percent of households (the pattern for the economic expansion of the 1960s) to one in which more than half go to the richest 1 percent."[17] The degree of American income inequality—of "economic polarization"—has stretched to a historic expanse.[18] Income inequality has reached its highest level since the 1920s, just before the Great Depression and the collapse of the republican democratic regime. Moreover, wealth inequality is just as bad as income inequality. As of 2007, the most affluent 1% of Americans controlled 35% of the nation's wealth, while the top 10% controlled nearly 75% of the wealth![19]

Unquestionably, there has been no "trickle down" to the less fortunate. If anything, America has developed a "trickle up" system. A greater percentage of the income and wealth goes to the already-rich rather than going to either the poor or the shrinking middle class.[20] Thomas Piketty has analyzed the causes of increasing income inequality. First, he draws on historical evidence to demonstrate that income inequality has increased because the rate of return on capital has exceeded the rate of growth of wages and output. That is, inequality has ballooned partly because a rentier class has been accruing greater income than the working class. The rich get richer without working. This phenomenon becomes more likely in slow-growing economies. Second, income inequality has increased because of the advent of "supersalaries": "extremely high remunerations at the summit of the wage hierarchy, particularly among top managers of large firms." In fact, Piketty shows that in the United States, while capital gains have contributed significantly to increasing inequality (approximately one-third of the increase since 1980), the incredible pay of top managers has primarily driven the growing expanse. For instance, CEO pay in the United States before the end of the Cold War stood at approximately 30 times the average pay for workers, while today CEO pay is nearly 300 times that of workers.[21]

Finally, Piketty emphasizes that skyrocketing income inequality does not arise because of unalterable market forces or deterministic laws of economics. Rather, "deeply political" choices produce inequality. Government tax policies obviously influence wealth distribution, but so do government policies regarding unions, executive pay, and financial markets. As Piketty puts it, politics can serve as an "amplifying mechanism" for increasing wealth. Benefiting from government policies, such as lower marginal tax rates, the rich use their enhanced power to push for additional policies that would further increase their wealth. To focus on one example, the supersalaries of top managers are not related to marginal productivity or managerial superiority. From the perspective of the corporate employers, the managers' salaries are economically irrational because the corporations do not accrue proportional benefits. CEOs and other corporate officials might receive supersalaries—but not because they are truly "supermanagers." Of course, the top managers act rationally, from their own economic standpoint, by maximizing the satisfaction of their own self-interest, granting themselves outrageous salaries and bonuses. But did not managers have the same incentives to maximize their own salaries in, let us say, 1970 as in 2010? In fact, no: Politics changed the incentives. Government tax policy now encourages managers to pursue supersalaries. In the 1970s, the top marginal tax rate was 70%, but as of 2012, the top rate had dropped to 35%, partly because the rich have supported officials and candidates willing to cut the rates. In recent years, then, managers have had strong financial incentives to maximize their own remunerations.[22]

Consequently, American income inequality has exploded partly because neoliberal policies in Democracy, Inc., are extractive. It is Robinhood in reverse: "[T]he riches accruing to the top have come at the *expense* of those down below."[23] Gains in American productivity have not generated increased income for the average American worker and household. The middle class, in particular, is being squeezed. As a recent Brookings Institute Project reported: "Many American families whose incomes are not low enough to officially place them in poverty live in economically precarious situations." These families are of an expanding and "struggling lower-middle class." Many of these families contain two wage earners, but they still need to fight merely to get by. "Though not officially poor, these individuals and families experience limited economic security. One major setback could thrust them into economic chaos."[24] To be sure, economic inequality is not unique to the United States. In many nations, the economically insecure and marginalized constitute more than 50% of the populations.[25] But the point of American exceptionalism is that, historically, the United States has maintained enough material equality to sustain a reasonable degree of political equality, which in turn has sustained the democratic culture. Now, though, the rich feast on the middle class, consumed like a blood-rare filet mignon, and then relax with an after-dinner liqueur.[26]

In the United States, it is worth emphasizing, the trickle up system is not race neutral. From 2000 to 2011, the income and wealth of African Americans and Hispanics shrank more than that of other Americans. In fact, as of 2009, the wealth gap between white and black households was an astronomical 20-fold. The median net worth (assets minus debts) of white households was over $113,000, while the median for black households was $5677. This incredible difference is a demonstrable legacy of slavery and subsequent racist policies.[27] According to one calculus, sustained racial oppression throughout American history has cost African

Americans a total of approximately $24 trillion, based on "lost wages, stolen land, educational impoverishment, and housing inequalities."[28]

The single largest factor contributing to the current wealth disparities between blacks and whites is home ownership, and the historical roots of the racial differences in home ownership are easily traced. When the Civil War and the Thirteenth Amendment ended slavery, racial segregation became the norm, de facto in the North and de jure in the South pursuant to Jim Crow laws. The Supreme Court deemed racially segregated public facilities to be constitutional in the infamous *Plessy v. Ferguson*, decided in 1896.[29] Meanwhile, discrimination in both the public and private spheres, including in educational opportunities, doomed most African Americans to choose between the lowest paying jobs or unemployment. Decades later, when Democrats gained national power in the 1930s and 1940s, they created many liberal social welfare programs. White southern Democrats, however, politically supported these New Deal laws only because the rest of the party succumbed to their demands for loopholes either excluding African Americans completely or minimizing their potential benefits. For instance, the National Labor Relations Act and the Social Security Act did not cover most agricultural and domestic service employees, positions widely held by black workers.[30] Similar loopholes riddled the GI Bill of Rights (the Servicemen's Readjustment Act), which created a comprehensive program of benefits for military veterans returning from World War II. In fact, John Rankin, an overtly racist Mississippi Democrat, chaired the House Committee on World War Legislation and controlled much of the initial drafting of bills creating veterans' benefits. The GI Bill provided the crucial means for many blue collar and previously poor workers to transition into home ownership and the middle class during the 1950s, yet blacks were largely excluded. The statutory benefits of course went to veterans, and during the war, the military forces had rejected a disproportionate number of black men. Many blacks nonetheless had served in the military and should have qualified for benefits. Regardless, they still often had to overcome state and local as well as private discrimination, as the federal government funded but did not administer many of the postwar programs. To take one example, under the GI Bill, the government would pay college tuition and fees for veterans, but colleges still controlled admissions and could discriminate racially when evaluating applicants. Most important in relation to home ownership and the long-term wealth gap, the GI Bill created a mortgage insurance program under which the government would guarantee low-interest home loans for veterans. Even so, the program required a prospective buyer to secure a loan from a bank or other private lending institution, and these lenders could and did discriminate on the basis of race. Many potential black homeowners were denied loans as a matter of course.[31] As of 1947, the Veterans' Administration (VA) had guaranteed 3229 loans in Mississippi, with only two going to African Americans. As of 1950, only one-in-ten VA mortgages in the New York City area had gone to blacks. As of 1953, the prototypical postwar suburb, Levittown, Long Island, which specialized in offering inexpensive starter homes for veterans, had a population of 70,000, with not a single African American. Consequently, while black families were thwarted again and again, many white families were able to buy houses during the postwar years and began to accrue equity or wealth, which was then passed on to the next generation. And to be clear, racism in housing and lending did not end after those years. In 1998, New York City banks were still denying loans to blacks at nearly double the rate of whites, even when the applicants had similar incomes.[32]

Despite this long history of persistent racism and discrimination, the politics of race hampers potential remedies. Many whites are either ignorant of or deny this history and become indignant when the government attempts or appears to act for the advantage of racial minorities. An oft-repeated refrain is that all Americans should be treated equally; no societal group should be singled out for favorable treatment. The government should be colorblind, in other words. Of course, this principled commitment to *formal* equality effaces history. Slavery, Jim Crow, lynchings, discrimination in employment and housing—all of which the government supported or blinked at (often with constitutional imprimatur)—all of it is instantly wiped from the slate. Privileges that historically accrued to whites and continue to this day are rendered invisible.[33] "The way to stop discrimination on the basis of race," John Roberts declared, "is to stop discriminating on the basis of race."[34] As Michael Eric Dyson says, "being white means never having to say you're white."[35]

In any event, exorbitant material inequality, racialized or not, threatens to crack the pillars of democratic culture.[36] For instance, gross inequality in a pluralist democratic regime will undermine commitment to the rule of law. Individuals obey the law because they accept it as legitimate, fear the punishment that might result from disobedience, or both accept the legitimacy and fear the punishment. Without the perception of rough material equality, sustaining a sense of reasonable political equality, government proclamations of legitimacy appear bankrupt. When massive sums of money infect the democratic and representative processes, citizens lose faith in the system. In the 2012 elections, when more than 6 billion dollars was spent, only .4% of the American population—that is, less than one-half of one percent of Americans—supplied 63.5% of the campaign contributions. In the 2014 mid-term elections, the percentages were even more extreme. In light of such disproportionate monetary contributions to the democratic process, average citizens fear "the political system is stacked" and mistrust their government. Citizens suspect (or know) they are not being fairly and equally represented. In such circumstances, people might realize they have little reason to obey the law other than fear. We could reasonably call such a nation a police state rather than a democracy.[37] In fact, the prison population of the United States is per capita larger than that of any other country, including Russia. It is approximately seven times as high as that of Europe as a whole. The American prison population has catapulted in size by an incredible 700% since 1970.[38] Unsurprisingly, several authors have linked neoliberal libertarian economic policies with the high incarceration rates.[39] More broadly, as Piketty puts it, extreme income and wealth inequalities "radically undermine the meritocratic values on which democratic societies are based."[40] According to an apocryphal quote from Louis Brandeis: "We may have democracy, or we may have wealth concentrated in the hands of a few, but we can't have both."[41]

Democracy, Inc., further threatens the democratic culture because it weakens the concept of national citizenship, the glue that binds individuals together in a national polity. Gross income inequality, again, is a contributing force as it diminishes individual allegiance to the nation. Statistics demonstrate that the poor and lower-middle class become disaffected and, consequently, less likely to vote than the wealthy. Democracy, Inc., systematically "works to depoliticize its citizenry." Without doubt, impoverished people are more apt to resort to crime and violence.[42] Moreover, multinational corporations care about profits, not borders. If anything, the national boundaries implicit in citizenship represent obstacles to corporations, which prefer the free flow of commercial goods to the most profitable markets, regardless of national identities. Corporate globalization threatens the very concept of a nation state. Renowned corporate advocate and management consultant, Kenichi Ohmae, has called the nation a "nostalgic fiction." From his perspective, "traditional nation states have become unnatural, even impossible, business units in a global economy."[43] Indeed, nowadays, a corporate officer who sacrificed profit for the well-being of any particular community—national or otherwise—would likely be deemed untrustworthy, if not daft. Milton Friedman has explicitly argued that the only social responsibility of business is to maximize profits. Any corporate effort to do otherwise, in his opinion, would be immoral. Friedman's views are not unusual. Business consultant and professor, Peter Drucker, declared, "If you find an executive who wants to take on social responsibilities, fire him. Fast."[44]

Corporations, in other words, care not one iota about promoting or sustaining national citizenship. Although the Supreme Court has deemed corporations to be persons for constitutional purposes, any real person with a corporation's single-minded desire for economic profit would be diagnosed a psychopath. Like a psychopath, corporations lack empathy for others, are manipulative of others (in the corporate quest for profit), and have delusions of grandeur (because their own profit or advantage is always most important). To the extent that citizens qua citizens survive in Democracy, Inc., they exist primarily "to be manipulated, managed, and intellectually massaged."[45] Corporations aim to produce consumers, not democratic citizens. These consumers tend to be "self-interested, exploitive, competitive, striving for inequalities, fearful of downward mobility." Sheldon Wolin has explained that, in Democracy, Inc., "[o]ne's neighbor [is] either a rival or a useful object. As the world of capital became steadily more enveloping and the claims of the political more anachronistic, capital became the standard of the 'real,' the 'true world.'"[46] In short, Democracy, Inc., endangers the democratic culture that has sustained American government for more than two centuries.

Robert Dahl succinctly conceptualizes the theoretical problem. The demos can threaten property rights because the indigent might use democratic power to take property from the wealthy. Meanwhile, property can threaten democracy because the wealthy might use economic power to seize political control. Consequently, the best way to preserve democratic culture and government is to maintain relative economic equality. Without extremes of poverty and wealth, the system will maintain balance and continue to function.[47]

The weakening of democratic culture and democratic government, though, is not merely a matter of theory. Over the past two centuries, the average life span of national constitutions is only 19 years.[48] Given this fact, recent developments in the United States are disturbing. In a *Journal of Democracy* article empirically grounded on survey results, the political scientists Roberto Stefan Foa and Yascha Mounk lamented: "In a world where most citizens fervently support democracy, where antisystem parties are marginal or nonexistent, and where major political forces respect the rules of the political game, democratic breakdown is extremely unlikely. *It is no longer certain, however, that this is the world we live in.*"[49] Another empirical study concluded that uncontrolled campaign spending, unleashed by *Citizens United* and its progeny, has undermined Americans' faith in democracy.[50] Unsurprisingly, then, in 2016, the otherwise disparate presidential campaigns of Bernie Sanders and Donald Trump both drew widespread support from Americans who distrusted the national government and Wall Street.[51]

Crucially, we are not looking at the possible undermining of only-democratic government. Bell, Habermas, and other scholars emphasize that the public and private spheres operate together as a system. American society is a democratic-capitalist system. If one part of the system fails or becomes too weak, then the entire system is threatened.[52] Quite simply, "no major country has sustained a market economy for multiple generations without also being democratic."[53] Thus, Joseph Stiglitz, an economist, emphasizes that "failures in politics and economics are related, and they reinforce each other."[54] Daron Acemoglu, an economist, and James A. Robinson, a political scientist and economist, jointly describe a "strong synergy between economic and political institutions." They explain that if either economic or political institutions are skewed—if they are not inclusive—then the entire societal system becomes unstable.[55] Yet, in any democratic-capitalist system, one should recognize, there are potential tensions or conflicts between the public and private spheres. The goals of actors in the respective spheres do not necessarily harmonize. The objectives of a profit-seeking corporate official, for instance, are unlikely to match those of a legislator focused on his or her constituents. Possibly, then, in the United States, such potential tensions between the public and private spheres have created weaknesses or instability in the political-economic system. But in the alternative, the tensions might engender strength in the proper circumstances. The tensile balance between the public and private spheres might well have created the flexibility that has enabled the American system to last more than two centuries despite enormous social and cultural changes.[56]

Because the public and private spheres are interconnected, if the private sphere subsumes the public realm, then the entire democratic-capitalist system will be threatened. If Democracy, Inc., and its neoliberal libertarian ideology undermine democratic culture—as seems to be happening—if the people lose their faith in democratic government—as appears to be occurring—then not only American democracy but also American capitalism will be endangered.[57] Government unequivocally needs the funding supplied from a functioning economic marketplace. The government cannot perform any task, whether road building, firefighting, public education, or anything else, without revenue derived from profit-driven economic actors. But contrary to laissez-faire dreaming, the economy needs a functioning democratic government. The government supports capitalism in multiple ways. Among its many functions, government regulates the money supply and credit; it supplies rules for contractual agreements; it educates and trains potential workers; it regulates land and resource use; and it builds and maintains roads, seaports, and airports. In short, government provides the hard and soft infrastructure that facilitates economic transactions. Without government infrastructure, economic transactions might be possible, but transaction costs would become astronomical. Dani Rodrik, an economist, reiterates the basic point: "Markets and states are complements." But Rodrik goes further, explaining that national markets depend on national government: "If you want more and better markets, you have to have more (and better) governance. Markets work best not where states are weakest, but where they are strong." In other words, a strong democratic government does more than provide infrastructure. Government can protect competition in the marketplace by, for instance, enacting and enforcing antitrust laws. Government can correct for the inequities that naturally flow from capitalist incentives by, for instance, providing sustenance during times of unemployment. And government can nurture the culture that sustains a continuing democracy by restricting the translation of economic power into political power. In sum, big multinational corporations need big democratic governments to maintain a healthy systemic balance.[58]

THE PRACTICAL EFFECTS OF LAISSEZ FAIRE IN HISTORY

Most important in terms of constitutional jurisprudence, the framers themselves clearly understood the need both to conceptualize separate public and private spheres and to recognize their systemic interrelationship. The framers feared for the nation's future when they arrived in Philadelphia for the convention. From their perspective, national survival depended on their successful drafting (and the subsequent ratification) of a constitution that would maintain a healthy balance between the public and private spheres. The framers had become pragmatic realists during the 1780s because, in their eyes, state governments had turned corrupt. The framers had learned that most people pursued their own passions and interests, whether acting in the economic marketplace or in governmental affairs. The people and their elected officials could not be trusted to act virtuously in pursuit of the common good. When individuals enjoy liberty, many if not most of them will seek to satisfy their own self-interest. If they contemplate government affairs at all, it is only to increase their own profits or wealth. In other words, the framers had seen during the 1780s, to their great disappointment, an alarming number of state citizens act like rational self-maximizers. And the framers recognized that this type of unchecked self-interested action could not be sustained. If the people continued their unchecked pursuit of self-interest in the public sphere, the American experiment in republican government and market economics would end in failure.[59]

History subsequent to the framing suggests the framers' perspicacity. In fact, the history of the early-twentieth century suggests that the United States in the early-twenty-first century faces a mounting crisis—a crisis of both democracy and capitalism—a crisis that would disappoint but not surprise the framers. Without doubt, the parallels between these two eras, separated by a century, are alarming, as numerous scholars in disciplines as diverse as economics, political science, history, anthropology, and economic sociology have recognized.[60] Laissez-faire ideology grew especially strong during the early-twentieth century, and neoliberal libertarianism, like laissez faire on steroids, has flexed its muscles in the early-twenty-first century. During both eras, the strength of laissez-faire ideology generated strong opposition to social welfare laws and other government policies that might impinge on the economic marketplace. Thus, during these two time periods, the dream of laissez faire moved closer to reality—though, during both times, businesses continued to seek and to accept government favors. Predictably, then, during both the early-twentieth and the early-twenty-first centuries, economic inequality increased to striking proportions.[61] And to be clear, gross inequality not only weakened democracy but also undermined the operation of the economic marketplace—witness the Great Depression of the twentieth century and the Great Recession of the twenty-first century. When Americans near the bottom of the income scale are so poor that they lack money to spend on consumer goods, then overall demand is reduced and unemployment rises. The rich are likely to funnel much of their extra wealth into financial investments rather than spending it on additional consumer goods; such investments therefore often do not boost demand, production, or employment. Moreover, during times of high inequality, the government is unlikely to invest adequately in hard and soft infrastructure. For instance, roads and bridges deteriorate and go unrepaired. The government is likely to reduce its support of scientific and social-scientific research—the type of support that helped create the Cold-War cities of knowledge. Overall, gross inequality undermines social cohesion, and social cohesion is a prerequisite for a well-tuned national economy.[62]

The predominance of laissez-faire ideology during both the early-twentieth and early-twenty-first centuries also generated persistent and overt attacks on democratic processes and government. For instance, nowadays, it is almost trite to criticize Congress as dysfunctional. Yet, the extreme party polarization that has crippled Congress in recent years eerily mirrors Karl Polanyi's 1944 description of European interwar democracies: A "clash of group interests" had paralyzed national institutions, thus creating "an immediate peril to society."[63] Moreover, rhetorical attacks on democracy can have serious consequences, as demonstrated by the early-twentieth century, when numerous democratic governments in Europe collapsed amidst calls for less interference with the marketplace. In the United States, many conservatives today attack democratic participation in ways that echo the early-twentieth-century. During both eras, voting restrictions have been justified as legitimate efforts to "preserve the purity of the ballot box," but the effect is to exclude certain societal groups, such as the poor and racial minorities. The disfranchisement laws tend to discriminate especially against those lacking money, leisure time, and bureaucratic know-how.[64] In recent years, more than 31 states have enacted laws restricting voting. For instance, the Voter Information Verification Act of North Carolina not only requires voters to present government-issued photo identification at the polls but also shortens the early voting period, ends pre-registration for 16- and 17-year-olds, and eliminates same-day voter registration. Under the Texas Voter Identification law, an individual who presents a concealed-gun permit can vote, but an individual with a student photo ID cannot.[65]

Lower courts have held some of these state laws to be illegal, but Republican party leaders and officials nonetheless suppressed thousands of votes in the 2016 elections by skirting the court decisions—for example, by reducing the number of early-polling and Election Day voting locations.[66] In fact, at candid moments, Republican officials have admitted that they support restrictive voter registration laws precisely to diminish Democratic voting. A Pew Center study discovered that "at least 51 million eligible U.S. citizens are unregistered, or more than 24% of the eligible population." For purposes of comparison, in Canada, more than 93% of eligible voters are registered. Texas alone has more unregistered voters than the populations of 20 states; the overwhelming majority of the unregistered Texas voters are racial minorities. To be clear, many American citizens do not vote *precisely because* they are purposefully discouraged or prevented from doing so, not because they are apathetic. And these missing votes matter; a study of the 2014 midterm elections concluded that disfranchisement laws potentially swung several gubernatorial and senate races.[67] Significantly, the early Roberts Court, which claimed in *Citizens United* to be concerned with protecting the democratic process, facilitated the passage of these disfranchisement laws by invalidating a key provision of the Voting Rights Act. Even when people can vote, it should be added, the political gerrymandering of legislative districts can skew voting power by creating safe districts.[68]

In sum, the history of the early-twentieth and early-twenty-first centuries supports those social and political theorists who reason that undue or improper mixing of the public and private spheres can undermine the entire societal system. More specifically, when one sphere undermines the operation of the other, or when either the private or public sphere languishes, then the entire democratic-capitalist system is threatened. Utopian dreams of an unregulated laissez-faire marketplace can weaken democratic governments. An inverse relationship exists: As demands for economic rationalism and laissez faire increase, confidence in government decreases. Yet, if the government or the economy becomes too weak, then the entire system can collapse. A pristine self-sufficient and self-regulating market economy has never existed and is literally impossible. Liberty cannot long continue in one sphere if it does not exist in the other. Despite laissez-faire ideology, the diminishment and ultimate destruction of democracy would be bad for business. Very bad. To be sure, democratic politics is messy and frustrating. The allure of a laissez-faire utopia is strong. But if the laissez-faire dream were realized—if the economic marketplace determined all, if democratic governance and politics were largely eliminated—then we would find ourselves in a dystopia, not a utopia. And while the framers did not get everything right—far from it—they recognized this crucial and fundamental principle: that the public and private spheres must simultaneously remain separated yet balanced.[69]

Notes

1. Sources in this chapter discussing economic developments, including globalization, include: Joel Bakan, The Corporation (2004); Barry Eichengreen, Golden Fetters: The Gold Standard and the Great Depression, 1919–1939 (1992); Jeffry A. Frieden, Global Capitalism (2006); Robert Heilbroner and William Milberg, The Making of Economic Society (10th ed. 1998); Kenichi Ohmae, The End of the Nation State (1995); Joseph E. Stiglitz, Globalization and Its Discontents (2002).

2. Helpful sources on the relationship between democracy and capitalism cited in this chapter include: Fred Block and Margaret R. Somers, The Power of Market Fundamentalism (2014); Samuel Bowles and Herbert Gintis, Democracy and Capitalism (1986); Robert A. Dahl, A Preface to Economic Democracy (1985); Paul Krugman, The Conscience of a Liberal (2007); Timothy K. Kuhner, Capitalism v. Democracy (2014); Thomas Piketty, Capital in the Twenty-first Century (Arthur Goldhammer trans., 2014); Karl Polanyi, The Great Transformation: The Political and Economic Origins of Our Time (2001 ed.); David F. Prindle, The Paradox of Democratic Capitalism (2006); Robert B. Reich, Saving Capitalism: For the Many, Not the Few (2015); Dani Rodrik, The Globalization Paradox (2011); Sidney A. Shapiro and Joseph P. Tomain, Achieving Democracy (2014); Joseph E. Stiglitz, The Price of Inequality (2013 ed.).

3. Richard A. Epstein, The Classical Liberal Constitution ix, 6–7, 37–38, 43, 45, 582 (2014); Randy Barnett, Restoring the Lost Constitution (2004); Randy Barnett, The Structure of Liberty (1998); see Paul D. Moreno, The American State From the Civil War to the New Deal 1–3 (2013) (arguing that founders believed that common good strictly limited government power and protected natural rights).

4. David G. Savage, *Scalia's views mixed with Kennedy's style: Meet Neil Gorsuch, Trump's pick for the Supreme Court*, L.A. Times, Jan. 31, 2017.

5. Roberto Stefan Foa and Yascha Mounk, *The Danger of Deconsolidation: The Democratic Disconnect*, 27 Journal of Democracy 5 (2016).

6. I do not mean to suggest implicitly that originalism sometimes provides clear and certain answers to constitutional issues. It does not. Stephen M. Feldman, *Constitutional Interpretation and History: New Originalism or Eclecticism?*, 28 Brigham Young University Journal of Public Law 283 (2014).

7. 558 U.S. at 354–356 (quoting The Federalist No. 10 (James Madison)); The Federalist No. 10 (James Madison).

8. 558 U.S. at 340–342 (free-speech protections extend to corporations).

9. *McCutcheon*, 134 S.Ct. 1434, 1467 (2014) (Breyer, J., dissenting); *Citizens United*, 558 U.S. at 426–428 (Stevens, J., dissenting); see Leo E. Strine, Jr. and Nicholas Walter, *Originalist or Original: The Difficulties of Reconciling Citizens United with Corporate Law History*, 91 Notre Dame Law Review 877 (2016) (*Citizens United* is inconsistent with an originalist approach). In *McCutcheon*, neither Roberts's plurality opinion nor Thomas's concurrence in the judgment invoked any originalist sources.

10. Daniel Bell, The Cultural Contradictions of Capitalism (1978; 1st ed. 1976); Jürgen Habermas, Between Facts and Norms: Contributions to a Discourse Theory of Law and Democracy 322 (William Rehg trans., 1996) [hereinafter Between]; Jürgen Habermas, 1 The Theory of Communicative Action 340–343 (Thomas McCarthy trans., 1984); see Hannah Arendt, The Human Condition 27–29 (1958); Benjamin R. Barber, Jihad vs. McWorld 239–246 (2001 ed.); Michael Walzer, Spheres of Justice: A Defense of Pluralism and Equality (1983); Jacob S. Hacker and Paul Pierson, Winner-Take-All Politics 74–75 (2010).

11. Walzer, supra note 10, at 298.

12. Bell, supra note 10, at xxiv–xxv, xxx–xxxi, 10–16, 23–25, 37, 54–65, 71–72, 196–198; Max Weber, The Protestant Ethic and the Spirit of Capitalism (Talcott Parsons trans., 1958).

13. Jürgen Habermas, Legitimation Crisis (Thomas McCarthy trans., 1975); Between, supra note 10, at 135.

14. John Winthrop, *A Modell of Christian Charity, reprinted in* The Puritans 195, 199 (Perry Miller and Thomas H. Johnson eds., 1963 ed.); John G. Gunnell, The Descent of Political Theory 241 (1993); Dorothy Ross, The Origins of American Social Science 468 (1991); G. Edward White, The Marshall Court and Cultural Change 1815–1835, at 6–9 (1991); see Stephen M. Feldman, Neoconservative Politics and the Supreme Court: Law, Power, and Democracy 54–68 (2013) [hereinafter Feldman, Neoconservative]; Kenneth Anderson, *Goodbye To All That? A Requiem For Neoconservatism*, 22 American University International Law Review 277, 288–290 (2007).

15. Francis Fukuyama, *The End of History?*, 16 The National Interest 3 (Summer 1989); Louis Hartz, The Liberal Tradition in America 50–64 (1955); Piketty, supra note 2, at 150–153. Democracy requires "a widespread sense of relative economic well-being, fairness, and opportunity, a condition derived not from absolute standards but from perceptions of relative advantage and deprivation." Dahl, supra note 2, at 46; Sanford Levinson, Framed: America's 51 Constitutions and the Crisis of Governance 232–233 (2012) (emphasizing "political culture").

16. Alexis de Tocqueville, Democracy in America 12 (Henry Reeve text, revised by Francis Bowen, edited by Phillips Bradley; Vintage Books ed. 1990). On the cultural foundations of democracy, see Edward Hallett Carr, The Twenty Years' Crisis, 1919–1939, at 27 (1962); John Lewis Gaddis, The Cold War: A New History 102 (2005).

17. Hacker and Pierson, supra note 10, at 16–17; Larry M. Bartels, Unequal Democracy 6–13 (2008); Piketty, supra note 2, at 24 (Figure: Income Inequality in the United States, 1910–2010); Facundo Alvaredo et al., *The Top 1 Percent in International and Historical Perspective*, 27 J. Economic Perspectives 3, 4 (Table: Top 1 Percent Income Shared in the United States); Emmanuel Saez, *Striking it Richer: The Evolution of Top Incomes in the United States (Updated with 2012 Preliminary Estimates)*, at 1–2; Chad Stone et al., *A Guide to Statistics on Historical Trends in Income Inequality*, Center on Budget and Policy Priorities 11 (December 5, 2013).

18. Kevin Phillips, Wealth and Democracy 127 (2002); Unequal, supra note 17, at 13.

19. Stiglitz, supra note 2, at 2–3, 9–10; Stone, supra note 17, at 1, 12–13.

20. Hacker and Pierson, supra note 10, at 19–20; Stiglitz, supra note 2, at 8–11, 31–32; see Reich, supra note 2, at xi–xii, 126–132 (emphasizing the decline of the middle class); Center for American Progress, *Report of the Commission on Inclusive Prosperity* 7 (Jan. 15, 2015) (unfettered markets threaten the middle class and weaken the nation).

21. Piketty, supra note 2, at 23–26, 166–167, 291–303, 571; Lawrence Mishel and Alyssa Davis, *CEO Pay Continues to Rise as Typical Workers Are Paid Less*, Economic Policy Institute Issue Brief #380 (June 12, 2014); Krugman, supra note 2, at 142; Stiglitz, supra note 2, at 26.

22. Piketty, supra note 2, at 20–21, 291, 314–315, 335; Hacker and Pierson, supra note 10, at 47–70; Krugman, supra note 2, at 7–9, 142–45; Phillips, supra note 18, at 201–248; Francis Fukuyama, *The Future of History: Can Liberal Democracy Survive the Decline of the Middle Class?*, 91 Foreign Affairs 53 (2012); Jeffrey A. Winters and Benjamin I. Page, *Oligarchy in the United States?*, 7 Perspectives on Politics 731 (2009); Tax Foundation, *U.S. Federal Individual Income Tax Rates History*,

1862–2013. High returns on capital are "a historical fact, not a logical necessity." Piketty, supra note 2, at 353.

23. Stiglitz, supra note 2, at 8 (emphasis in original); Piketty, supra note 2 at 23–27, 291–335, 350–353; David Harvey, A Brief History of Neoliberalism 29–31 (2005).

24. Melissa S. Kearney and Benjamin H. Harris, *A Dozen Facts About America's Struggling Lower-Middle Class,* Brookings Institute Hamilton Project 1, 3 (December 2013); Ian Dew-Becker and Robert Gordon, *Where Did the Productivity Growth Go? Inflation Dynamics and the Distribution of Income* (National Bureau of Economic Research Working Paper No. 11842); Organization for Economic Cooperation and Development, *Divided We Stand: Why Inequality Keeps Rising* (2011).

25. Fran Tonkiss, Contemporary Economic Sociology 163–165 (2006).

26. Theda Skocpol and Alexander Hertel-Frenandez, *The Koch Network and Republican Party Extremism,* 14 Perspectives on Politics 681 (2016) (emphasizing the political influence of the Koch brothers); Ganesh Sitaraman, *Economic Structure and Constitutional Structure: An Intellectual History,* 94 Texas Law Review 1301 (2016) (emphasizing the importance of the middle class to our constitutional system).

27. Thomas Shapiro et al., *The Roots of the Widening Racial Wealth Gap: Explaining the Black-White Economic Divide,* Institute on Assets and Social Policy (Feb. 2013); Rakesh Kochhar et al., *Wealth Gaps Rise to Record Highs Between Whites, Blacks, Hispanics,* Pew Research Center (July 26, 2011); Thomas W. Mitchell, *Growing Inequality and Racial Economic Gaps,* 56 Howard Law Journal 849, 850–852, 857–861 (2013); Piketty, supra note 2, at 161–162.

28. Carol Anderson, White Rage: The Unspoken Truth of Our Racial Divide 99 (2016); Danny Vinik, *The Economics of Reparations: Why Congress Should Meet Ta Nehisi Coates's Modest Demand,* New Republic, May 21, 2014; Joe R. Feagin, *Documenting the Costs of Slavery, Segregation, and Contemporary Racism: Why Reparations Are in Order for African Americans,* 20 Harvard BlackLetter Law Journal 49 (2004).

29. 163 U.S. 537 (1896).

30. Ira Katznelson, When Affirmative Action was White 22, 43–46 (2005); Michael K. Brown, et al., Whitewashing Race 28–30 (2003); Legislative History of the National Labor Relations Act, 1935, at 1058–1059 (1985 Commemorative ed.).

31. Servicemen's Readjustment Act of 1944 (June 22, 1944), 58 Stat. 284; Lizabeth Cohen, A Consumers' Republic 169–171 (2003); Brown, supra note 30, at 75–77; Thomas J. Sugrue, Sweet Land of Liberty 38, 43–44 (2008).

32. Derrick Bell, Race, Racism, and American Law 591–594 (2d ed. 1980); Brown, supra note 30, at 72; Cohen, supra note 31, at 171, 217; Katznelson, supra note 30, at 114-15, 122–129, 164; Manning Marable, The Great Wells of Democracy 60 (2002); see Matthew Desmond, Evicted (2016) (exploring connections between race and the growing rate of tenant evictions).

33. Michael Eric Dyson, Tears We Cannot Stop 53 (2017). "[B]eing white offers you benefits, understanding, forgiveness where needed." Id. at 79.

34. Parents Involved v. Seattle School District No. 1, 551 U.S. 701, 748 (2007) (invalidating public school affirmative action programs). If anything, Trump's election buried Americans even deeper in the blindness of colorblindness, an utter national disregard for institutional racism. "Donald Trump is the literal face of white innocence without consciousness, white privilege without apology." Dyson, supra note 33, at 109.

35. Dyson, supra note 33, at 65. For additional discussions of the influence of race on American politics, including the sometimes subtle invocation of white resentment or rage, see Anderson, supra note 28; Ian Haney Lopez, Dog Whistle Politics: How Coded Racial Appeals Have Reinvented Racism and Wrecked the Middle Class (2014). Dyson writes: "Black and white people don't merely have different experiences; we seem to occupy different universes, with worldviews that are fatally opposed to one another." Dyson, supra note 33, at 3

36. Racism has always been a crack in the democratic culture. Anderson, supra note 28, at 6.

37. Stiglitz, supra note 2, at 151, 157; Richard A. Clucas and Melody Ellis Valdini, The Character of Democracy 9-11, 16–17, 103 (2015); Martin Gilens, Affluence and Influence (2012). Statistics are drawn from the OpenSecrets.org website (see especially Donor Demographics).

38. Information on prison populations is drawn from the following: Robert A. Ferguson, Inferno 2 (2014); Roy Walmsley, World Prison Population List (10th ed. 2013); ACLU, The Prison Crisis https://www.aclu.org/files/assets/massincarceration_problems.pdf.

39. Bernard E. Harcourt, The Illusion of Free Markets 31–32, 42–43 (2011); Nicola Lacey, The Prisoners' Dilemma 170–173 (2008); Loic Wacquant, Punishing the Poor 1–3 (2009); James Q. Whitman, The Free Market and the Prison, 125 Harvard Law Review 1212, 1213–1217 (2012).

40. Piketty, supra note 2, at 1.

41. Peter Scott Campbell, Democracy v. Concentrated Wealth: In Search of a Louis D. Brandeis Quote, 16 Green Bag 2d 251 (2013).

42. Sheldon S. Wolin, Politics and Vision 592 (Expanded ed. 2004) [hereinafter Vision]; Chris Hedges, Death of the Liberal Class 6, 9 (2010); Phillips, supra note 18, at 391; Stiglitz, supra note 2, at 167.

43. Ohmae, supra note 1, at 5, 12; Barber, supra note 10, at 7–8, 13; Tonkiss, supra note 25, at 56–61.
44. Bakan, supra note 1, at 35 (quoting Drucker); Milton Friedman, *The Social Responsibility of Business is to Increase its Profits*, The New York Times Magazine (Sept. 13, 1970); Bakan, supra note 1, at 34; Phillips, supra note 18, at 148, 412–413.
45. David S. Allen, Democracy, Inc. 147 (2005); Bakan, supra note 1, at 56–57.
46. Vision, supra note 42, at 597. Reich argues that America needs to get past the myth of a free market—the market does not exist without or prior to government—and adjust the rules of capitalism itself so that its fruits are fairly shared. Reich, supra note 2, at 3–7, 85, 153–157, 183.
47. Dahl, supra note 2, at 68–71.
48. Zachary Elkins et al., Endurance of National Constitutions 129 (2009).
49. Foa and Mounk, supra note 5, at 16 (emphasis added).
50. Rebecca L. Brown and Andrew D. Martin, *Rhetoric and Reality: Testing the Harm of Campaign Spending*, 90 New York University Law Review 1066 (2015); see Joseph Fishkin and William Forbath, *Reclaiming Constitutional Political Economy: An Introduction to the Symposium on the Constitution and Economic Inequality*, 94 Texas Law Review 1287 (2016) (connecting growing economic inequality to the endangerment of American constitutionalism); Michael Kent Curtis and Eugene D. Mazo, *Campaign Finance and the Ecology of Democratic Speech*, 103 Kentucky Law Journal 529 (2015) (emphasizing threat to democracy).
51. Tamara Keith, *5 Ways Bernie Sanders and Donald Trump are More Alike Than You Think*, NPR, Feb. 8, 2016; Molly Ball, *What Trump and Sanders Have in Common*, The Atlantic (Notes), Jan. 6, 2016.
52. Stiglitz, supra note 1, at xiii.
53. Barry R. Weingast, *Capitalism, Democracy, and Countermajoritarian Institutions*, 23 Supreme Court Economic Review 255, 257 (2015).
54. Stiglitz, supra note 2, at 1.
55. Daron Acemoglu and James A. Robinson, Why Nations Fail 3–4, 81–82 (2012).
56. Bowles and Gintis, supra note 2, at 3–7; Kuhner, supra note 2, at 24; Prindle, supra note 2, at x, 2; Weingast, supra note 53, at 257 (emphasizing the trade-offs or tensions between capitalism and democracy). A Weberian perspective suggests that systemic tensions can create strength rather than weakness. Stephen M. Feldman, *An Interpretation of Max Weber's Theory of Law: Metaphysics, Economics, and the Iron Cage of Constitutional Law*, 16 Law & Social Inquiry 205, 216, 242–248 (1991).
57. Lawrence Lessig, Republic, Lost (2012). Thus, Reich emphasizes the current danger to capitalism and our "social fabric" rather than to democratic government. Reich, supra note 2, at xii, 153–157, 163.

58. Rodrik, supra note 2, at xviii, 14–16 (emphasis omitted); Acemoglu and Robinson, supra note 55, at 76; Heilbroner and Milberg, supra note 1, at 114–117; Reich, supra note 2, at 3–7, 153–154; Shapiro and Tomain, supra note 2, at xiii, 137–138; Stiglitz, supra note 2, at 66, 116; Fred Block and Peter Evans, *The State and the Economy, in* The Handbook of Economic Sociology 505, 506 (2d ed. 2005); Fred Block, *Introduction, in* Polanyi, supra note 2, at xxvi–xxvii.

59. Richard Beeman, Plain, Honest Men 3–21 (2009); Forrest McDonald, Novus Ordo Seclorum 94–96, 138–142, 177–179 (1985); Jennifer Nedelsky, Private Property and the Limits of American Constitutionalism 30, 125–126 (1990); Gordon S. Wood, The Creation of the American Republic, 1776–1787, at 403–425 (1969).

60. Harvey, supra note 23, at 153, 188–189 (anthropologist); Rodrik, supra note 2, at xvi (economist); Joseph E. Stiglitz, *Foreword, in* Polanyi, supra note 2, at vii, xiv (economist); Fred Block, *Introduction, in* Polanyi, supra note 2, at xviii, xxxiii–xxxiv (economic sociologist); see Christopher Clark, The Sleepwalkers: How Europe Went to War in 1914, at xxvii–xxviii (2012) (historian paralleling political situations of early-twentieth and early-twenty-first centuries); Frieden, supra note 1, at xv–xvii, 391 (political scientist paralleling globalization of early-twentieth and early-twenty-first centuries); Margaret MacMillan, The War that Ended Peace xxxii (2013) (historian doing same).

61. Stiglitz, supra note 2, at 106; Emmanuel Saez, *Income Inequality: Evidence and Policy Implications*, Arrow Lecture, Stanford (Jan. 2013); Thomas Piketty and Emmanuel Saez, *Income Inequality in the United States, 1913–1998*, 118 Q. J. Economics 1 (2003).

62. Heilbroner and Milberg, supra note 1, at 102–104; Stiglitz, supra note 2, at 104–147, 219; see Harvey, supra note 23, at 188–189; Council of Economic Advisers, *Supporting Research and Development to Promote Economic Growth: The Federal Government's Role* (Oct. 1995) (discussing how federal investment on research benefits the economy).

63. Polanyi, supra note 2, at 244. For discussions of polarization, see Feldman, Neoconservative, supra note 14, at 43–45; Morris P. Fiorina et al., Culture War? The Myth of a Polarized America (2005).

64. Alexander Keyssar, *The Squeeze on Voting*, International Herald Tribune (Feb. 15, 2012); Anderson, supra note 28, at 144–154; Stiglitz, supra note 2, at 163; Walter Dean Burnham, *Democracy in Peril: The American Turnout Problem and the Path to Plutocracy*, The Roosevelt Institute, Working Paper No. 5, at 2–11 (December 1, 2010).

65. Brennan Center for Justice, *Summary of Voter ID Laws Passed Since 2011*, at 13–14 (Nov. 12, 2013); Rick Lyman, *Texas' Stringent Voter ID Law Makes a Dent at Polls*, New York Times, Nov. 6, 2013; Aaron Blake, *North Carolina Governor Signs Extensive Voter ID Law*, Washington Post (Aug. 12, 2013).

66. N. Carolina State Conference of NAACP v. McCrory, 831 F.3d 204 (4th Cir. 2016) (holding that North Carolina law violated equal protection and the Voting Rights Act); Veasey v. Abbott, 830 F.3d 216 (5th Cir. 2016) (holding that Texas law violated Voting Rights Act); Gabrielle Gurley, *Voter Suppression Works Too Well*, The American Prospect 15 (Winter 2017) (explaining effectiveness of voter suppression measures despite court rulings); Michael Wines, *After a Fraught Election, Questions Over the Impact of a Balky Voting Process*, NYTimes (Nov. 12, 2016) (same).

67. Pew Center on the States, *Inaccurate, Costly, and Inefficient: Evidence that America's Voter Registration System Needs an Upgrade* 1–2 (Feb. 14, 2012); Ben Jealous and Ryan P. Haygood, Center for American Progress, *The Battle to Protect the Vote: Voter Suppression Efforts in Five States and Their Effect on the 2014 Midterm Elections* (Dec. 2014); Burnham, supra note 64, at 25; Ari Berman, *Texas's Jim Crow Voting Laws*, The Nation 14 (Oct. 31, 2016) (discussing Texas and methods used to discourage or prevent voter registration); see Justin Levitt, *The Truth About Voter Fraud* 6 (Brennan Center for Justice, 2007) (quoting the former political director for the Republican Party of Texas as to desire to cut Democratic voting); Alan Wolfe, *Voting Wrongs*, New Republic (Oct. 11, 2016) (quoting conservative activist Paul Weyrich to same effect).

68. Shelby County v. Holder, 133 S.Ct. 2612 (2013); Anderson, supra note 28, at 148–154 (on the ramifications of *Shelby County*); Zachary Roth, The Great Suppression: Voting Rights, Corporate Cash, and the Conservative Assault on Democracy (2016) (on the Republican attack on democracy); Daryl J. Levinson and Richard H. Pildes, *Separation of Parties, Not Powers*, 119 Harvard Law Review 2311, 2379–2381 (2006) (how to prevent safe districts).

69. Block and Somers, supra note 2, at 10–11, 34–35, 79, 101; Polanyi, supra note 2, at 3–4, 25, 145, 240–244; Block, supra note 58, at xxiii–xxvii; Neil J. Smelser and Richard Swedberg, *The Sociological Perspective on the Economy*, *in* The Handbook of Economic Sociology 3, 7, 13–15 (1994).

CHAPTER 8

Will We Save the American Constitutional System?

The early-twentieth and early-twenty-first centuries parallel each other to a frightening degree, yet the two eras differ significantly—though, at this time, it is too soon to determine the ultimate importance of those differences. In the twentieth century, American democracy tumbled into crisis, as did many European democracies. During that time, numerous Americans considered whether fascism or communism might prove superior to democracy. Yet, while most European democracies collapsed, American democracy survived. At least two factors contributed to the sustenance of American democracy. First, the nation's strong democratic culture, despite being eroded by gross economic inequality, provided a foundation for the reformation of American democratic institutions and practices: Pluralist democracy supplanted republican democracy.[1] The new pluralist democratic regime was, in many ways, stronger than its republican democratic predecessor. Political participation was more widespread, and the New Deal manifestation of pluralist democracy emphasized the interconnection of government and capitalism. Government, it was widely recognized, could be used to bolster the economy and to correct for marketplace imperfections. For the moment, then, utopian dreams of laissez faire were buried in the nation's unconscious. Government power expanded and further centralized at the national level, and the economy entered into a period of sustained prosperity.

Hence, today, an important question arises concerning the strength of our democratic culture. It was strong enough to help sustain democracy in the 1920s and 1930s, but is it strong enough today to withstand the

© The Author(s) 2017   227
S.M. Feldman, *The New Roberts Court, Donald Trump, and Our Failing Constitution*, DOI 10.1007/978-3-319-56451-7_8

massive and growing economic inequality—compounded by the ever-present racism—that now besets the nation? The empirical evidence does not breed optimism. Only around 30% of individuals born since 1980 in the United States believe it is "essential" for them "to live in a democracy." Among this group, a remarkable 24% "considered democracy to be a 'bad' or 'very bad' way of running the country."[2] In a survey conducted in early October 2016, an incredible 40% of Americans agreed, "I have lost faith in American democracy."[3] Given such evidence, political scientists Foa and Mounk see a "crisis of democratic legitimacy." Voters manifest this crisis when they "endorse single-issue movements, vote for populist candidates, or support 'antisystem' parties [or candidates] that define themselves in opposition to the status quo."[4] The election of Donald Trump as president only reinforces Foa and Mounk's conclusions, and to be sure, Trump's authoritarian tendencies and Cabinet appointments of billionaires and multi-millionaires does not augur well either for our democratic culture or the economic prospects of the middle and lower classes.[5]

A second factor contributing to the sustenance of American democracy in the early-twentieth century was that many Americans, liberals and conservatives alike, eventually perceived the dangers threatening the United States. By the late 1930s, the perilous position of the nation had grown conspicuous, partly because external threats (other countries) obviously endangered the nation's security. To be sure, the long-running Great Depression had shaken the nation's confidence, but the rise of the Nazi and Japanese war machines tangibly imperiled the existence of democracy. When war arrived, the nation responded. Indeed, even when it came to democratic theory, intellectuals responded. Numerous American political and constitutional theorists from the late-1930s through the 1950s, scholars like Dewey and Dahl, recognized the threat to democratic government (from World War II and then the Cold War) and openly defended it by articulating pluralist democratic theory.[6]

But in the twenty-first century, at least before the 2016 election, few Americans seemed to recognize the dangers threatening our democratic-capitalist system. An increasing number of people realized that growing economic inequality presents serious problems, but still, too many Americans seemed oblivious to the deepening danger.[7] One reason for this blindness was that the Cold War had ended. The Cold War itself had spurred the advancement of both democracy and capitalism. The two, democratic governance and capitalist economics, were bonded in joined battle against Soviet communism. The United States wielded its democratic principles and capitalist prosperity as linked weapons against the Soviets. Thus, when the Soviet Union collapsed, it seemed only a matter of time before democracy and capitalism would together rule the world. Of course, Americans soon had to worry about terrorism, but few see terrorism as an existential threat to the nation—not in the way that Soviet communism had been. But in the American Cold War victory, hidden dangers lurked, as neoliberal libertarianism was unleashed, and Democracy, Inc., emerged.[8]

Neoliberal libertarians—laissez-faire ideologues—consistently ignore market problems while emphasizing government failures. Ironically, these libertarians are tied as strongly to their utopian ideals of the marketplace as the Soviets were tied to their utopian visions of a proletarian revolution. Both the libertarians and the communists believe that capitalism cannot coexist with extensive social welfare laws intruding into the economic market. The communists favored social welfare, so they sought the end of capitalism. The libertarians favor capitalism, so they have sought to end or minimize social welfare laws and other democratic intrusions on the marketplace. But utopian thinking, in general, obscures history. Utopians do not learn from experience. When a critic accused Keynes of changing his mind about the benefits of free trade, he purportedly replied: "When the facts change, I change my mind—what do you do, sir?" Unlike Keynes, though, neoliberal libertarians do not adjust their theories to fit the evidence. Instead, they insist that the future will adhere to the theory—if only the government will get out of the way![9]

Neoliberal libertarians persistently conceptualize the economic marketplace in ideal terms while casting government and political decision making in the worst possible lights. Moreover, conservatives work hard—and spend much money—to persuade the public to perceive the marketplace and government in such extreme terms. To take a specific illustration, many Americans report liking Medicare, a government insurance program covering medical expenses for Americans aged 65 and older. A 2013 poll concluded that 54% of Americans had a favorable opinion of Medicare. For those Americans 65 and older, the number favoring Medicare rose to 88%. Yet, the same poll concluded that only 29% of Americans had a favorable opinion of government-provided health insurance. Apparently, some Americans believe Medicare is a type of private enterprise; furthermore, some condemn similar proposed government programs as socialism. More generally, neoliberal libertarians proclaim that interest groups constantly manipulate legislatures and capture administrative agencies—because government cannot be rational since it does not operate in accord with marketplace price mechanisms. Those same libertarians persistently seek to slash funding of government programs, and then complain loudly when the underfunded programs fail to perform adequately.[10]

To be sure, many of the libertarian complaints about government have elements of truth—and therefore need to be confronted—but simultaneously, neoliberal libertarians rarely even acknowledge that markets are imperfect. Indeed, markets might be riddled with imperfections and inefficiencies for many reasons, including inadequate knowledge, high transaction costs, and purposeful corporate maneuvering (as corporations seek to maximize their own profits). Yet, many neoliberal libertarians will attribute any and all market failures to government interference. In fact, while government should not be judged solely by the norm of economic efficiency, it is worth underscoring that government sometimes works more efficiently than private enterprises. For instance, many might be surprised to learn that public-sector wages are lower than private-sector wages for comparable workers. Moreover, studies show that (government-run) Medicare is more efficient than private medical insurance (based on administrative costs), and Social Security is more efficient than private life insurance annuities. As Joseph Stiglitz puts it, government intervention sometimes enhances efficiency and makes "*everyone* better off."[11]

Hence, the current threat to our democratic-capitalist system is magnified precisely because so many Americans, particularly those strongly influenced by neoliberal libertarianism, do not even perceive the danger. And given the longevity of the American constitutional system, the stability of democratic government can be easily overestimated. Only around two dozen nations "have sustained democracy since 1950." Economist and political scientist Barry R. Weingast notes that, as an empirical matter, "most democracies that exist today are likely to succumb to a form of authoritarian government in the next generation."[12] Once we acknowledge that democratic governments do not necessarily last forever, then we should be not only surprised but alarmed to learn that "explicit support for authoritarian regime forms is ... on the rise." Amazingly, 32% of American citizens would like to have a "strong leader" who does not need to bother with elections. Even worse, one in six citizens believe "it would be a 'good' or 'very good' thing for the 'army to rule.'" These sentiments tend to be the strongest among the wealthy and the young (millennials).[13] Given these widespread sentiments, the election of the autocratic Trump was equal parts predictable—despite pre-election polls favoring Hillary Clinton—and frightening. Trump's election epitomized the private subsuming of the public sphere so characteristic of Democracy, Inc. A billionaire TV reality star known primarily for his marketplace brand and without demonstrable knowledge of American history, the Constitution, or political nuance in domestic and foreign affairs rose to demagogic status and became president. Yet, the cloud of Trump's election and initial presidential actions had a silver lining: At least some Americans realized that he presented a grave peril to our constitutional system.[14] We would be seriously mistaken, however, if we believed that Trump alone threatens our democratic-capitalist system. Trump's election was a product of Democracy, Inc., and the degradation of our democratic culture. To be sure, Trump's impulsiveness, personal defensiveness, and authoritarian tendencies intensify the crisis, but even if the United States survives his presidency, the underlying dangers of Democracy, Inc., will likely remain.

Insofar as growing inequality contributes to loss of confidence in democratic government, the good news is that at least some conservatives acknowledge that inequality has increased in recent decades. Nevertheless, these conservatives typically brush aside this fact with one of two responses. First, they simply dismiss inequality as relatively unimportant.[15] Second they decree that such inequality inevitably results from market forces—contrary to Piketty's empirical study. Edward Lazear, chair of the President's Council of Economic Advisers from 2006 to 2009, intertwined both responses in a 2006 presentation. He admitted that income inequality had been increasing but then insisted that one should not mistakenly view this fact in the "pejorative way that the rich are getting richer at the expense of the poor." In fact, he claimed that increasing inequality was "good news" because it reflected "an increase in returns to 'investing in skills'—workers completing more school, getting more training, and acquiring new capabilities." But "[w]hat accounts for this divergence of earnings for the skilled and earnings for the unskilled?" Lazear asked. "Most economists believe that fundamentally this is traceable to technological change that has occurred over the past two or three decades. In our technologically-advanced society, skill has higher value than it does in a less technologically-advanced society." From this standpoint, democratic government has no answer for inequality because it is inevitable rather than political. If government tries to help, then it will necessarily create worse problems. If there are any solutions, they will arise naturally from the self-regulating economic marketplace—or at least that is what conservatives generally claim.[16]

A favorite conservative political ploy is to claim that liberal social programs produce unintended detrimental effects.[17] For example, the neoconservative icon Irving Kristol criticized welfare as a "liberal and compassionate social policy [that] has bred all sorts of unanticipated and perverse consequences." Welfare, according to Kristol, generated numerous "social pathologies—crime, juvenile delinquency, illegitimacy, drug addiction, and alcoholism, along with the destruction of a once functioning public school system."[18] But the tables are turned on conservatives in this instance. Many conservatives, especially neoliberal libertarians, persistently celebrate the marketplace and attack democratic government. The conservatives, though, are spawning an unintended consequence: Namely, if democratic government is undermined, then the entire democratic-capitalist system is endangered.

Conservatives appear to be ensnared in their own game of the so-called prisoner's dilemma. In the classic prisoner's dilemma of game theory, two prisoners who committed a crime together must decide whether to confess. The prosecutor presents each prisoner with the identical deal. Confess first and get a light sentence, though the other prisoner will get a heavy sentence. If both confess simultaneously, then they both get heavy sentences. Naturally, each prisoner assumes the other one will act in his or her self-interest by confessing imminently. Each prisoner, then, acts to protect his or her own interest by immediately confessing, and they both get long sentences. Thus, more generally, a prisoner's dilemma is any situation where individual rational action—that is, conduct in accord with rational self-maximization—leads to collective loss or disaster.[19]

In any democratic-capitalist system, individual economic actors are likely to pursue their own self-interest in the private sphere. That is, from an economic standpoint, individuals act as rational self-maximizers by seeking to increase their own profits while decreasing their own costs. Economic elites—or in other words, the wealthy—will naturally try to manipulate the system to their own personal advantage—and they often wield sufficient economic power to do so.[20] From this perspective, government regulation and limited markets can only get in the way of profits—unless, of course, the rich can manipulate the government to increase their rents or profits even higher. Mostly, though, economic elites will try to constrain the government and to emphasize globalization to enhance their opportunities for aggrandizing wealth. In other words, the rational self-maximizer seems likely to become a laissez-faire dreamer on both the domestic and international fronts. In the United States, the rise of laissez-faire ideology was and is predictable, both at the turn into the twentieth century and now, as we have turned into the twenty-first century. Government, quite simply, appears to interfere with rational economic action and profit. But what appears profitable for the individual is not necessarily good or useful for society. Instead, the rational economic actions of individuals (or corporations) can contribute to the weakening and even ultimate downfall of the democratic-capitalist system.[21]

In a democratic-capitalist system, the government must act to maintain the health of the economic marketplace and the system as a whole. The University of Chicago economist Luigi Zingales, an unabashed free-market enthusiast, underscores this basic point. He argues that some government regulations are economically inefficient in the short term and therefore appear to be anti-business, but they are nonetheless necessary to maintain the competitive free market. From his perspective, a competitive free market generates enormous social benefits, but businesses frequently seek to reduce or undermine competition in order to increase profits. To create profitable anti-competitive advantages, a business might try to use its economic power directly (in the marketplace) to defeat potential competitors. Or, quite often, a business will attempt to translate its economic power into political power and then manipulate the government to generate rents or increased profits. In fact, Zingales writes: "The worst outcome is a scenario in which firms' market power transcends the industry they operate in and becomes political power." Zingales adds that, since the end of the Cold War, businesses have increasingly sought to use "political influence" to mold government for their own economic advantage. Therefore, we need democratic government to prevent such anti-competitive actions—to control profit-hungry businesses and to keep the marketplace open and free. For example, from Zingales's viewpoint, antitrust laws interfere with some businesses but are nonetheless pro-market because they help preserve competition, reducing the number of monopolies.[22]

Meanwhile, another economist, Dani Rodrik, reasons that national democratic governance and the rational pursuit of economic profits inevitably conflict in a global marketplace. Rodrik has described a "fundamental political trilemma of the world economy: we cannot simultaneously pursue democracy, national determination, and economic globalization." Given that *global* democracy seems highly unlikely at this point in time, nation-states such as the United States will remain the only hope for democratic governance. If so, according to Rodrik's analysis, then Americans must choose between democratic politics and deep globalization (or, as Rodrik sometimes calls it, hyperglobalization). We cannot simultaneously retain the United States as an independent and self-determined nation governed by democratic politics while also participating fully in a global economy. Full participation in a global economic marketplace requires that a nation follow market rules that will inevitably conflict with certain domestic political agendas, such as those related to labor relations, environmental controls, corporate taxes, and so on. In fact, these market rules sometimes are not merely implicit but are explicitly written into law. Within a decade after the end of the Cold War, nations had already entered into more than a thousand bilateral investment treaties (BITs), typically agreements between economically developed and developing countries. There now exist thousands of BITs as well as hundreds of regional trade agreements (RTAs), such as NAFTA. Many BITs and RTAs purportedly constrain nations that seek to regulate foreign corporate business activities, with the nations potentially incurring legal damages. "BITs and RTAs," as explained by Rodrik, "usually allow foreign investors to sue host governments in an international tribunal for damages when new domestic regulations have adverse effects on the investors' profits." Under NAFTA, for instance, corporations have won multi-million dollar awards because of environmental regulations. BITs and RTAs can also shield corporations from liabilities. In a recent case, Ecuadorian citizens sought to sue Chevron for causing environmental devastation of a rain forest. Ecuador and the United States, however, had previously agreed to a BIT, and Chevron successfully invoked its arbitration clause as a potential barrier against the lawsuit. Because BITs and RTAs, in general, create legal barricades protecting corporate profits from government regulations, they provide additional incentives to corporations to seek globalization—as if there were not enough already. But BITs and RTAs are merely one example of Rodrik's political trilemma, albeit an unusually clear and concrete one. Even apart from BITs and RTAs, Rodrik shows that the logic of deep globalization—the corporate quest for (global) profits—necessarily contravenes the logic of democratic governance.[23]

In short, Democracy, Inc., is inherently unstable. The American democratic-capitalist system is teetering on the edge of an abyss, but too many Americans are staring up at the sky to see the danger. The ideology of Democracy, Inc., tells us to look upward, to quest for profits and only profits, and to ignore or denounce the government.[24] And unfortunately, the early Roberts Court conservatives were swept up in this ideology. They blithely protected economic liberty in accord with the utopian dreams of the neoliberal libertarians. Moreover, those same conservative justices occasionally invoked originalist methods and sources to support their interpretations of the Constitution, yet the framers were anything but utopians.[25] The framers had moved beyond the idealism of the Revolutionary era and had become pragmatic realists. This realism extended to economic transactions. Gouverneur Morris, who probably emphasized economic-based interests more than any other framer, explained: "Men must be treated as men, and not as machines, much less as philosophers, and least of all things as reasonable creatures, seeing that in effect they reason not to direct, but to excuse their conduct."[26] Meanwhile, Hamilton, in a letter to Robert Morris discussing the nation's finances, explained: "A great source of error in disquisitions of this nature, is the judging of events by abstract calculations; which, though geometrically true, are false as they relate to the concerns of beings governed more by passion and prejudice than by an enlightened sense of their interests. A degree of illusion mixes itself in all the affairs of society."[27] In other words, Hamilton not only warned Morris, broadly, against the illusions or ideals of utopian thinking but also cautioned him, specifically, about assuming that individuals truly base economic transactions on rational calculations. Individuals are swayed as much by their passions and prejudices as by a rational assessment of their own interests. Regardless, whether individuals are influenced more by passions or (economic) interests, the framers never suggested that government should be subordinated to private-sphere machinations.

Indeed, the framers deserve great praise for their insights into public–private interrelationships. When they arrived in Philadelphia for the constitutional convention, they had observed republican government up close, at the state level, for barely more than a decade. Based on that brief experience, they had largely shed their utopian ideals, which had animated the state constitutions, and had become pragmatic realists. Their insights into human nature and citizens' attitudes toward property and economic wealth, on the one side, and government, on the other, were shrewd, original, and sagacious. Their conceptualization of separate public and private spheres, in relative balance, was a remarkable and long-lasting achievement. They successfully created a government–market system that allows individuals to enjoy a degree of liberty in a private or economic realm while simultaneously cooperating in a political community which respects, to some degree, both liberty and equality.[28]

The early Roberts Court conservatives, however, do not deserve all the blame for the current state of constitutional jurisprudence and the danger threatening our nation. Political and historical context shapes actors. The justices lived and worked in the context of Democracy, Inc., in which many people, especially conservatives, accepted the ideology of neoliberal libertarianism. The conservative justices followed mainstream conservative principles, even if they contravened the framers' vision. But the framers, too, were products of their political and historical times. True, they realistically assessed human motivations and astutely analyzed the 1780s. But the framers made mistakes—some terrible ones—at least partly because of their context. And those mistakes now threaten to undermine the long-term achievement of the framers' goals: maintaining a public–private balance that insures democratic government and protects individual rights, including property rights. In short, the framers themselves must bear some of the blame for the current endangerment of the United States.

The framers recognized the complexity of human nature. They recognized that individuals were motivated not only by passions and interests but also by virtue and reason. They even recognized that the pursuit of self-interest might be useful in the private sphere but harmful in the public sphere. Yet, ironically, the framers did not fully appreciate the complexity of their own motivations. The framers, we might say, did not recognize how their own interests and prejudices, imbued by their cultural, religious, economic, and political backgrounds, shaped their perceptions of government principles and institutions. At the very end of the Philadelphia convention, Benjamin Franklin astutely observed that "when you assemble a number of men to have the advantage of their joint wisdom, you inevitably assemble with those men, all their prejudices, their passions, their errors of opinion, their local interests, and their selfish views." Yet Franklin immediately backtracked: "It therefore astonishes me, Sir, to find this system approaching so near to perfection as it does."[29]

Despite Franklin's optimism, the framers had proven themselves to be all-too-human. For instance, the framers—all white men, mostly Protestant, and mostly wealthy—readily relegated black slaves to the status of property. Blinded by racism and a desire to protect their own property interests—many owned slaves—the framers poisoned the American political-economic system with a disease that still infects the nation today, as evidenced by the dramatic wealth disparities between black and white households. As Michael Eric Dyson laments, "[s]lavery casts a long shadow across our lives.... continu[ing] to haunt us in a racial gulf that seems impossible to overcome."[30] More broadly, the framers did not appreciate the degree to which the rich, people largely like themselves, could threaten the liberty and property of others, including the poor. The framers feared that the poor would form self-interested factions that would try to control the government to pursue their own selfish advantages. The poor might unjustly seek debt relief—as in Shays's Rebellion—but the wealthy, of course, would have little reason to do so. The wealthy, from the framers' perspective, were an unlikely source of factionalism and government corruption. Instead, most framers believed a virtuous elite would emerge largely from among the wealthiest men.[31] To put this in different words, the framers conceptualized separate public and private spheres. They sought to construct a system that would protect both spheres. But when they mused about corruption, they primarily envisioned the poor—because of their private-sphere poverty—banding together to seize control of government and then using it to threaten the property rights of the wealthy. The poor would use political or public-sphere power to intrude illegitimately into the private sphere.

To be sure, the framers designed a Constitution that, they believed, could overcome self-interest in general, not only the self-interest of the poor. Yet, they did not devote sufficient attention to the types of corruption that could originate with the wealthy. Significantly, in this regard, Gouverneur Morris was one framer who, along with Benjamin Franklin, warned that the rich could be as self-interested as the poor. At the convention, Morris stated: "The Rich will strive to establish their dominion and enslave the rest [of the people]. They always did. They always will."[32] Morris, however, was pessimistic about most people, rich and poor alike. He worried that the poor—"the ignorant and the dependent"—would likely sell their votes.[33] In fact, Morris proposed that the

Senate be composed of wealthy aristocrats chosen for life, even though he believed the rich would use their power to manipulate the people. "We should remember that the people never act from reason alone," he explained. "The rich will take advantage of [the people's] passions and make these the instruments for oppressing them."[34] But Morris and Franklin were outliers in their emphases on economic class-based interests, in general, and on the powerful self-interest of the wealthy, more specifically. Madison and most of the other framers did not acknowledge that the wealthy might be just as likely as the poor—maybe even more likely—to seek control of the government for their own advantages. The framers fretted about the poor banding together into democratic majorities, but they did not fully grasp how private-sphere power—wealth itself—might be used to control government. The framers, flawed like other people, failed to recognize the degree to which their own passions and interests obscured the rational pursuit of their goals for the nation. Overall, then, the framers failed to construct or insert sufficient protections shielding government power from private-sphere overreaching—regardless of the source.[35]

Looking at this from an alternative angle, the American Revolution and the Constitution, as several historians have emphasized, unleashed social and cultural forces that would change America in ways beyond the anticipation of the founding generation.[36] The protection of liberty in the public and private spheres, the protection of property in the private sphere, and the guarantee of republican democratic government with at least a degree of equality in the public sphere combined to create a dynamic society. In particular, the founders created a country that would unleash an enormous amount of commercial energy, a private-sphere power that would seemingly continue to grow from decade to decade, from century to century. Thus, the framers aimed for a balance between the private and public spheres, between property rights and government power, but they unwittingly triggered forces that would ineluctably change the nation, engendering a commercial republic that would eventually arrive at Democracy, Inc. They might have aimed for balance, but they failed to create systemic structures that would maintain it in the long run. Ultimately, from this perspective, the framers must bear some of the blame for the development and constitutionalization of Democracy, Inc.[37]

What, then, can be done at this point in time? I am not arguing, it is worth emphasizing, that the American democratic-capitalist system will necessarily collapse in the near future. Rather, I maintain that the current emphasis on the private sphere and slighting of the public sphere—combined with Trump's presidency—seriously threaten the American democratic-capitalist system.[38] Will it collapse? I certainly hope not, but I also hope for and urge action that will ameliorate the danger. Other commentators have recommended various legislative and constitutional solutions.[39] For instance, some advocate for a constitutional amendment overturning *Citizens United*.[40] I would support most such reforms. Basically, any legislative or constitutional restriction on spending in politics, particularly on political campaigns, would likely improve on the status quo. A framework or program that would equalize funding for candidates running for the same office would be ideal. To be sure, an equalizing program would face internal or definitional problems. An obvious one: How would an individual qualify as a 'candidate' who deserved (or qualified for) equalized funding? Two far larger obstacles loom, however, for potential campaign finance reforms. First, any legislation would need to pass constitutional muster in the courts, possibly in the Supreme Court. While legislative restrictions on political spending would be difficult to enact, they would at least seem possible, especially at the state level (at least in some states). But any such statutes would then have to survive the judicial gauntlet, and in light of *Citizens United* and its progeny, they would likely be invalidated. Second, the odds of adopting a constitutional amendment, whether overturning *Citizens United* or otherwise, seem infinitesimally remote. The nation and Congress are too politically polarized to attain the supermajoritarian consensus needed to amend the Constitution.

Yet, the possibility of constitutional amendment is worth pausing over. First, Americans do not appear to be opposed in principal to constitutional amendments. To the contrary, states have held more than 200 constitutional conventions and have ratified more than 6000 amendments.[41] Second, as I have argued, when it comes to the Constitution and our democratic-capitalist system, *Citizens United* is only part of the problem. To be sure, *Citizens United* manifests and bolsters a neoliberal libertarian interpretation of the Constitution, but *Citizens United* is only one prong in the Court's constitutional protection of wealth and the economic marketplace. Many of the early Roberts Court's neoliberal decisions invoked the First-Amendment Free-Speech Clause, but the conservative justices have relied more broadly on numerous authoritative texts, including other constitutional provisions, federal rules, statutes, and case precedents.[42] Moreover, many elected officials as well as other citizens have supported a neoliberal libertarian approach. The result is Democracy, Inc., with its gross income and wealth disparity and crumbling democratic culture. The danger to our constitutional system is so serious, the dysfunctions of the system so distinct, that perhaps we need to consider the need for an entirely new constitutional system. The Constitution does not preclude this possibility. Article V, which contains the burdensome procedures for amending the Constitution, includes provisions for calling a new constitutional convention. Such a convention could be used to consider one or two amendments—such as a provision overruling *Citizens United*—but a convention could also consider a full rewrite of the Constitution.

There are many reasons to wish we could write a new Constitution.[43] The current weakness of our democratic-capitalist system and the possibility that it could collapse into authoritarianism is, of course, most important. But there are other reasons (some of which contribute to the weakness of the system). As structural matters, the Senate and the Electoral College are prominent constitutional problems. A premise of pluralist democracy is equal citizenship, the opportunity for each and every citizen to have an equal vote with all other citizens. The Supreme Court constitutionalized this premise in 1964 with the maxim of one person, one vote.[44] But the makeup of the Senate unequivocally and outrageously violates this maxim.[45] For instance, California has a population of 38.8 million, while Wyoming has a population of less than 586,000. Yet, each state has two senators. Quite simply, then, the vote of a Wyoming citizen is far weightier than that of a Californian—roughly 70 times heavier. Defenders of the Senate would respond that this inequality is the result of political compromise, namely between the large states and the small states at the constitutional convention. But at the time of the framing and ratification, 691,737 people lived in the most populous state, Virginia, while 59,096 lived in the least populous state, Delaware.[46] A Delaware vote, at the time, was therefore 11.7 times weightier than a Virginia vote. In terms of population, at least, the current voting inequality is far more egregious than the framing-era voting inequality. Moreover, at the time of the framing, states precluded massive segments of the American population from voting. In that era of republican democracy, an equal vote was not considered to be as crucial as it is today under pluralist democracy. Under pluralist democratic principles, the Senate as currently constituted is indefensible.[47]

Regardless, this voting inequality is baked into the constitutional system. Article I grants each state two senators, while Article V limits possible amendments related to that grant.[48] In particular, Article V states "that no State, without its Consent, shall be deprived of it's equal Suffrage in the Senate." This constitutionally mandated voting inequality in the Senate then contributes to the inequalities of the Electoral College (Article II grants each state electors "equal to the [state's] whole Number of Senators and Representatives").[49] As numerous commentators emphasized after the 2016 election, Hillary Clinton easily won the popular vote, receiving nearly 3 million more votes than Donald Trump, but Trump won the election by garnering a majority of the Electoral College votes (306 to Clinton's 232). Needless to say, Electoral College results such as this cannot be squared with the idea that American government is based on the consent of the governed. It is worth recalling, then, that Madison himself favored a direct popular vote for president but realized that slave states preferred an Electoral College because it would bloat their voting power. Indeed, as Michael Klarman emphasizes, the Electoral College, the makeup of the Senate, and many other aspects of the Constitution resulted from numerous assumptions and political compromises that might have made sense to the framers in 1787 but are highly questionable today.[50]

If these structural problems were insufficient to make one wish for a new Constitution, then one might consider the breakdown of the traditional norms needed for basic government functioning—the crumbling of democratic culture, in other words. As the American constitutional system evolved into a two-party pluralist democratic system, it depended on the willingness of each party to negotiate and compromise with the other. The system could function only because each party accepted "the idea of legitimate opposition." As Harvard professors of government, Steven Levitsky and Daniel Ziblatt, explain: "In a democracy, partisan rivals must fully accept one another's right to exist, to compete and to govern. Democrats and Republicans may disagree intensely, but they must view one another as loyal Americans and accept that the other side will occasionally win elections and lead the country."[51] But many members of the Republican party stopped recognizing the legitimacy of Democratic opposition years ago. When Republicans refused to accept that Barack Obama was born in this country and eligible to be president, they betrayed our constitutional system. After all, from the Republican perspective, how could they possibly negotiate and compromise with

Obama and the Democrats if he was not a legitimate president? Hence, Mitch McConnell, then the Senate Minority Leader, unsurprisingly admitted in 2010: "The single most important thing we want to achieve is for President Obama to be a one-term president."[52] Given Republican attitudes, it is no wonder that many Republican-controlled state legislatures have passed voter identification laws that prevent Democratic voters from casting a ballot. Republican intransigence has so completely undermined our democratic culture that the national government can barely function, as evidenced by the Republican Senate's 10-month refusal to consider President Obama's nominee, Merrick Garland, for a vacant Supreme Court seat created by Justice Scalia's death.[53]

Despite the strong case that can be made for a second constitutional convention and a new Constitution, hesitation might be prudent. Without doubt, our national Constitution has serious defects and our democratic-capitalist system is in ill repair. But the framing of a new Constitution would be a political act, as was the framing of the original Constitution. And given the state of our current polarized politics, a constitutional convention might produce a new document that would make us yearn for the old one. Would all citizens be granted an equal right to vote? Would women's interests and rights be fully respected? What about LBGT rights? Would there be an accounting for the structural racism that has been embedded in the system since the original framing? I for one cannot claim to be confident that the basic government structures and human rights necessary for a functioning democracy would be recognized and protected. For instance, even among young adults, ages 18 to 29, fewer than 50% believe that "basic necessities, such as food and shelter," and "basic health insurance" are rights that "government should provide to those unable to afford them," according to an April 2016 poll.[54]

A few words should be added about procedure. Article V provides procedures for calling a convention but does not specify procedures for conducting one. Obviously, the process for framing any proposed constitution would be crucial. Indeed, in reviewing Madison's notes from the Philadelphia constitutional convention, the multiple, persistent, and vehement disagreements—between large-and small-population states; between slave and "mostly free states;" between northern and southern and middle-Atlantic states—leave the reader amazed that the overwhelming majority of delegates ultimately agreed on any single Constitution. Although many of delegates feared that the nation was collapsing, the convention appeared on the verge of failure multiple times (and ratification was far from a certainty).[55] If, today, the United States were to hold a new constitutional convention, would the delegates even agree that the nation should remain unified? Or would many delegates support some type of division? With regard to ratification, Article V provides that three-fourths of the states must ratify any constitutional changes (whether single amendments or more)—with state legislatures or state conventions indicating assent. But this ratification process grants each state one vote, thus effectively reiterating the gross voting inequality of the Senate. The preferred process for ratification would be a nationwide referendum in which each citizen has one vote, though this approach would contravene Article V. In any event, given the nation's extreme political polarization, the procedural obstacles to the framing and ratification of a new constitution might be too large to overcome.[56]

Regardless, all this talk of a new Constitution does not diminish the current danger to our democratic-capitalist system. Assuming that a new constitutional convention will not be called, one national institution that nonetheless could feasibly act to ameliorate the danger is the Supreme Court. The Court stands in a unique institutional and official position in our democratic-capitalist system because the justices enjoy lifetime appointments. While they are not politically isolated—not by a long shot—they are politically insulated, if only because they do not have to run for reelection. In this time of crisis, when American constitutional government is imperiled, the new Roberts Court must choose: Will it reverse course and protect our democratic-capitalist system, or will it continue to uphold the Republicans' neoliberal libertarian fantasy?[57]

To be certain, the new Court is likely to follow the early Roberts Court. Gorsuch, the new justice, is likely to decide cases as Scalia would have done. Gorsuch greatly admired Scalia, viewing him as a "lion of the law." And like Scalia, Gorsuch claims to be an originalist, ostensibly interpreting the Constitution "according to its original public meaning."[58] In an empirical ranking of Supreme Court justices according to their political ideologies, political scientists Lee Epstein, Andrew D. Martin, and Kevin Quinn unequivocally rank Gorsuch as conservative, to the right of Roberts, Alito, and Scalia.[59] They predict that Gorsuch will "be a reliable conservative, 'voting to limit gay rights, uphold restrictions on abortion and invalidate affirmative action programs.'"[60]

Most important in relation to Democracy, Inc., Gorsuch's extra-judicial writings and prior judicial opinions suggest he will fall into line with the other pro-business conservatives on the Court. For instance, in a 2005 essay, he worried about "the filing of frivolous securities fraud class actions."[61] In a 2011 case, the Tenth Circuit Court of Appeals upheld an Occupational Safety and Health Review Commission finding that a corporation violated a safety regulation and caused an employee's death. Gorsuch, though, dissented and would have held for the corporation. "Administrative agencies enjoy remarkable powers in our legal order," he explained. "Still, there remains one thing even federal administrative agencies cannot do. Even they cannot penalize private persons and companies without *some* evidence the law has been violated."[62] In another case, decided in 2016, the Tenth Circuit upheld a Department of Labor Administrative Review Board decision. TransAm Trucking, Inc., instructed its driver, Maddin, to remain with his unheated truck after the trailer brakes failed because of subzero temperatures. Maddin instead unhitched the trailer and drove his truck to a gas station. TransAm fired him for disobeying orders. The Board found that Maddin's actions were protected under the Surface Transportation Assistance Act. Gorsuch dissented, reasoning that the Board had decided erroneously. "It might be fair to ask whether TransAm's decision [to discharge Maddin] was a wise or kind one," he wrote. "But it's not our job to answer questions like that. Our only task is to decide whether the decision was an illegal one." According to Gorsuch, the meaning of the statute was "perfectly plain," and it did not cover this situation. Maddin should have stayed in his unheated truck despite the freezing temperatures.[63]

If the new Justice Gorsuch performs largely like a Scalia clone, which seems highly likely, then the Court will probably continue following its recent course despite the dangers. Yet, because most of the key cases that protect and bolster Democracy, Inc., including *Citizens United*, are decided by five-to-four votes, if only one conservative justice were to switch his vote, then the Court might reverse direction. Perhaps Gorsuch will deny expectations and diverge from Scalia's path, or perhaps Roberts, who has voiced concern for the Court's institutional role and reputation, will realize that the Court has no legitimate function if the democratic-capitalist system collapses.[64] Of course, even if one conservative begins to consistently vote with the progressive justices, the Court alone cannot save the nation. But the Court can act in two interrelated ways that would help protect our constitutional system. First, the Court can act symbolically. Historians and legal scholars have debated the degree to which *Brown v. Board of Education* effectively undermined racial segregation,[65] but few question the symbolic importance that *Brown* played in the Cold War (and at least some historians argue that *Brown* served as an inspirational symbol for civil rights protestors).[66] During the Cold War, the Court's *Brown* decision allowed the national government to plunge ahead in its battle against the Soviet Union by claiming that the rule of law governed in America. All Americans, even racial minorities, were protected equally—or at least, the national government could proclaim as much while pointing to *Brown*.

Today, the nation needs one or more Supreme Court decisions that are clarion calls, symbolically instructing the nation: Our democratic-capitalist system is, in fact, endangered. Americans can still save the nation, but we need to acknowledge the danger and act to counter it. The Court can shine a spotlight on Democracy, Inc., and its risks to our nationhood. The Court can emphasize the importance of democratic culture and decide cases that nurture democracy and its fair and open processes. The Court can rally citizens and government officials to step back and stop the mad dash for profits regardless of long-term consequences. In short, the Court can help the nation come to its senses.

Second, guided by the three-pronged critique articulated in the previous chapter, the new Court can begin to undo the judicial imprimatur that the conservative justices have given Democracy, Inc. The framing and originalist sources, social and political theory, and the practical effects of laissez faire in history all point toward the need for a judicial repudiation of neoliberal libertarianism and the reinstitution of a balance between the public and private spheres. To achieve these goals, the Court needs to move in multiple directions. For instance, the Court should overturn the non-constitutional decisions that limit individual access to the courts and that otherwise insulate corporations from liability. In the future, the Court should interpret federal rules and statutes to balance the power of ordinary individuals and the government, on the one side, against that of corporations and the super-rich, on the other.

In the realm of constitutional cases, the Court should overturn decisions that impose judicial limits on congressional power. The key congressional power case under the early Roberts Court was *National Federation of Independent Business v. Sebelius*, the *Affordable Care Act Case*.[67] In that decision, the Court restricted Congress's power under both the Commerce and Spending Clauses. The conservative justices extended formalist reasoning that the Rehnquist Court had previously introduced in a series of cases involving the Tenth Amendment, Congress's commerce power, and Congress's Fourteenth Amendment, section five, power.[68] When the justices follow a formalist approach, they claim to discern the existence, content, and boundaries of certain preexisting categories of actions or events without inquiring into their real-world consequences. For instance, in the *ACA* case, Roberts distinguished the category of commercial activity from the category of commercial inactivity. He reasoned that the Commerce Clause empowers Congress to regulate activity but not inactivity. He then categorized the individual mandate provision in the ACA—requiring individuals to buy minimum health insurance or pay a penalty—as a regulation of inactivity. The mandate would force inactive individuals to buy into (or become active in) the health insurance market. Consequently, according to Roberts, Congress had exceeded its commerce power. Roberts did not consider, though, how the failure to buy insurance affected the health care market more broadly.[69]

The new Roberts Court should reject this type of formalist reasoning and instead return to the approach the Court followed from 1937 to 1992, years when the Court upheld every challenged congressional exercise of its commerce power with only one exception, a 1976 case that the Court soon overruled.[70] During that era of 55 years, the Court deferred to the democratic process. Limits on congressional power arose from the ballot box rather than from judicial imposition. As the Court explained in 1985, "the fundamental limitation that the constitutional scheme imposes on the Commerce Clause ... is one of process rather than one of result."[70] In following this approach to congressional power, the Court allowed the democratic process to strike the appropriate balance between public and private power.[71]

If the Court defers to the democratic process, however, the Court also needs to insure that private wealth and partisan manipulation do not warp that process. The Court needs to actively protect democracy. To do so, the Court must affirmatively protect voting rights and prevent the partisan gerrymandering of congressional and state legislative districts. The new Court will probably rule on the legality of the restrictive voter registration laws that Republican-controlled state legislatures have enacted in recent years (such as the North Carolina and Texas laws discussed in Chap. 7). If the Court were to reverse the lower courts and uphold these laws, even greater restrictions on voting would likely flow from conservative state legislatures.[72]

The Court also needs to stop using the First Amendment, especially the Free-Speech Clause, as a constitutional shield for wealth and the economic marketplace. The Court should therefore retreat from its protection of commercial advertising and return to its pre-1970s approach.[73] From that earlier perspective, advertising is a marketplace activity subject to government regulation. As such, advertising should not necessarily be restricted even if doing so is constitutionally permissible. Rather, decisions regarding the regulation of advertising should arise from the democratic process. The Court, in other words, should defer to legislative decisions and not judicially block regulations.

When it comes to the First Amendment, though, the new Court's most urgent task will be the overturning of *Citizens United*. The Court needs to stop interfering with legislative efforts by the people and their representatives to correct for the current and dangerous imbalance between the public and private spheres. Remember, *Citizens United* and its progeny invalidated legislative actions that Congress and various states had enacted in attempting to control the power of private-sphere wealth in political campaigns. And in fact, Congress and state legislatures had enacted numerous campaign finance regulations going back more than a century, at least to the 1880s.[74] Thus, as I stated, it is reasonable to presume that state legislatures could enact new campaign finance regulations. Were prior legislative enactments perfect in attaining their goals? Certainly not. Would they have diminished the power of wealth in politics? Perhaps, to a degree. But that possibility—diminishing the political power of wealth—is precisely what the early Roberts Court would not abide. The new Roberts Court can do better.

In theory, the new Court could interpret the Constitution to prohibit the spending of excessive wealth on politics. For instance, one could reasonably conclude that the principle of "one person, one vote," requires that all citizens have an opportunity to exercise relatively equal political power. More than a decade ago, Justice Breyer at least suggested such a line of reasoning in a concurrence: "[R]estrictions upon the amount any one individual can contribute to a particular candidate seek to protect the integrity of the electoral process—the means through which a free society democratically translates political speech into concrete governmental action."[75] But the Court need not take such affirmative (and unlikely) steps to protect equal participation. Instead, the Court merely needs to stop interpreting free expression as if it protects the spending of money on politics. To do so, the justices need to stop behaving like unwitting participants in their own prisoner's dilemma, blinded by self-interest and neoliberal libertarian ideology. The justices need to recognize the danger looming over the nation and to reinstitute the public–private balance envisioned by the framers.

But what exactly constitutes the public sphere under a pluralist democratic system? Under republican democracy, the definition of the common good helped identify the public sphere: Government could regulate or otherwise act within a realm that reached as far as the common good. That is, government could act for the common good but not beyond. Since the emergence of pluralist democracy in the 1930s, however, the concept of the common good has become problematic, if not completely repudiated. What, then, is the public sphere under pluralist democracy and its descendants (consumers' democracy and Democracy, Inc.)?

To be clear, I am not advocating for a so-called "republican revival," in which the United States would return to a republican democratic type of government.[76] First, the republican democratic system had serious weaknesses, none more significant than its propensity for legitimating exclusions from the polity. While under republican democracy an ostensible lack of virtue supposedly justified diminished political rights for women, racial minorities, and other peripheral groups, pluralist democracy is built on the presumption that all citizens should be free to participate in the political process. Second, the republican democratic regime was grounded on a rural, agrarian, and relatively homogeneous American society that no longer exists and cannot be recreated. Whether or not republican democracy truly fit the United States of the late-eighteenth and nineteenth centuries, it clearly does not fit the urban-suburban-exurban, post-industrial informational, and heterogeneous American society of the twenty-first century.

Again, then, what is the public sphere if it cannot be tied to the concept of the common good under republican democracy? Under pluralist democracy, the public sphere should be defined by the reach of government. What is the scope or reach of government power? As discussed above, it should be defined through the democratic process itself. Unquestionably, though, in the era of Democracy, Inc., when the wealthy, especially corporations, wield enormous power, the government must exercise expansive power to maintain a reasonable balance between the public and private spheres. The framers astutely recognized the need for such balance. A market economy is necessary for individual liberty and generally leads to productivity. But strong democratic government is necessary to protect competition in the marketplace, to correct for the inequities that naturally flow from capitalist incentives, and to nurture the culture that sustains a continuing democracy.[77] Government must have the power to limit the translation of economic power into political power. The private cannot be allowed to subsume the public. To protect our American democratic-capitalist system, to maintain the balance between government power and private rights, the Supreme Court must stop interpreting the Constitution as a shield for the unconstrained exercise of economic power.[78]

Finally, I realize that many neoliberal libertarians will be tempted to dismiss my argument summarily. Some might accuse me of being a socialist or even a communist. But that is not my intent. I do not favor central planning or government ownership of the means of production. Rather, for three interrelated reasons, I argue against an interpretation of the Constitution that follows neoliberal libertarian (or laissez-faire) ideology and facilitates private-sphere dominance of the public sphere. First, the constitutional framers sought to create a political-economic system in which the public and private remained relatively balanced. Second, numerous political and social theorists persuasively reason that a political-economic system will be endangered if one sphere dominates the other. Third, the history of the early-twentieth century suggests that the framers and the theorists are correct. When laissez faire reared its head in the United States and Europe—when the private dominated the public—it eventually caused practical and serious problems not only for democratic governments but also for capitalist economies. Similar problems are apparent today.

Rodrik uses the well-known metaphorical comparison of foxes and hedgehogs to describe economists. "The fox knows many things, but the hedgehog knows one big thing."[79] As Rodrik explains, many economists are hedgehogs. They reduce every problem to fit their rigid worldview. The solution for all ills is to allow the economic marketplace free rein. Minimize or eliminate the government. But some economists are foxes. They see complexities in many social problems and therefore try to draw on multiple sources in crafting solutions. They believe in the competitive free market, but they do not believe the market, standing alone, can solve all our difficulties. Clearly, neoliberal libertarians, whether they are economists or not, are hedgehogs. I am not an economist, but I am siding with the foxes, as did the constitutional framers. The public sphere should not eclipse the private, but likewise, the private should not subsume the public. Neither corporations nor government should dominate. The goal is a reasonable balance. In a democratic-capitalist system, big business requires big government. When multinational corporations disappear, then we can discuss returning the national government to its late-eighteenth century size.

NOTES

1. Helpful sources on the relationship between democracy and capitalism cited in this chapter include: Fred Block and Margaret R. Somers, The Power of Market Fundamentalism (2014); Paul Krugman, The Conscience of a Liberal (2007); Timothy K. Kuhner, Capitalism v. Democracy (2014); Thomas Piketty, Capital in the Twenty-first Century (Arthur Goldhammer trans., 2014); Karl Polanyi, The Great Transformation: The Political and Economic Origins of Our Time (2001 ed.); Robert B. Reich, Saving Capitalism: For the Many, Not the Few (2015); Dani Rodrik, The Globalization Paradox (2011); Sidney A. Shapiro and Joseph P. Tomain, Achieving Democracy (2014); Joseph E. Stiglitz, The Price of Inequality (2013 ed.); Luigi Zingales, A Capitalism for the People (2012); Barry R. Weingast, Capitalism, Democracy, and Countermajoritarian Institutions, 23 Sup. Ct. Econ. Rev. 255 (2015).
2. Roberto Stefan Foa and Yascha Mounk, The Danger of Deconsolidation: The Democratic Disconnect, 27 J. of Democracy 5, 7–8 (2016).
3. Nathaniel Persily and Jon Cohen, Are Americans Losing Faith in Democracy—And in Each Other, The Washington Post, Oct. 14, 2016.
4. Foa and Mounk, supra note 2, at 6–7; Sanford V. Levinson & William D. Blake, When Americans Think About Constitutional Reform: Some Data and Reflections, 77 Ohio St. L.J. 211, 212–213 (2016) (noting that increasing number of Americans question the soundness of the Constitution).
5. Roberto Stefan Foa and Yascha Mounk, The Signs of Deconsolidation, _ Journal of Democracy _ (forthcoming); Don Lee, Trump to Preside Over the Richest Cabinet in U.S. History, L. A. Times, Jan. 16, 2017. On Trump's authoritarian tendencies, see Ruth Ben-Ghiat, Donald Trump's Authoritarian Politics of Memory, The Atlantic, Jan. 22, 2017; Jason Stanley, Beyond Lying: Donald Trump's Authoritarian Reality, New York Times, Nov. 4, 2016.
6. Ira Katznelson, Desolation and Enlightenment 1–8, 126–128, 156–158 (2003).
7. Stiglitz, supra note 1 (focusing on costs of inequality); Foa and Mounk, supra note 2, at 6 (arguing that a "wide range of leading scholars"

believe that support for democracy "remains robust"); Joseph Fishkin and William E. Forbath, *The Anti-Oligarchy Constitution*, 94 B.U. L. Rev. 669 (2014). The attention focused on Thomas Piketty's *Capital in the Twentieth-First Century* underscores the increasing attention being paid to inequality and its consequences. Piketty, supra note 1; e.g., Paul Krugman, *The Piketty Panic*, New York Times (April 25, 2014); Robert M. Solow, *Thomas Piketty is Right: Everything You Need to Know About 'Capital in the Twenty-First Century'*, New Republic (April 23, 2014).

8. Zingales, supra note 1, at 252 ("intellectual hegemony of capitalism" after the Cold-War victory led to "complacency and extremism"); Foa and Mounk, supra note 2, at 15–16 (citizens began to lose trust in democracy when it became the "only game in town").

9. Rodrik, supra note 1, at 84 (quoting Keynes); Block and Somers, supra note 1, at 34; Jeffry A. Frieden, Global Capitalism 276 (2006); John Lewis Gaddis, The Cold War: A New History 116–117 (2005) (communist utopianism).

10. Kathy Frankovic, *Americans Distrust Government Health Care—Except If It's Medicare*, Economist/YouGov Poll (Nov. 7, 2013); Jacob Sattler, *Clear Majority Want No Medicare, Social Security or Education Cuts*, The National Memo (Jan. 25, 2013) (poll showing eight out of ten Americans, aged 65 and older, approve of Medicare); Philip Rucker, *Sen. Demint of S.C. Is Voice of Opposition to Health-Care Reform*, Washington Post (July 28, 2009); Stiglitz, supra note 1, at 189, 200, 204, 216–220.

11. Joseph E. Stiglitz, Globalization and Its Discontents xii (2002) (emphasis in original); Rodrik, supra note 1, at xii, xxi, 61–62, 134; Stiglitz, supra note 1, at 55, 72, 220. Many political scientists focus on problems in the democratic process. E.g., Polarized Politics: Congress and the President in a Partisan Era (Jon R. Bond and Richard Fleisher eds., 2000); Interest Group Politics (Allen J. Cigler and Burdett A. Loomis eds., 1983).

12. Weingast, supra note 1, at 258; Zachary Elkins et al., Endurance of National Constitutions 129 (2009) (average constitutions endure for 19 years).

13. Foa and Mounk, supra note 2, at 12–13.

14. David Frum, *How to Build an Autocracy*, The Atlantic, March 2017; Tom Ashcroft, *Guarding Against Authoritarianism*, NPR On Point, Jan. 31, 2017; Daron Acemoglu, *We Are the Last Defense Against Trump*, Foreign Policy, Jan. 18, 2017.

15. Ramesh Ponnuru and Yuval Levin, *Unequal to the Challenge*, National Review (Feb. 10, 2014), at 26; Scott Winship, *Inequality and the Fate of Capitalism*, National Review (May 19, 2014), at 31.

16. Edward Lazear, Chair, President's Council of Economic Advisers, *The State of the U.S. Economy and Labor Market*, Remarks at the Hudson

Institute (May 2, 2006); Krugman, supra note 1, at 132–133 (little empirical support for claim that inequality is increasing because of market forces).

17. Albert O. Hirschman, The Rhetoric of Reaction 135, 164–168 (1991).

18. Irving Kristol, Neoconservatism: The Autobiography of an Idea 48 (1995); Irving Kristol, *A Conservative Welfare State* (June 14, 1993), *reprinted in* The Neocon Reader 143, 146 (Irwin Stelzer ed., 2004).

19. Adrian Vermeule, *Foreword: System Effects and the Constitution*, 123 Harv. L. Rev. 4, 6 (2009); Michael A. Fitts, *The Vices of Virtue: A Political Party Perspective on Civic Virtue Reforms of the Legislative Process*, 136 U. Pa. L. Rev. 1567, 1585 n.51 (1988).

20. Daron Acemoglu and James A. Robinson, Why Nations Fail 82–87 (2012).

21. Edward Hallett Carr, The 20 Years' Crisis, 1919–1939, at 7–8 (1962); Reich, supra note 1, at 157 (individual actions of the wealthy are rational within the system but undermine the system overall).

22. Zingales, supra note 1, at 5, 28–32, 36–39, 44, 80; Piketty, supra note 1, at 20–22, 573–575; Thomas B. Nachbar, *The Antitrust Constitution*, 99 Iowa L. Rev. 57 (2013) (antitrust should protect freedom to use property in the marketplace rather than economic efficiency).

23. Rodrik, supra note 1, at xviii, 197–198, 200–205; Republic of Ecuador v. Chevron Corp., 638 F.3d 384 (2d Cir. 2011); Andrew T. Guzman, *Why LDCS Sign Treaties That Hurt Them: Explaining the Popularity of Bilateral Investment Treaties*, 38 Va. J. Int'l L. 639 (1998); Andrew B. Steinberg, *Bilateral Investment Treaties and International Air Transportation*, 76 J. Air L. & Commerce 457 (2011); see Block and Somers, supra note 1, at 17; Stiglitz, supra note 9, at 175–177; *cf.*, Frieden, supra note 9, at 461 (explaining Robert Mundell's impossibility theorem, emphasizing a tension among "capital mobility, a stable exchange rate, and monetary independence"). Rodrik advocates for "a 'thin' version of globalization—to reinvent the Bretton Woods compromise for a different era." Rodrik, supra note 1, at 205.

24. Reich warns against the danger to the American "social fabric." Reich, supra note 1, at 163. Moreover, some participants in the Occupy Wall Street movement had their eyes on the ground rather than in the sky.

25. Sources cited in this chapter on the founding include: Richard Beeman, Plain, Honest Men 359–368 (2009); Michael J. Klarman, The Framers' Coup: The Making of the United States Constitution (2016); Pauline Maier, Ratification (2010); Jennifer Nedelsky, Private Property and the Limits of American Constitutionalism (1990); Gordon S. Wood, The Radicalism of the American Revolution (1991) [hereinafter Radicalism];

The Records of the Federal Convention of 1787 (Max Farrand ed., 1966 reprint of 1937 rev. ed.) [hereinafter Farrand].

26. Nedelsky, supra note 25, at 76 (quoting Morris).

27. Hamilton Letter to Morris (1780), *in* 3 The Works of Alexander Hamilton (Henry Cabot Lodge ed., 1904); see Alexander Hamilton, *Report on Manufactures* (Communicated to the House of Representatives, December 5, 1791), 2 Annals of Congress 971, 973 (1791–1793) (rejecting utopianism).

28. See Lawrence D. Brown and Lawrence R. Jacobs, The Private Abuse of the Public Interest 2–3 (2008) (calling for pragmatism and realism rather than adherence to economic theory or idealism).

29. 2 Farrand, supra note 25, at 642 (Sept. 17, 1787).

30. Michael Eric Dyson, Tears We Cannot Stop 3 (2017).

31. Beeman, supra note 25, at 66–67, 114; Nedelsky, supra note 25, at 142–144.

32. 1 Farrand, supra note 25, at 512 (July 2, 1787); 2 Farrand, supra note 25, at 249 (Aug. 10, 1787) (Franklin). "Wealth tends to corrupt the mind and to nourish its love of power, and to stimulate it to oppression. History proves this to be the spirit of the opulent." 2 Farrand, supra note 25, at 52 (July 19, 1787) (Morris discussing need for executive to protect against legislative tyranny).

33. 2 Farrand, supra note 25, at 202–203 (Aug. 7, 1787).

34. 1 Farrand, supra note 25, at 514 (July 2, 1787); Beeman, supra note 25, at 48.

35. Nedelsky, supra note 25, at 65, 142–149, 201–203; see Klarman, supra note 25, at 596–616 (emphasizing that the framing and ratification resulted from ordinary politics and strategic manipulations).

36. Gordon S. Wood, Empire of Liberty: A History of the Early Republic, 1789–1815, at 1–4 (2009); Radicalism, supra note 25, at 3–8; Joyce Appleby, Capitalism and a New Social Order: The Republican Vision of the 1790s (1984); see Nedelsky, supra note 25, at 1–14; Douglas A. Irwin & Richard Sylla, *The Significance of the Founding Choices: Editors' Introduction*, *in* Founding Choices: American Economic Policy in the 1790s 1, 14 (2011) (policy choices embedded in the Constitution and its early implementation gave "the United States a governmental and financial system conducive to economic growth).

37. One might defend the framers by emphasizing that they could not have foreseen the enormous technological and social changes that would transform the nation. True enough. But they might have anticipated the possibility of transformations that would necessitate constitutional amendment. Nonetheless, they created an unwieldy amendment process that is near-impossible to overcome. U.S. Const. art. V.

38. Roberto Stefan Foa and Yascha Mounk, *The Signs of Deconsolidation*,—J. of Democracy—(forthcoming) (arguing that, even with Trump's election, it is too early to determine whether American democracy is seriously endangered).

39. Kuhner, supra note 1, at 14–23; Spencer Overton, *The Participation Interest*, 100 Geo. L.J. 1259 (2012) (encouraging more people to contribute to political campaigns).

40. Kuhner, supra note 1, at 286–288; Robert Weissman, *Let the People Speak: The Case for a Constitutional Amendment to Remove Corporate Speech from the Ambit of the First Amendment*, 83 Temp. L. Rev. 979 (2011).

41. "[T]he fifty states have held 233 constitutional conventions, adopted 146 constitutions, and ratified over 6000 amendments to their current constitutions." John J. Dinan, The American State Constitutional Tradition 1 (2006).

42. On the many ways the Roberts Court has undermined democracy, see Stephen E. Gottlieb, Unfit for Democracy: The Roberts Court and the Breakdown of American Politics 203 (2016); see Elizabeth Sepper, *Free Exercise Lochnerism*, 115 Colum. L. Rev. 1453 (2015) (arguing that the Court has used the Free Exercise Clause to protect business).

43. For more extensive arguments in favor of rewriting the Constitution, see Sanford Levinson, Framed: America's 51 Constitutions and the Crisis of Governance (2012) [hereinafter Framed]; Sanford Levinson, Our Undemocratic Constitution (2006) [hereinafter Undemocratic]. For another sharp criticism of our Constitution, see Louis Michael Seidman, On Constitutional Disobedience (2012).

44. Reynolds v. Sims, 377 U.S. 533 (1964); Wesberry v. Sanders, 376 U.S. 1 (1964); Robert A. Dahl, A Preface to Economic Democracy 59 (1985) ("votes must be allocated equally among citizens").

45. Undemocratic, supra note 43, at 50–59.

46. These populations are from 1790. The Statistical History of the United States from Colonial Times to the Present 13 (1965) (Table: Population for States: 1790 to 1950).

47. Robert A. Dahl, How Democratic Is the American Constitution? 48–54 (2001) (emphasizing that the Senate alone renders the constitutional system grossly undemocratic).

48. U.S. Const., Art. I, § 3, cl. 1.

49. U.S. Const., Art. II, § 1, cl. 2; Undemocratic, supra note 43, at 82–90.

50. Dahl, supra note 47, at 79-89 (criticizing the Electoral College for undermining democracy); Framed, supra note 43, at 75–76 (emphasizing the centrality of the 'consent of the governed' to the American system and its origins in the Declaration of Independence); Klarman, supra note 25, at 604, 628–631.

51. Steven Levitsky and Daniel Ziblatt, *Is Donald Trump a Threat to Democracy?*, New York Times, Dec. 16, 2016.

52. Mitch McConnell, The National Journal, Nov. 4, 2010.

53. Zachary Roth, The Great Suppression: Voting Rights, Corporate Cash, and the Conservative Assault on Democracy (2016). Another recent Republican attack on democratic culture arose when the Republican-controlled legislature of North Carolina, in cooperation with the outgoing Republican governor, attempted to strip much of the executive power from the newly elected Democratic governor. Richard Fausset, *North Carolina Governor Signs Law Limiting Successor's Power*, New York Times, Dec. 16, 2016. Mann and Ornstein emphasize that Republicans and Democrats are not equally at fault in undermining our democratic culture and system. Thomas E. Mann and Norman J. Ornstein, It's Even Worse Than It Looks xiv–xv, xxiv, 18–19, 102–103 (2012); Norman J. Ornstein, *Yes, Polarization Is Asymmetric—and Conservatives Are Worse*, The Atlantic, June 19, 2014.

54. Harvard Public Opinion Project, Executive Summary, *Survey of Young American's Attitudes Toward Politics and Public Service*, 29th ed., April 25, 2016.

55. Klarman, supra note 25, at 397–398, 599; 2 Farrand, supra note 25, at 4–8 (July 14, 1787) (Wilson, Martin, King, and Strong in a tense exchange over equality and representation, which led Martin, King, and Strong all to suggest the dissolution of the Union might be the preferred result); Klarman, supra note 25, at 127, 596 (on possible failure of the convention); Maier, supra note 25, at 68–69 (ratification in doubt).

56. Undemocratic, supra note 43, at 173–174 (arguing that Article V articulates possible but not exclusive procedures for calling a new constitutional convention); id. at 176–177 (discussing the ambiguity of the ratification process and recommending "a national referendum"); Akhil Reed Amar, *Popular Sovereignty and Constitutional Amendment, in* Responding to Imperfection 89, 89 (Sanford Levinson ed., 1995) (recommending the same).

57. Neil S. Siegel, *The Distinctive Role of Justice Samuel Alito: From A Politics of Restoration to A Politics of Dissent*, 126 Yale Law Journal Forum 164, 165 n.3 (2016) (noting how Alito follows the Republican party agenda).

58. Neil Gorsuch, *Of Lions and Bears, Judges and Legislators, and the Legacy of Justice Scalia*, 66 Case W. Res. L. Rev. 905, 905–906, 920 (2016); Cordova v. City of Albuquerque, 816 F.3d 645, 661 (10th Cir. 2016) (Gorsuch, Circuit Judge, concurring in the judgment).

59. Lee Epstein, Andrew D. Martin, and Kevin Quinn, *President-Elect Trump and his Possible Justices* (Dec. 15, 2016). For rankings of prior Supreme Court justices based on political ideology, see Lee Epstein et al., The

Behavior of Federal Judges 106–116 (2013), which includes comparisons with the Martin-Quinn scores (accounting for changes over time) http://mqscores.wustl.edu/index.php, and the Segal-Cover scores (quantifying Court nominees' perceived political ideologies at the time of appointment) http://www.sunysb.edu/polsci/jsegal/qualtable.pdf (data drawn from Jeffrey Segal and Albert Cover, *Ideological Values and the Votes of Supreme Court Justices*, 83 Am. Pol. Sci. Rev. 557–565 (1989); updated in Lee Epstein and Jeffrey A. Segal, Advice and Consent: The Politics of Judicial Appointments (2005)).

60. Alicia Parlapiano and Karen Yourish, *Where Neil Gorsuch Would Fit on the Supreme Court*, New York Times, Feb. 1, 2017; see, e.g., Little Sisters of the Poor v. Burwell, Order, No. 13-1540, Sept. 3, 2015 (Gorsuch joining dissent from order denying en banc hearing in case holding that the Affordable Care Act's contraception mandate did not violate religious liberty).

61. Neil M. Gorsuch and Paul B. Matey, *Settlements In Securities Fraud Class Actions: Improving Investor Protection*, Washington Legal Foundation Critical Legal Issues Working Paper Series 35 (April 2005); Sam Hananel and Laurie Kellman, *Gorsuch Has Record as Business-Friendly Judge*, The Register-Guard, Feb. 7, 2017.

62. Compass Envtl., Inc. v. Occupational Safety and Health Review Comm'n, 663 F.3d 1164, 1170 (10th Cir. 2011) (Gorsuch, J., dissenting).

63. TransAm Trucking, Inc. v. Admin. Review Bd., U.S. Department of Labor, 833 F.3d 1206, 1215–16 (10th Cir. 2016) (Gorsuch, J., dissenting).

64. Brent Kendall and Jess Bravin, *John Roberts Looks to Steer Supreme Court Through Political Winds*, Wall Street Journal , Feb. 19, 2016; Lincoln Caplan, *John Roberts's Court*, The New Yorker, June 29, 2015.

65. Michael J. Klarman, From Jim Crow to Civil Rights (2004); Gerald N. Rosenberg, The Hollow Hope: Can Courts Bring About Social Change? (1991).

66. Mary L. Dudziak, Cold War Civil Rights (2000); Derrick A. Bell, *Brown v. Board of Education and the Interest-Convergence Dilemma*, 93 Harv. L. Rev. 518, 523–525 (1980). For historians arguing for the symbolic importance of *Brown*, see Richard Kluger, Simple Justice 758–761 (1975) (emphasizing the importance of *Brown* for social change); Kenneth W. Mack, *Law and Local Knowledge in the History of the Civil Rights Movement*, 125 Harv. L. Rev. 1018 (2012); Paul Finkelman, *Civil Rights in Historical Context: In Defense of Brown*, 118 Harv. L. Rev. 973 (2005).

67. 132 S. Ct. 2566 (2012).

68. United States v. Morrison, 529 U.S. 598 (2000) (invalidating the Violence Against Women Act under both the Commerce Clause and the Fourteenth Amendment, section 5); City of Boerne v. Flores, 521 U.S. 527 (1997) (focusing on Fourteenth Amendment, section 5); United States v. Lopez, 514 U.S. 549 (1995) (focusing on Commerce Clause); New York v. United States, 505 U.S. 144 (1992) (focusing on Tenth Amendment).

69. 132 S. Ct. at 2586–2587; see id. at 2611 (Ginsburg, J., concurring in part and dissenting in part) (explaining that health care providers raised prices and insurance companies increased premiums to cover for the costs of the uninsured).

70. National League of Cities v. Usery, 426 U.S. 833 (1976), *overruled by* Garcia v. San Antonio Metro. Transit Auth., 469 U.S. 528 (1985).

71. Garcia v. San Antonio Metropolitan Transit Authority, 469 U.S. 528, 554 (1985).

72. N. Carolina State Conference of NAACP v. McCrory, 831 F.3d 204 (4th Cir. 2016) (holding that North Carolina law violated equal protection and the Voting Rights Act); Veasey v. Abbott, 830 F.3d 216 (5th Cir. 2016) (holding that Texas law violated Voting Rights Act).

73. Valentine v. Chrestensen, 316 U.S. 52 (1942).

74. Kuhner, supra note 1, at 9.

75. Nixon v. Shrink Missouri Government PAC, 528 U.S. 377, 401 (2000) (Breyer, J., concurring); Stephen Breyer, *Our Democratic Constitution*, 77 N.Y.U. L. Rev. 245, 252–253 (2002) (emphasizing democratic participation).

76. In the 1980s and early 1990s, numerous constitutional scholars explored how civic republican political theory might reshape constitutional jurisprudence. *Frank Michelman, Law's Republic*, 97 Yale L.J. 1493 (1988); see G. Edward White, *Reflections on the "Republican Revival": Interdisciplinary Scholarship in the Legal Academy*, 6 Yale L.J. and Human. 1 (1994).

77. One could define public goods, from an economic standpoint, as those goods or needs that individual rational economic actors would not be motivated to pursue or produce. Thus, cleaning up pollution would be a public good. Shapiro and Tomain, supra note 1, at 139–140.

78. Reich, supra note 1, at 157 (advocating for the cultivation of power that can countervail the wealthy in politics).

79. Rodrik, supra note 1, at 114; id. at 114–123. Rodrik drew from Isaiah Berlin who had drawn from the Greek poet Archilochus. Isaiah Berlin, *The Hedgehog and the Fox, reprinted in* The Hedgehog and the Fox: An Essay on Tolstoy 1, 1 (Henry Hardy ed., 2d ed. 2013).

INDEX

© The Editor(s) (if applicable) and The Author(s) 2017
S.M. Feldman, *The New Roberts Court, Donald Trump, and Our Failing Constitution*, DOI 10.1007/978-3-319-56451-7

CPSIA information can be obtained
at www.ICGtesting.com
Printed in the USA
LVOW13s0716011117

554462LV00031B/317/P